Cram101 Textbook Outlines to accompany:

Effective Small Business Management

Scarborough and Zimmer, 7th Edition

An Academic Internet Publishers (AIPI) publication (c) 2007.

You have a discounted membership at www.Cram101.com with this book.

Get all of the practice tests for the chapters of this textbook, and access in-depth reference material for writing essays and papers. Here is an example from a Cram101 Biology text:

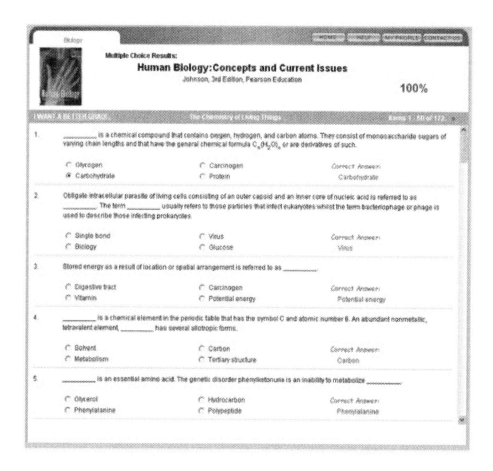

When you need problem solving help with math, stats, and other disciplines, www.Cram101.com will walk through the formulas and solutions step by step.

With Cram101.com online, you also have access to extensive reference material.

You will nail those essays and papers. Here is an example from a Cram101 Biology text:

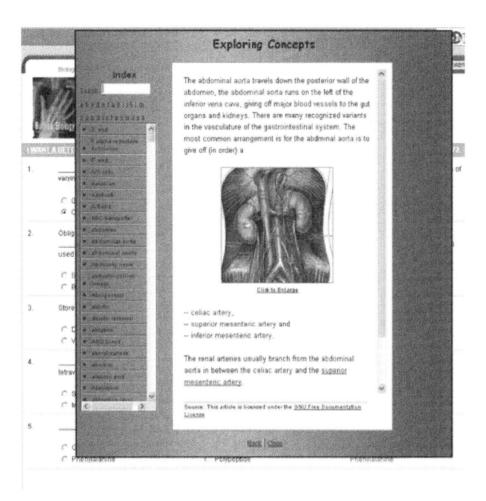

Learning System

Cram101 Textbook Outlines is a learning system. The notes in this book are the highlights of your textbook, you will never have to highlight a book again.

How to use this book. Take this book to class, it is your notebook for the lecture. The notes and highlights on the left hand side of the pages follow the outline and order of the textbook. All you have to do is follow along while your intructor presents the lecture. Circle the items emphasized in class and add other important information on the right side. With Cram101 Textbook Outlines you'll spend less time writing and more time listening. Learning becomes more efficient.

Cram101.com Online

Increase your studying efficiency by using Cram101.com's practice tests and online reference material. It is the perfect complement to Cram101 Textbook Outlines. Use self-teaching matching tests or simulate in-class testing with comprehensive multiple choice tests, or simply use Cram's true and false tests for quick review. Cram101.com even allows you to enter your in-class notes for an integrated studying format combining the textbook notes with your class notes.

Visit **www.Cram101.com**, click Sign Up at the top of the screen, and enter **DK73DW1739** in the promo code box on the registration screen. Access to www.Cram101.com is normally $9.95, but because you have purchased this book, your access fee is only $4.95. Sign up and stop highlighting textbooks forever.

Effective Small Business Management
Scarborough and Zimmer, 7th

CONTENTS

Small business	Small business refers to a business that is independently owned and operated, is not dominant in its field of operation, and meets certain standards of size in terms of employees or annual receipts.
Drawback	Drawback refers to rebate of import duties when the imported good is re-exported or used as input to the production of an exported good.
Entrepreneurship	The assembling of resources to produce new or improved products and technologies is referred to as entrepreneurship.
Entrepreneur	The owner/operator. The person who organizes, manages, and assumes the risks of a firm, taking a new idea or a new product and turning it into a successful business is an entrepreneur.
Contribution	In business organization law, the cash or property contributed to a business by its owners is referred to as contribution.
Economy	The income, expenditures, and resources that affect the cost of running a business and household are called an economy.
American Dream	The American Dream is the belief held by many in the United States of America that through hard work, courage, and determination one can achieve a better life for oneself, usually through financial prosperity.
Economic development	Increase in the economic standard of living of a country's population, normally accomplished by increasing its stocks of physical and human capital and improving its technology is an economic development.
Service	Service refers to a "non tangible product" that is not embodied in a physical good and that typically effects some change in another product, person, or institution. Contrasts with good.
Market	A market is, as defined in economics, a social arrangement that allows buyers and sellers to discover information and carry out a voluntary exchange of goods or services.
Big Business	Big business is usually used as a pejorative reference to the significant economic and political power which large and powerful corporations (especially multinational corporations), are capable of wielding.
Incorporation	Incorporation is the forming of a new corporation. The corporation may be a business, a non-profit organization or even a government of a new city or town.
Corporation	A legal entity chartered by a state or the Federal government that is distinct and separate from the individuals who own it is a corporation. This separation gives the corporation unique powers which other legal entities lack.
Interest	In finance and economics, interest is the price paid by a borrower for the use of a lender's money. In other words, interest is the amount of paid to "rent" money for a period of time.
Technology	The body of knowledge and techniques that can be used to combine economic resources to produce goods and services is called technology.
Downsizing	The process of eliminating managerial and non-managerial positions are called downsizing.
Competitive advantage	A business is said to have a competitive advantage when its unique strengths, often based on cost, quality, time, and innovation, offer consumers a greater percieved value and there by differtiating it from its competitors.
Management	Management characterizes the process of leading and directing all or part of an organization, often a business, through the deployment and manipulation of resources. Early twentieth-century management writer Mary Parker Follett defined management as "the art of getting things done through people."
Hierarchy	A system of grouping people in an organization according to rank from the top down in which all subordinate managers must report to one person is called a hierarchy.
Balance	In banking and accountancy, the outstanding balance is the amount of money owned, (or due), that

	remains in a deposit account (or a loan account) at a given date, after all past remittances, payments and withdrawal have been accounted for. It can be positive (then, in the balance sheet of a firm, it is an asset) or negative (a liability).
Business incubator	An innovation that provides shared office space, management support services, and management advice to entrepreneurs is a business incubator.
Capital	Capital generally refers to financial wealth, especially that used to start or maintain a business. In classical economics, capital is one of four factors of production, the others being land and labor and entrepreneurship.
Factors of production	Economic resources: land, capital, labor, and entrepreneurial ability are called factors of production.
Production	The creation of finished goods and services using the factors of production: land, labor, capital, entrepreneurship, and knowledge.
Information technology	Information technology refers to technology that helps companies change business by allowing them to use new methods.
Profit	Profit refers to the return to the resource entrepreneurial ability; total revenue minus total cost.
Marketing	Promoting and selling products or services to customers, or prospective customers, is referred to as marketing.
Industry	A group of firms that produce identical or similar products is an industry. It is also used specifically to refer to an area of economic production focused on manufacturing which involves large amounts of capital investment before any profit can be realized, also called "heavy industry".
Holding	The holding is a court's determination of a matter of law based on the issue presented in the particular case. In other words: under this law, with these facts, this result.
Stock	In financial terminology, stock is the capital raized by a corporation, through the issuance and sale of shares.
Foundation	A Foundation is a type of philanthropic organization set up by either individuals or institutions as a legal entity (either as a corporation or trust) with the purpose of distributing grants to support causes in line with the goals of the foundation.
Forbes	David Churbuck founded online Forbes in 1996. The site drew attention when it uncovered Stephen Glass' journalistic fraud in The New Republic in 1998, a scoop that gave credibility to internet journalism.
Business opportunity	A business opportunity involves the sale or lease of any product, service, equipment, etc. that will enable the purchaser-licensee to begin a business
Research and development	The use of resources for the deliberate discovery of new information and ways of doing things, together with the application of that information in inventing new products or processes is referred to as research and development.
Byproduct	A byproduct is a secondary or incidental product deriving from a manufacturing process or chemical reaction, and is not the primary product or service being produced.
Mistake	In contract law a mistake is incorrect understanding by one or more parties to a contract and may be used as grounds to invalidate the agreement. Common law has identified three different types of mistake in contract: unilateral mistake, mutual mistake, and common mistake.
Financial analysis	Financial analysis is the analysis of the accounts and the economic prospects of a firm.
Optimizers	Computer model and software that allow media buyers to make decisions about the value of various audience segments in a media schedule are optimizers.

Business plan	A detailed written statement that describes the nature of the business, the target market, the advantages the business will have in relation to competition, and the resources and qualifications of the owner is referred to as a business plan.
Operation	A standardized method or technique that is performed repetitively, often on different materials resulting in different finished goods is called an operation.
Cash flow	In finance, cash flow refers to the amounts of cash being received and spent by a business during a defined period of time, sometimes tied to a specific project. Most of the time they are being used to determine gaps in the liquid position of a company.
Gain	In finance, gain is a profit or an increase in value of an investment such as a stock or bond. Gain is calculated by fair market value or the proceeds from the sale of the investment minus the sum of the purchase price and all costs associated with it.
Controlling	A management function that involves determining whether or not an organization is progressing toward its goals and objectives, and taking corrective action if it is not is called controlling.
Developing country	Developing country refers to a country whose per capita income is low by world standards. Same as LDC. As usually used, it does not necessarily connote that the country's income is rising.
Users	Users refer to people in the organization who actually use the product or service purchased by the buying center.
Instrument	Instrument refers to an economic variable that is controlled by policy makers and can be used to influence other variables, called targets. Examples are monetary and fiscal policies used to achieve external and internal balance.
Enterprise	Enterprise refers to another name for a business organization. Other similar terms are business firm, sometimes simply business, sometimes simply firm, as well as company, and entity.
Product line	A group of products that are physically similar or are intended for a similar market are called the product line.
Publicity	Publicity refers to any information about an individual, product, or organization that's distributed to the public through the media and that's not paid for or controlled by the seller.
Saks Fifth Avenue	Saks Fifth Avenue is a chain of upscale department stores that is a owned and operated by Saks Fifth Avenue Enterprises, a subsidiary of Saks Incorporated. It competes on a price level on par with Neiman Marcus, Bergdorf Goodman and above Bloomingdale's and Nordstrom. Saks Fifth Avenue is headquartered in New York City.
Fund	Independent accounting entity with a self-balancing set of accounts segregated for the purposes of carrying on specific activities is referred to as a fund.
Glass ceiling	Glass ceiling refers to a term that refers to the many barriers that can exist to thwart a woman's rise to the top of an organization; one that provides a view of the top, but a ceiling on how far a woman can go.
Franchise	A contractual right to sell certain products or services, use certain trademarks, or perform activities in a geographical region is called a franchise.
Trust	An arrangement in which shareholders of independent firms agree to give up their stock in exchange for trust certificates that entitle them to a share of the trust's common profits.
Wage	The payment for the service of a unit of labor, per unit time. In trade theory, it is the only payment to labor, usually unskilled labor. In empirical work, wage data may exclude other compenzation, which must be added to get the total cost of employment.
Failure rate	Failure rate is the frequency with an engineered system or component fails, expressed for example in failures per hour. Failure rate is usually time dependent. In the special case when the likelihood of

Go to **Cram101.com** for the Practice Tests for this Chapter.

failure remains constant as time passes, failure rate is simply the inverse of the mean time to failure, expressed for example in hours per failure.

Administration	Administration refers to the management and direction of the affairs of governments and institutions; a collective term for all policymaking officials of a government; the execution and implementation of public policy.
Independent business	In business, an independent business as a term of distinction generally refers to privately-owned companies (as opposed to those companies owned publicly through a distribution of shares on the market).
Wells Fargo	Following completion of the First Security acquisition, Wells Fargo had total assets of $263 billion. Its strategy echoed that of the old Norwest: making selective acquisitions and pursuing cross-selling of an ever-wider array of credit and investment products to its vast customer base.
Remainder	A remainder in property law is a future interest created in a transferee that is capable of becoming possessory upon the natural termination of a prior estate created by the same instrument.
Labor	People's physical and mental talents and efforts that are used to help produce goods and services are called labor.
Investment	Investment refers to spending for the production and accumulation of capital and additions to inventories. In a financial sense, buying an asset with the expectation of making a return.
Security	Security refers to a claim on the borrower future income that is sold by the borrower to the lender. A security is a type of transferable interest representing financial value.
Realization	Realization is the sale of assets when an entity is being liquidated.
Nike	Because Nike creates goods for a wide range of sports, they have competition from every sports and sports fashion brand there is. Nike has no direct competitors because there is no single brand which can compete directly with their range of sports and non-sports oriented gear, except for Reebok.
Dell Computer	Dell Computer, formerly PC's Limited, was founded on the principle that by selling personal computer systems directly to customers, PC's Limited could best understand their needs and provide the most effective computing solutions to meet those needs.
Michael Dell	Michael Dell is the founder of Dell, Inc., the world's largest computer manufacturer which revolutionized the home computer industry.
Mary Kay Ash	Mary Kay Ash (May 12, 1908–November 22, 2001) was a U.S. businesswoman and the founder of one of the largest direct sellers of skin care and color cosmetics in the world.
Option	A contract that gives the purchaser the option to buy or sell the underlying financial instrument at a specified price, called the exercise price or strike price, within a specific period of time.
Economic growth	Economic growth refers to the increase over time in the capacity of an economy to produce goods and services and to improve the well-being of its citizens.
Gross domestic product	Gross domestic product refers to the total value of new goods and services produced in a given year within the borders of a country, regardless of by whom.
Domestic	From or in one's own country. A domestic producer is one that produces inside the home country. A domestic price is the price inside the home country. Opposite of 'foreign' or 'world.'.
Hilton Hotels	Since its founding in 1919, Hilton Hotels has grown to become the America's first coast-to-coast hotel chain, placing special emphasis on business travel, but owning and operating a number of resorts and leisure-oriented hotels as well. Hilton Hotels became the first international hotel chain with the opening of the Caribe Hilton in San Juan, Puerto Rico.
Customer service	The ability of logistics management to satisfy users in terms of time, dependability, communication, and convenience is called the customer service.

Go to **Cram101.com** for the Practice Tests for this Chapter.

Exporter	A firm that sells its product in another country is an exporter.
Export	In economics, an export is any good or commodity, shipped or otherwise transported out of a country, province, town to another part of the world in a legitimate fashion, typically for use in trade or sale.
Generation x	Generation x refers to the 15 percent of the U.S. population born between 1965 and 1976 a period also known as the baby bust.
Slowdown	A slowdown is an industrial action in which employees perform their duties but seek to reduce productivity or efficiency in their performance of these duties. A slowdown may be used as either a prelude or an alternative to a strike, as it is seen as less disruptive as well as less risky and costly for workers and their union.
Bond	Bond refers to a debt instrument, issued by a borrower and promising a specified stream of payments to the purchaser, usually regular interest payments plus a final repayment of principal.
Principal	In agency law, one under whose direction an agent acts and for whose benefit that agent acts is a principal.
Revenue	Revenue is a U.S. business term for the amount of money that a company receives from its activities, mostly from sales of products and/or services to customers.
Economic freedom	Freedom to engage in economic transactions, without government interference but with government support of the institutions necessary for that freedom, including rule of law, sound money, and open markets is referred to as economic freedom.
Asset	An item of property, such as land, capital, money, a share in ownership, or a claim on others for future payment, such as a bond or a bank deposit is an asset.
Cottage industry	A cottage industry is an industry – primarily manufacturing – which includes many producers, working from their homes, typically part time.
Firm	An organization that employs resources to produce a good or service for profit and owns and operates one or more plants is referred to as a firm.
Financial control	A process in which a firm periodically compares its actual revenues, costs, and expenses with its projected ones is called financial control.
Preparation	Preparation refers to usually the first stage in the creative process. It includes education and formal training.
Competitor	Other organizations in the same industry or type of business that provide a good or service to the same set of customers is referred to as a competitor.
Zoning	Government restrictions on the use of private property in order to ensure the orderly growth and development of a community and to protect the health, safety, and welfare of citizens is called zoning.
Business rule	A business rule describes an operation, definition and constraint that apply to an organization in achieving its goals. For example a business rule might state that no credit check is to be performed on return customers.
Insurance	Insurance refers to a system by which individuals can reduce their exposure to risk of large losses by spreading the risks among a large number of persons.
Policy	Similar to a script in that a policy can be a less than completely rational decision-making method. Involves the use of a pre-existing set of decision steps for any problem that presents itself.
Agent	A person who makes economic decisions for another economic actor. A hired manager operates as an agent for a firm's owner.
Personal finance	Personal finance is the application of the principles of financial economics to an individual's (or a

Go to **Cram101.com** for the Practice Tests for this Chapter.

	family's) financial decisions.
Wall Street Journal	Dow Jones & Company was founded in 1882 by reporters Charles Dow, Edward Jones and Charles Bergstresser. Jones converted the small Customers' Afternoon Letter into The Wall Street Journal, first published in 1889, and began delivery of the Dow Jones News Service via telegraph. The Journal featured the Jones 'Average', the first of several indexes of stock and bond prices on the New York Stock Exchange.
Journal	Book of original entry, in which transactions are recorded in a general ledger system, is referred to as a journal.
Assessment	Collecting information and providing feedback to employees about their behavior, communication style, or skills is an assessment.
Authority	Authority in agency law, refers to an agent's ability to affect his principal's legal relations with third parties. Also used to refer to an actor's legal power or ability to do something. In addition, sometimes used to refer to a statute, case, or other legal source that justifies a particular result.
Gap	In December of 1995, Gap became the first major North American retailer to accept independent monitoring of the working conditions in a contract factory producing its garments. Gap is the largest specialty retailer in the United States.
Restructuring	Restructuring is the corporate management term for the act of partially dismantling and reorganizing a company for the purpose of making it more efficient and therefore more profitable.
Strike	The withholding of labor services by an organized group of workers is referred to as a strike.
Microsoft	Microsoft is a multinational computer technology corporation with 2004 global annual sales of US$39.79 billion and 71,553 employees in 102 countries and regions as of July 2006. It develops, manufactures, licenses, and supports a wide range of software products for computing devices.
Market research	Market research is the process of systematic gathering, recording and analyzing of data about customers, competitors and the market. Market research can help create a business plan, launch a new product or service, fine tune existing products and services, expand into new markets etc. It can be used to determine which portion of the population will purchase the product/service, based on variables like age, gender, location and income level. It can be found out what market characteristics your target market has.
Credit	Credit refers to a recording as positive in the balance of payments, any transaction that gives rise to a payment into the country, such as an export, the sale of an asset, or borrowing from abroad.
Innovation	Innovation refers to the first commercially successful introduction of a new product, the use of a new method of production, or the creation of a new form of business organization.
Monopoly	A monopoly is defined as a persistent market situation where there is only one provider of a kind of product or service.
Peak	Peak refers to the point in the business cycle when an economic expansion reaches its highest point before turning down. Contrasts with trough.
Unemployment rate	The unemployment rate is the number of unemployed workers divided by the total civilian labor force, which includes both the unemployed and those with jobs (all those willing and able to work for pay).
Great Depression	The period of severe economic contraction and high unemployment that began in 1929 and continued throughout the 1930s is referred to as the Great Depression.
Depression	Depression refers to a prolonged period characterized by high unemployment, low output and investment, depressed business confidence, falling prices, and widespread business failures. A milder form of business downturn is a recession.
Property	Assets defined in the broadest legal sense. Property includes the unrealized receivables of a cash

Go to **Cram101.com** for the Practice Tests for this Chapter.

	basis taxpayer, but not services rendered.
Mortgage	Mortgage refers to a note payable issued for property, such as a house, usually repaid in equal installments consisting of part principle and part interest, over a specified period.
Appeal	Appeal refers to the act of asking an appellate court to overturn a decision after the trial court's final judgment has been entered.
Consignment	Consignment refers to a bailment for sale. The consignee does not undertake the absolute obligation to sell or pay for the goods.
Royalties	Remuneration paid to the owners of technology, patents, or trade names for the use of same name are called royalties.
Leadership	Management merely consists of leadership applied to business situations; or in other words: management forms a sub-set of the broader process of leadership.
Bankruptcy	Bankruptcy is a legally declared inability or impairment of ability of an individual or organization to pay their creditors.
Effective manager	Leader of a team that consistently achieves high performance goals is an effective manager.
Margin	A deposit by a buyer in stocks with a seller or a stockbroker, as security to cover fluctuations in the market in reference to stocks that the buyer has purchased but for which he has not paid is a margin. Commodities are also traded on margin.
Undercapital-zation	Undercapitalization refers to any situation where a business owner cannot acquire the capital they need. Usually, this refers to a business that cannot afford current operational expenses due to a lack of capital, which can trigger bankruptcy.
Accounts receivable	Accounts receivable is one of a series of accounting transactions dealing with the billing of customers which owe money to a person, company or organization for goods and services that have been provided to the customer. This is typically done in a one person organization by writing an invoice and mailing or delivering it to each customer.
Accounts payable	A written record of all vendors to whom the business firm owes money is referred to as accounts payable.
Expense	In accounting, an expense represents an event in which an asset is used up or a liability is incurred. In terms of the accounting equation, expenses reduce owners' equity.
Strategic management	A philosophy of management that links strategic planning with dayto-day decision making. Strategic management seeks a fit between an organization's external and internal environments.
Strategic plan	The formal document that presents the ways and means by which a strategic goal will be achieved is a strategic plan. A long-term flexible plan that does not regulate activities but rather outlines the means to achieve certain results, and provides the means to alter the course of action should the desired ends change.
Advertising campaign	A comprehensive advertising plan that consists of a series of messages in a variety of media that center on a single theme or idea is referred to as an advertising campaign.
Marketing Plan	Marketing plan refers to a road map for the marketing activities of an organization for a specified future period of time, such as one year or five years.
Advertising	Advertising refers to paid, nonpersonal communication through various media by organizations and individuals who are in some way identified in the advertising message.
Assignment	A transfer of property or some right or interest is referred to as assignment.
Personnel	A collective term for all of the employees of an organization. Personnel is also commonly used to refer

to the personnel management function or the organizational unit responsible for administering personnel programs.

Inventory	Tangible property held for sale in the normal course of business or used in producing goods or services for sale is an inventory.
Organizational structure	Organizational structure is the way in which the interrelated groups of an organization are constructed. From a managerial point of view the main concerns are ensuring effective communication and coordination.
Complexity	The technical sophistication of the product and hence the amount of understanding required to use it is referred to as complexity. It is the opposite of simplicity.
Time magazine	Time magazine was co-founded in 1923 by Briton Hadden and Henry Luce, making it the first weekly news magazine in the United States.
Inventory control	Inventory control, in the field of loss prevention, are systems designed to introduce technical barriers to shoplifting.
Working capital	The dollar difference between total current assets and total current liabilities is called working capital.
Accumulation	The acquisition of an increasing quantity of something. The accumulation of factors, especially capital, is a primary mechanism for economic growth.
Management team	A management team is directly responsible for managing the day-to-day operations (and profitability) of a company.
Chief executive officer	A chief executive officer is the highest-ranking corporate officer or executive officer of a corporation, or agency. In closely held corporations, it is general business culture that the office chief executive officer is also the chairman of the board.
Walt Disney	As the co-founder of Walt Disney Productions, Walt became one of the most well-known motion picture producers in the world. The corporation he co-founded, now known as The Walt Disney Company, today has annual revenues of approximately US $30 billion.
Disney	Disney is one of the largest media and entertainment corporations in the world. Founded on October 16, 1923 by brothers Walt and Roy Disney as a small animation studio, today it is one of the largest Hollywood studios and also owns nine theme parks and several television networks, including the American Broadcasting Company (ABC).
Thomas Edison	Thomas Edison was one of the first inventors to apply the principles of mass production to the process of invention, and can therefore be credited with the creation of the first industrial research laboratory. He developed many devices which greatly influenced life in the 20th century.
Niche	In industry, a niche is a situation or an activity perfectly suited to a person. A niche can imply a working position or an area suited to a person who occupies it. Basically, a job where a person is able to succeed and thrive.
Mutual fund	A mutual fund is a form of collective investment that pools money from many investors and invests the money in stocks, bonds, short-term money market instruments, and/or other securities. In a mutual fund, the fund manager trades the fund's underlying securities, realizing capital gains or loss, and collects the dividend or interest income.
Case study	A case study is a particular method of qualitative research. Rather than using large samples and following a rigid protocol to examine a limited number of variables, case study methods involve an in-depth, longitudinal examination of a single instance or event: a case. They provide a systematic way of looking at events, collecting data, analyzing information, and reporting the results.
Distribution	Distribution in economics, the manner in which total output and income is distributed among individuals or factors.

Go to **Cram101.com** for the Practice Tests for this Chapter.
And, **NEVER** highlight a book again!

Union	A worker association that bargains with employers over wages and working conditions is called a union.
Public relations	Public relations refers to the management function that evaluates public attitudes, changes policies and procedures in response to the public's requests, and executes a program of action and information to earn public understanding and acceptance.
Market share	That fraction of an industry's output accounted for by an individual firm or group of firms is called market share.
Long run	In economic models, the long run time frame assumes no fixed factors of production. Firms can enter or leave the marketplace, and the cost (and availability) of land, labor, raw materials, and capital goods can be assumed to vary.
Trade association	An industry trade group or trade association is generally a public relations organization founded and funded by corporations that operate in a specific industry. Its purpose is generally to promote that industry through PR activities such as advertizing, education, political donations, political pressure, publishing, and astroturfing.
Information system	An information system is a system whether automated or manual, that comprises people, machines, and/or methods organized to collect, process, transmit, and disseminate data that represent user information.
Lender	Suppliers and financial institutions that lend money to companies is referred to as a lender.
Supply	Supply is the aggregate amount of any material good that can be called into being at a certain price point; it comprises one half of the equation of supply and demand. In classical economic theory, a curve representing supply is one of the factors that produce price.
Financial statement	Financial statement refers to a summary of all the transactions that have occurred over a particular period.
Accounting	A system that collects and processes financial information about an organization and reports that information to decision makers is referred to as accounting.
Consultant	A professional that provides expert advice in a particular field or area in which customers occassionaly require this type of knowledge is a consultant.
Free enterprise	Free enterprise refers to a system in which economic agents are free to own property and engage in commercial transactions.
Demographic	A demographic is a term used in marketing and broadcasting, to describe a demographic grouping or a market segment.
Preference	The act of a debtor in paying or securing one or more of his creditors in a manner more favorable to them than to other creditors or to the exclusion of such other creditors is a preference. In the absence of statute, a preference is perfectly good, but to be legal it must be bona fide, and not a mere subterfuge of the debtor to secure a future benefit to himself or to prevent the application of his property to his debts.
Service economy	Service economy can refer to one or both of two recent economic developments. One is the increased importance of the service sector in industrialized economies. Also used to refer to the relative importance of service in a product offering.
Family business	A family business is a company owned, controlled, and operated by members of one or several families. Many companies that are now publicly held were founded as family businesses. Many family businesses have non-family members as employees, but, particularly in smaller companies, the top positions are often allocated to family members.
Tactic	A short-term immediate decision that, in its totality, leads to the achievement of strategic goals is called a tactic.
Brief	Brief refers to a statement of a party's case or legal arguments, usually prepared by an attorney. Also

Go to **Cram101.com** for the Practice Tests for this Chapter.

	used to make legal arguments before appellate courts.
Trend	Trend refers to the long-term movement of an economic variable, such as its average rate of increase or decrease over enough years to encompass several business cycles.
Driving force	The key external pressure that will shape the future for an organization is a driving force. The driving force in an industry are the main underlying causes of changing industry and competitive conditions.
Maturity	Maturity refers to the final payment date of a loan or other financial instrument, after which point no further interest or principal need be paid.

Go to **Cram101.com** for the Practice Tests for this Chapter.

Entrepreneur	The owner/operator. The person who organizes, manages, and assumes the risks of a firm, taking a new idea or a new product and turning it into a successful business is an entrepreneur.
Short run	Short run refers to a period of time that permits an increase or decrease in current production volume with existing capacity, but one that is too short to permit enlargement of that capacity itself (eg, the building of new plants, training of additional workers, etc.).
Small business	Small business refers to a business that is independently owned and operated, is not dominant in its field of operation, and meets certain standards of size in terms of employees or annual receipts.
Market	A market is, as defined in economics, a social arrangement that allows buyers and sellers to discover information and carry out a voluntary exchange of goods or services.
Intellectual capital	Intellectual capital makes an organization worth more than its balance sheet value. For many years, intellectual capital and goodwill meant the same thing. Today, intellectual capital management is far broader. It seeks to explain how knowledge, collaboration, and process-engagement create decisions and actions that lead to cost allocations, productivity, and finally financial performance.
Economy	The income, expenditures, and resources that affect the cost of running a business and household are called an economy.
Capital	Capital generally refers to financial wealth, especially that used to start or maintain a business. In classical economics, capital is one of four factors of production, the others being land and labor and entrepreneurship.
Factor of production	Factor of production refers to economic resources used in production such as land, labor, and capital.
Production	The creation of finished goods and services using the factors of production: land, labor, capital, entrepreneurship, and knowledge.
Human capital	Human capital refers to the stock of knowledge and skill, embodied in an individual as a result of education, training, and experience that makes them more productive. The stock of knowledge and skill embodied in the population of an economy.
Patent	The legal right to the proceeds from and control over the use of an invented product or process, granted for a fixed period of time, usually 20 years. Patent is one form of intellectual property that is subject of the TRIPS agreement.
Goodwill	Goodwill is an important accounting concept that describes the value of a business entity not directly attributable to its tangible assets and liabilities.
Foundation	A Foundation is a type of philanthropic organization set up by either individuals or institutions as a legal entity (either as a corporation or trust) with the purpose of distributing grants to support causes in line with the goals of the foundation.
General Electric	In 1876, Thomas Alva Edison opened a new laboratory in Menlo Park, New Jersey. Out of the laboratory was to come perhaps the most famous invention of all—a successful development of the incandescent electric lamp. By 1890, Edison had organized his various businesses into the Edison General Electric Company.
Management	Management characterizes the process of leading and directing all or part of an organization, often a business, through the deployment and manipulation of resources. Early twentieth-century management writer Mary Parker Follett defined management as "the art of getting things done through people."
Jack Welch	In 1986, GE acquired NBC. During the 90s, Jack Welch helped to modernize GE by emphasizing a

Go to **Cram101.com** for the Practice Tests for this Chapter.

shift from manufacturing to services. He also made hundreds of acquisitions and made a push to dominate markets abroad. Welch adopted the Six Sigma quality program in late 1995.

Competitor	Other organizations in the same industry or type of business that provide a good or service to the same set of customers is referred to as a competitor.
Strategic management	A philosophy of management that links strategic planning with dayto-day decision making. Strategic management seeks a fit between an organization's external and internal environments.
Matching	Matching refers to an accounting concept that establishes when expenses are recognized. Expenses are matched with the revenues they helped to generate and are recognized when those revenues are recognized.
Competitive advantage	A business is said to have a competitive advantage when its unique strengths, often based on cost, quality, time, and innovation, offer consumers a greater percieved value and there by differtiating it from its competitors.
Early adopters	Early adopters refers to the 13.5 percent of the population who are leaders in their social setting and act as an information source on new products for other people.
Marketing	Promoting and selling products or services to customers, or prospective customers, is referred to as marketing.
Targeting	In advertizing, targeting is to select a demographic or other group of people to advertise to, and create advertisements appropriately.
Niche	In industry, a niche is a situation or an activity perfectly suited to a person. A niche can imply a working position or an area suited to a person who occupies it. Basically, a job where a person is able to succeed and thrive.
Competitive Strategy	An outline of how a business intends to compete with other firms in the same industry is called competitive strategy.
Revenue	Revenue is a U.S. business term for the amount of money that a company receives from its activities, mostly from sales of products and/or services to customers.
Customer service	The ability of logistics management to satisfy users in terms of time, dependability, communication, and convenience is called the customer service.
Core competency	A company's core competency are things that a firm can (alsosns) do well and that meet the following three conditions. 1. It provides customer benefits, 2. It is hard for competitors to imitate, and 3. it can be leveraged widely to many products and market. A core competency can take various forms, including technical/subject matter knowhow, a reliable process, and/or close relationships with customers and suppliers. It may also include product development or culture such as employee dedication. Modern business theories suggest that most activities that are not part of a company's core competency should be outsourced.
Team building	A term that describes the process of identifying roles for team members and helping the team members succeed in their roles is called team building.
Consideration	Consideration in contract law, a basic requirement for an enforceable agreement under traditional contract principles, defined in this text as legal value, bargained for and given in exchange for an act or promise. In corporation law, cash or property contributed to a corporation in exchange for shares, or a promise to contribute such cash or property.
Business plan	A detailed written statement that describes the nature of the business, the target market, the advantages the business will have in relation to competition, and the resources and qualifications of the owner is referred to as a business plan.
Innovation	Innovation refers to the first commercially successful introduction of a new product, the use

Go to **Cram101.com** for the Practice Tests for this Chapter.

of a new method of production, or the creation of a new form of business organization.

Service	Service refers to a "non tangible product" that is not embodied in a physical good and that typically effects some change in another product, person, or institution. Contrasts with good.
Core	A core is the set of feasible allocations in an economy that cannot be improved upon by subset of the set of the economy's consumers (a coalition). In construction, when the force in an element is within a certain center section, the core, the element will only be under compression.
Forming	The first stage of team development, where the team is formed and the objectives for the team are set is referred to as forming.
Gain	In finance, gain is a profit or an increase in value of an investment such as a stock or bond. Gain is calculated by fair market value or the proceeds from the sale of the investment minus the sum of the purchase price and all costs associated with it.
Controlling	A management function that involves determining whether or not an organization is progressing toward its goals and objectives, and taking corrective action if it is not is called controlling.
Inventory	Tangible property held for sale in the normal course of business or used in producing goods or services for sale is an inventory.
Electronic data interchange	Electronic data interchange refers to the direct exchange between organizations of data via a computer-to-computer interface.
Purchasing	Purchasing refers to the function in a firm that searches for quality material resources, finds the best suppliers, and negotiates the best price for goods and services.
Product line	A group of products that are physically similar or are intended for a similar market are called the product line.
Organization structure	The system of task, reporting, and authority relationships within which the organization does its work is referred to as the organization structure.
Big Business	Big business is usually used as a pejorative reference to the significant economic and political power which large and powerful corporations (especially multinational corporations), are capable of wielding.
Mistake	In contract law a mistake is incorrect understanding by one or more parties to a contract and may be used as grounds to invalidate the agreement. Common law has identified three different types of mistake in contract: unilateral mistake, mutual mistake, and common mistake.
Organizational structure	Organizational structure is the way in which the interrelated groups of an organization are constructed. From a managerial point of view the main concerns are ensuring effective communication and coordination.
Operation	A standardized method or technique that is performed repetitively, often on different materials resulting in different finished goods is called an operation.
Continuous process	An uninterrupted production process in which long production runs turn out finished goods over time is called continuous process.
Strategic planning	The process of determining the major goals of the organization and the policies and strategies for obtaining and using resources to achieve those goals is called strategic planning.
Mission statement	Mission statement refers to an outline of the fundamental purposes of an organization.

Go to **Cram101.com** for the Practice Tests for this Chapter.

Option	A contract that gives the purchaser the option to buy or sell the underlying financial instrument at a specified price, called the exercise price or strike price, within a specific period of time.
Strategic plan	The formal document that presents the ways and means by which a strategic goal will be achieved is a strategic plan. A long-term flexible plan that does not regulate activities but rather outlines the means to achieve certain results, and provides the means to alter the course of action should the desired ends change.
Action plan	Action plan refers to a written document that includes the steps the trainee and manager will take to ensure that training transfers to the job.
Lender	Suppliers and financial institutions that lend money to companies is referred to as a lender.
Market share	That fraction of an industry's output accounted for by an individual firm or group of firms is called market share.
Shares	Shares refer to an equity security, representing a shareholder's ownership of a corporation. Shares are one of a finite number of equal portions in the capital of a company, entitling the owner to a proportion of distributed, non-reinvested profits known as dividends and to a portion of the value of the company in case of liquidation.
Context	The effect of the background under which a message often takes on more and richer meaning is a context. Context is especially important in cross-cultural interactions because some cultures are said to be high context or low context.
Alignment	Term that refers to optimal coordination among disparate departments and divisions within a firm is referred to as alignment.
Firm	An organization that employs resources to produce a good or service for profit and owns and operates one or more plants is referred to as a firm.
Social responsibility	Social responsibility is a doctrine that claims that an entity whether it is state, government, corporation, organization or individual has a responsibility to society.
Profit	Profit refers to the return to the resource entrepreneurial ability; total revenue minus total cost.
Scope	Scope of a project is the sum total of all projects products and their requirements or features.
Market segments	Market segments refer to the groups that result from the process of market segmentation; these groups ideally have common needs and will respond similarly to a marketing action.
Business opportunity	A business opportunity involves the sale or lease of any product, service, equipment, etc. that will enable the purchaser-licensee to begin a business
Core business	The core business of an organization is an idealized construct intended to express that organization's "main" or "essential" activity.
Cisco Systems	While Cisco Systems was not the first company to develop and sell a router (a device that forwards computer traffic from one network to another), it did create the first commercially successful multi-protocol router to allow previously incompatible computers to communicate using different network protocols.
Corporation	A legal entity chartered by a state or the Federal government that is distinct and separate from the individuals who own it is a corporation. This separation gives the corporation unique powers which other legal entities lack.
Compaq	Compaq was founded in February 1982 by Rod Canion, Jim Harris and Bill Murto, three senior managers from semiconductor manufacturer Texas Instruments. Each invested $1,000 to form the

Go to **Cram101.com** for the Practice Tests for this Chapter.

company. Their first venture capital came from Ben Rosen and Sevin-Rosen partners. It is often told that the architecture of the original PC was first sketched out on a placemat by the founders while dining in the Houston restaurant, House of Pies.

Interest rate	The rate of return on bonds, loans, or deposits. When one speaks of 'the' interest rate, it is usually in a model where there is only one.
Recession	A significant decline in economic activity. In the U.S., recession is approximately defined as two successive quarters of falling GDP, as judged by NBER.
Interest	In finance and economics, interest is the price paid by a borrower for the use of a lender's money. In other words, interest is the amount of paid to "rent" money for a period of time.
Agent	A person who makes economic decisions for another economic actor. A hired manager operates as an agent for a firm's owner.
Domestic	From or in one's own country. A domestic producer is one that produces inside the home country. A domestic price is the price inside the home country. Opposite of 'foreign' or 'world.'.
Industry	A group of firms that produce identical or similar products is an industry. It is also used specifically to refer to an area of economic production focused on manufacturing which involves large amounts of capital investment before any profit can be realized, also called "heavy industry".
Demographic	A demographic is a term used in marketing and broadcasting, to describe a demographic grouping or a market segment.
Trend	Trend refers to the long-term movement of an economic variable, such as its average rate of increase or decrease over enough years to encompass several business cycles.
Key Success Factor	A Key Success Factor is a factor in a given market that is a necessary condition for success.
Success factor	The term success factor refers to the characteristics necessary for high performance; knowledge, skills, abilities, behaviors.
Variable	A variable is something measured by a number; it is used to analyze what happens to other things when the size of that number changes.
Labor	People's physical and mental talents and efforts that are used to help produce goods and services are called labor.
Startup	Any new company can be considered a startup, but the description is usually applied to aggressive young companies that are actively courting private financing from venture capitalists, including wealthy individuals and investment companies.
Southwest airlines	Southwest Airlines is a low-fare airline in the United States. It is the third-largest airline in the world, by number of passengers carried, and the largest in the United States by number of passengers carried domestically.
Airbus	In 2003, for the first time in its 33-year history, Airbus delivered more jet-powered airliners than Boeing. Boeing states that the Boeing 777 has outsold its Airbus counterparts, which include the A340 family as well as the A330-300. The smaller A330-200 competes with the 767, outselling its Boeing counterpart.
Technology	The body of knowledge and techniques that can be used to combine economic resources to produce goods and services is called technology.
Accounting	A system that collects and processes financial information about an organization and reports that information to decision makers is referred to as accounting.

Go to **Cram101.com** for the Practice Tests for this Chapter.

Secondary market	Secondary market refers to the market for securities that have already been issued. It is a market in which investors trade back and forth with each other.
Wall Street Journal	Dow Jones & Company was founded in 1882 by reporters Charles Dow, Edward Jones and Charles Bergstresser. Jones converted the small Customers' Afternoon Letter into The Wall Street Journal, first published in 1889, and began delivery of the Dow Jones News Service via telegraph. The Journal featured the Jones 'Average', the first of several indexes of stock and bond prices on the New York Stock Exchange.
Journal	Book of original entry, in which transactions are recorded in a general ledger system, is referred to as a journal.
Distribution	Distribution in economics, the manner in which total output and income is distributed among individuals or factors.
Tangible	Having a physical existence is referred to as the tangible. Personal property other than real estate, such as cars, boats, stocks, or other assets.
Credit	Credit refers to a recording as positive in the balance of payments, any transaction that gives rise to a payment into the country, such as an export, the sale of an asset, or borrowing from abroad.
Competitive intelligence	Competitive Intelligence is defined as business intelligence focusing on the external competitive environment.
Consultant	A professional that provides expert advice in a particular field or area in which customers occassionaly require this type of knowledge is a consultant.
Tactic	A short-term immediate decision that, in its totality, leads to the achievement of strategic goals is called a tactic.
Trade show	A type of exhibition or forum where manufacturers can display their products to current as well as prospective buyers is referred to as trade show.
Credit report	Information about a person's credit history that can be secured from a credit bureau is referred to as credit report.
Knowledge management	Sharing, organizing and disseminating information in the simplest and most relevant way possible for the users of the information is a knowledge management.
Leverage	Leverage is using given resources in such a way that the potential positive or negative outcome is magnified. In finance, this generally refers to borrowing.
Customer database	Customer database refers to a computer database specifically designed for storage, retrieval, and analysis of customer data by marketers.
Asset	An item of property, such as land, capital, money, a share in ownership, or a claim on others for future payment, such as a bond or a bank deposit is an asset.
Knowledge base	Knowledge base refers to a database that includes decision rules for use of the data, which may be qualitative as well as quantitative.
Brain drain	Brain drain refers to the migration of skilled workers out of a country. First applied to the migration of British-trained scientists, physicians, and university teachers in the early 1960's, mostly to the United States.
Intranet	Intranet refers to a companywide network, closed to public access, that uses Internet-type technology. A set of communications links within one company that travel over the Internet but are closed to public access.
Productivity	Productivity refers to the total output of goods and services in a given period of time divided by work hours.

Welfare	Welfare refers to the economic well being of an individual, group, or economy. For individuals, it is conceptualized by a utility function. For groups, including countries and the world, it is a tricky philosophical concept, since individuals fare differently.
Hierarchy	A system of grouping people in an organization according to rank from the top down in which all subordinate managers must report to one person is called a hierarchy.
Broker	In commerce, a broker is a party that mediates between a buyer and a seller. A broker who also acts as a seller or as a buyer becomes a principal party to the deal.
Stock	In financial terminology, stock is the capital raized by a corporation, through the issuance and sale of shares.
Advertising	Advertising refers to paid, nonpersonal communication through various media by organizations and individuals who are in some way identified in the advertising message.
Budget	Budget refers to an account, usually for a year, of the planned expenditures and the expected receipts of an entity. For a government, the receipts are tax revenues.
Forbes	David Churbuck founded online Forbes in 1996. The site drew attention when it uncovered Stephen Glass' journalistic fraud in The New Republic in 1998, a scoop that gave credibility to internet journalism.
Margin	A deposit by a buyer in stocks with a seller or a stockbroker, as security to cover fluctuations in the market in reference to stocks that the buyer has purchased but for which he has not paid is a margin. Commodities are also traded on margin.
Cost leadership	Organization's ability to achieve lower costs relative to competitors through productivity and efficiency improvements, elimination of waste, and tight cost control is cost leadership.
Michael Porter	Michael Porter is a leading contributor to strategic management theory, Porter's main academic objectives focus on how a firm or a region, can build a competitive advantage and develop competitive strategy. Porter's strategic system consists primarily of 5 forces analysis, strategic groups, the value chain, and market positioning stratagies.
Leadership	Management merely consists of leadership applied to business situations; or in other words: management forms a sub-set of the broader process of leadership.
Cost Leadership Strategy	Using a serious commitment to reducing expenses that, in turn, lowers the price of the items sold in a relatively broad array of market segments is called cost leadership strategy.
Price floor	Price floor refers to a government-imposed lower limit on the price that may be charged for a product. If that limit is binding, it implies a situation of excess supply, which the government may need to purchase to keep price from falling below the floor.
Buyer	A buyer refers to a role in the buying center with formal authority and responsibility to select the supplier and negotiate the terms of the contract.
Price war	Price war refers to successive and continued decreases in the prices charged by firms in an oligopolistic industry. Each firm lowers its price below rivals' prices, hoping to increase its sales and revenues at its rivals' expense.
No frills	No frills is the term used to describe any service or product for which the non-essential features have been removed.
Manufacturing costs	Costs incurred in a manufacturing process, which consist of direct material, direct labor, and manufacturing overhead are referred to as manufacturing costs.
Overhead cost	An expenses of operating a business over and above the direct costs of producing a product is an overhead cost. They can include utilities (eg, electricity, telephone), advertizing and marketing, and any other costs not billed directly to the client or included in the price of

	the product.
Manufacturing	Production of goods primarily by the application of labor and capital to raw materials and other intermediate inputs, in contrast to agriculture, mining, forestry, fishing, and services a manufacturing.
Cost driver	Cost driver refers to a factor related to an activity that changes the volume or characteristics of that activity, and in doing so changes its costs. An activity can have more than one cost driver.
Customer loyalty	Marketers tend to define customer loyalty as making repeat purchases. Some argue that it should be defined attitudinally as a strongly positive feeling about the brand.
Positioning	The art and science of fitting the product or service to one or more segments of the market in such a way as to set it meaningfully apart from competition is called positioning.
Loyalty	Marketers tend to define customer loyalty as making repeat purchases. Some argue that it should be defined attitudinally as a strongly positive feeling about the brand.
Differentiation Strategy	Differentiation strategy requires innovation and significant points of difference in product offerings, brand image, higher quality, advanced technology, or superior service in a relatively broad array of market segments.
Profit margin	Profit margin is a measure of profitability. It is calculated using a formula and written as a percentage or a number. Profit margin = Net income before tax and interest / Revenue.
Brand loyalty	The degree to which customers are satisfied, like the brand, and are committed to further purchase is referred to as brand loyalty.
Brand	A name, symbol, or design that identifies the goods or services of one seller or group of sellers and distinguishes them from the goods and services of competitors is a brand.
Total revenue	Total revenue refers to the total number of dollars received by a firm from the sale of a product; equal to the total expenditures for the product produced by the firm; equal to the quantity sold multiplied by the price at which it is sold.
Homogeneous	In the context of procurement/purchasing, homogeneous is used to describe goods that do not vary in their essential characteristic irrespective of the source of supply.
Principal	In agency law, one under whose direction an agent acts and for whose benefit that agent acts is a principal.
Authority	Authority in agency law, refers to an agent's ability to affect his principal's legal relations with third parties. Also used to refer to an actor's legal power or ability to do something. In addition, sometimes used to refer to a statute, case, or other legal source that justifies a particular result.
Switching costs	Switching costs is a term used in microeconomics, strategic management, and marketing to describe any impediment to a customer's changing of suppliers. In many markets, consumers are forced to incur costs when switching from one supplier to another. These costs are called switching costs and can come in many different shapes.
Emerging market	The term emerging market is commonly used to describe business and market activity in industrializing or emerging regions of the world.
Market niche	A market niche or niche market is a focused, targetable portion of a market. By definition, then, a business that focuses on a niche market is addressing a need for a product or service that is not being addressed by mainstream providers.
Control process	A process involving gathering processed data, analyzing processed data, and using this information to make adjustments to the process is a control process.

Key Performance Indicator	A Key Performance Indicator is a financial and non-financial metric used to quantify objectives to reflect the strategic performance of an organization.
Balanced scorecard	A framework for implementing strategy by translating an organization's mission and strategy into a set of performance measures is called balanced scorecard.
Comprehensive	A comprehensive refers to a layout accurate in size, color, scheme, and other necessary details to show how a final ad will look. For presentation only, never for reproduction.
Business model	A business model is the instrument by which a business intends to generate revenue and profits. It is a summary of how a company means to serve its employees and customers, and involves both strategy (what an business intends to do) as well as an implementation.
Customer satisfaction	Customer satisfaction is a business term which is used to capture the idea of measuring how satisfied an enterprise's customers are with the organization's efforts in a marketplace.
Return on investment	Return on investment refers to the return a businessperson gets on the money he and other owners invest in the firm; for example, a business that earned $100 on a $1,000 investment would have a ROI of 10 percent: 100 divided by 1000.
Financial measure	A financial measure is often used as a very simple mechanism to describe the performance of a business or investment. Because they are easily calculated they can not only be used to compare year on year results but also to compare and set norms for a particular type of business or investment.
Investment	Investment refers to spending for the production and accumulation of capital and additions to inventories. In a financial sense, buying an asset with the expectation of making a return.
Instrument	Instrument refers to an economic variable that is controlled by policy makers and can be used to influence other variables, called targets. Examples are monetary and fiscal policies used to achieve external and internal balance.
Complexity	The technical sophistication of the product and hence the amount of understanding required to use it is referred to as complexity. It is the opposite of simplicity.
Bottom line	The bottom line is net income on the last line of a income statement.
Policy	Similar to a script in that a policy can be a less than completely rational decision-making method. Involves the use of a pre-existing set of decision steps for any problem that presents itself.
Control system	A control system is a device or set of devices that manage the behavior of other devices. Some devices or systems are not controllable. A control system is an interconnection of components connected or related in such a manner as to command, direct, or regulate itself or another system.
Competitive market	A market in which no buyer or seller has market power is called a competitive market.
Evaluation	The consumer's appraisal of the product or brand on important attributes is called evaluation.
Objective setting	Objective setting is the setting of specific goals which are part of the overall business plan for employees to reach. Performance in reaching these goals is outlined, monitored and measured by the organization.
Assignable	Capable of being lawfully assigned or transferred to another is the assignable.
Brief	Brief refers to a statement of a party's case or legal arguments, usually prepared by an attorney. Also used to make legal arguments before appellate courts.
Devise	In a will, a gift of real property is called a devise.

| Harvard Business Review | Harvard Business Review is a research-based magazine written for business practitioners, it claims a high ranking business readership and enjoys the reverence of academics, executives, and management consultants. It has been the frequent publishing home for well known scholars and management thinkers. |

Go to **Cram101.com** for the Practice Tests for this Chapter.

Partnership	In the common law, a partnership is a type of business entity in which partners share with each other the profits or losses of the business undertaking in which they have all invested.
Corporation	A legal entity chartered by a state or the Federal government that is distinct and separate from the individuals who own it is a corporation. This separation gives the corporation unique powers which other legal entities lack.
Limited liability	Limited liability is a liability that is limited to a partner or investor's investment. Shareholders in a corporation or in a limited liability company cannot lose more money than the value of their shares if the corporation runs into debt, as they are not personally responsible for the corporation's obligations.
Joint venture	Joint venture refers to an undertaking by two parties for a specific purpose and duration, taking any of several legal forms.
S corporation	One designation for a small business corporation is a S corporation.
Liability	A liability is a present obligation of the enterprise arizing from past events, the settlement of which is expected to result in an outflow from the enterprise of resources embodying economic benefits.
Limited liability company	Limited liability company refers to a form of entity allowed by all of the states. The entity is taxed as a partnership in which all members or owners of the limited liability company are treated much like limited partners.
Form of ownership	Distinguishes retail outlets based on whether individuals, corporate chains, or contractual systems own the outlet is called form of ownership.
Entrepreneur	The owner/operator. The person who organizes, manages, and assumes the risks of a firm, taking a new idea or a new product and turning it into a successful business is an entrepreneur.
Firm	An organization that employs resources to produce a good or service for profit and owns and operates one or more plants is referred to as a firm.
Option	A contract that gives the purchaser the option to buy or sell the underlying financial instrument at a specified price, called the exercise price or strike price, within a specific period of time.
Financial liability	A financial liability is something that is owed to another party. This is typically contrasted with an asset which is something of value that is owned.
Capital	Capital generally refers to financial wealth, especially that used to start or maintain a business. In classical economics, capital is one of four factors of production, the others being land and labor and entrepreneurship.
Exchange	The trade of things of value between buyer and seller so that each is better off after the trade is called the exchange.
Downturn	A decline in a stock market or economic cycle is a downturn.
Conversion	Conversion refers to any distinct act of dominion wrongfully exerted over another's personal property in denial of or inconsistent with his rights therein. That tort committed by a person who deals with chattels not belonging to him in a manner that is inconsistent with the ownership of the lawful owner.
Liquidated	Damages made certain by the prior agreement of the parties are called liquidated.
Buyer	A buyer refers to a role in the buying center with formal authority and responsibility to select the supplier and negotiate the terms of the contract.
Sole	A sole proprietorship is a business which legally has no separate existence from its owner.

Go to **Cram101.com** for the Practice Tests for this Chapter.

proprietorship	Hence, the limitations of liability enjoyed by a corporation do not apply.
Consideration	Consideration in contract law, a basic requirement for an enforceable agreement under traditional contract principles, defined in this text as legal value, bargained for and given in exchange for an act or promise. In corporation law, cash or property contributed to a corporation in exchange for shares, or a promise to contribute such cash or property.
Business plan	A detailed written statement that describes the nature of the business, the target market, the advantages the business will have in relation to competition, and the resources and qualifications of the owner is referred to as a business plan.
Net income	Net income is equal to the income that a firm has after subtracting costs and expenses from the total revenue. Expenses will typically include tax expense.
Service	Service refers to a "non tangible product" that is not embodied in a physical good and that typically effects some change in another product, person, or institution. Contrasts with good.
Revenue	Revenue is a U.S. business term for the amount of money that a company receives from its activities, mostly from sales of products and/or services to customers.
Internal Revenue Service	In 1862, during the Civil War, President Lincoln and Congress created the office of Commissioner of Internal Revenue and enacted an income tax to pay war expenses. The position of Commissioner still exists today. The Commissioner is the head of the Internal Revenue Service.
Marketing	Promoting and selling products or services to customers, or prospective customers, is referred to as marketing.
Marketing communication	The communication components of marketing, which include public relations, advertising, personal selling, and sales promotion is a marketing communication.
Business strategy	Business strategy, which refers to the aggregated operational strategies of single business firm or that of an SBU in a diversified corporation refers to the way in which a firm competes in its chosen arenas.
Discount	The difference between the face value of a bond and its selling price, when a bond is sold for less than its face value it's referred to as a discount.
Advertising	Advertising refers to paid, nonpersonal communication through various media by organizations and individuals who are in some way identified in the advertising message.
Brand	A name, symbol, or design that identifies the goods or services of one seller or group of sellers and distinguishes them from the goods and services of competitors is a brand.
Operation	A standardized method or technique that is performed repetitively, often on different materials resulting in different finished goods is called an operation.
License	A license in the sphere of Intellectual Property Rights (IPR) is a document, contract or agreement giving permission or the 'right' to a legally-definable entity to do something (such as manufacture a product or to use a service), or to apply something (such as a trademark), with the objective of achieving commercial gain.
Jurisdiction	The power of a court to hear and decide a case is called jurisdiction. It is the practical authority granted to a formally constituted body or to a person to deal with and make pronouncements on legal matters and, by implication, to administer justice within a defined area of responsibility.
Trade name	A commercial legal name under which a company does business is referred to as the trade name.
Service mark	A mark that distinguishes the services rather than the product of the holder from those of

Go to **Cram101.com** for the Practice Tests for this Chapter.

	its competitors is a service mark.
Trademark	A distinctive word, name, symbol, device, or combination thereof, which enables consumers to identify favored products or services and which may find protection under state or federal law is a trademark.
Competitor	Other organizations in the same industry or type of business that provide a good or service to the same set of customers is referred to as a competitor.
Incentive	An incentive is any factor (financial or non-financial) that provides a motive for a particular course of action, or counts as a reason for preferring one choice to the alternatives.
Expense	In accounting, an expense represents an event in which an asset is used up or a liability is incurred. In terms of the accounting equation, expenses reduce owners' equity.
Profit	Profit refers to the return to the resource entrepreneurial ability; total revenue minus total cost.
Market	A market is, as defined in economics, a social arrangement that allows buyers and sellers to discover information and carry out a voluntary exchange of goods or services.
Asset	An item of property, such as land, capital, money, a share in ownership, or a claim on others for future payment, such as a bond or a bank deposit is an asset.
Brief	Brief refers to a statement of a party's case or legal arguments, usually prepared by an attorney. Also used to make legal arguments before appellate courts.
C corporation	C corporation refers to a separate taxable entity, subject to the rules of Subchapter C of the Code. This business form may create a double taxation effect relative to its shareholders.
Accounting	A system that collects and processes financial information about an organization and reports that information to decision makers is referred to as accounting.
General partnership	A partnership that is owned by one or more general partners. Creditors of a general partnership can collect amounts owed them from both the partnership assets and the assets of the partners individually.
Malfeasance	Malfeasance refers to the doing of an act that a person ought not to do at all. It is to be distinguished from misfeasance; the improper doing of an act that a person might lawfully do.
Plaintiff	A plaintiff is the party who initiates a lawsuit (also known as an action) before a court. By doing so, the plaintiff seeks a legal remedy, and if successful, the court will issue judgment in favour of the plaintiff and make the appropriate court order.
Statute	A statute is a formal, written law of a country or state, written and enacted by its legislative authority, perhaps to then be ratified by the highest executive in the government, and finally published.
Fund	Independent accounting entity with a self-balancing set of accounts segregated for the purposes of carrying on specific activities is referred to as a fund.
Collateral	Property that is pledged to the lender to guarantee payment in the event that the borrower is unable to make debt payments is called collateral.
Capital requirement	The capital requirement is a bank regulation, which sets a framework on how banks and depository institutions must handle their capital. The categorization of assets and capital is highly standardized so that it can be risk weighted.
Financial capital	Common stock, preferred stock, bonds, and retained earnings are financial capital. Financial capital appears on the corporate balance sheet under long-term liabilities and equity.

Go to **Cram101.com** for the Practice Tests for this Chapter.

Contract	A contract is a "promise" or an "agreement" that is enforced or recognized by the law. In the civil law, a contract is considered to be part of the general law of obligations.
Inventory	Tangible property held for sale in the normal course of business or used in producing goods or services for sale is an inventory.
Management accounting	Management accounting measures and reports financial and nonfinancial information that helps managers make decisions to fulfill the goals of an organization. It focuses on internal reporting.
Management	Management characterizes the process of leading and directing all or part of an organization, often a business, through the deployment and manipulation of resources. Early twentieth-century management writer Mary Parker Follett defined management as "the art of getting things done through people."
Creditor	A person to whom a debt or legal obligation is owed, and who has the right to enforce payment of that debt or obligation is referred to as creditor.
Contribution	In business organization law, the cash or property contributed to a business by its owners is referred to as contribution.
Partnership agreement	A document that defines the specific terms of a partnership or business relationship, such as how much work each partner will do and how the profits are divided is a partnership agreement.
Interest	In finance and economics, interest is the price paid by a borrower for the use of a lender's money. In other words, interest is the amount of paid to "rent" money for a period of time.
Complete information	Complete information refers to the assumption that economic agents know everything that they need to know in order to make optimal decisions. Types of incomplete information are uncertainty and asymmetric information.
Arbitration	Arbitration is a form of mediation or conciliation, where the mediating party is given power by the disputant parties to settle the dispute by making a finding. In practice arbitration is generally used as a substitute for judicial systems, particularly when the judicial processes are viewed as too slow, expensive or biased. Arbitration is also used by communities which lack formal law, as a substitute for formal law.
Trust	An arrangement in which shareholders of independent firms agree to give up their stock in exchange for trust certificates that entitle them to a share of the trust's common profits.
Complement	A good that is used in conjunction with another good is a complement. For example, cameras and film would complement eachother.
Foundation	A Foundation is a type of philanthropic organization set up by either individuals or institutions as a legal entity (either as a corporation or trust) with the purpose of distributing grants to support causes in line with the goals of the foundation.
Synergistic effect	In media buying, combining a number of complementary types of media that create advertising awareness greater than the sum of each is called synergistic effect.
Technology	The body of knowledge and techniques that can be used to combine economic resources to produce goods and services is called technology.
Logistics	Those activities that focus on getting the right amount of the right products to the right place at the right time at the lowest possible cost is referred to as logistics.
Commerce	Commerce is the exchange of something of value between two entities. It is the central mechanism from which capitalism is derived.
Undercapital-	Undercapitalization refers to any situation where a business owner cannot acquire the capital

zation	they need. Usually, this refers to a business that cannot afford current operational expenses due to a lack of capital, which can trigger bankruptcy.
General partners	Partners in a limited partnership who invest capital, manage the business, and are personally liable for partnership debts are referred to as general partners.
General partner	An owner who has unlimited liability and is active in managing the firm is a general partner. The individual or firm that organizes and manages the limited partnership. For example a hedge fund.
Limited partner	An owner of a limited partnership who has no right to manage the business but who possesses liability limited to his capital contribution to the business is referred to as limited partner.
Limited partnership	A partnership in which some of the partners are limited partners. At least one of the partners in a limited partnership must be a general partner.
Investment	Investment refers to spending for the production and accumulation of capital and additions to inventories. In a financial sense, buying an asset with the expectation of making a return.
Unlimited liability	Absence of any limits on the maximum amount that an individual may become legally required to pay is called unlimited liability.
Red tape	Red tape is a derisive term for excessive regulations or rigid conformity to formal rules that are considered redundant or bureaucratic and hinders or prevents action or decision-making.
Shares	Shares refer to an equity security, representing a shareholder's ownership of a corporation. Shares are one of a finite number of equal portions in the capital of a company, entitling the owner to a proportion of distributed, non-reinvested profits known as dividends and to a portion of the value of the company in case of liquidation.
Double taxation	The taxation of both corporate net income and the dividends paid from this net income when they become the personal income of households a double taxation.
Attachment	Attachment in general, the process of taking a person's property under an appropriate judicial order by an appropriate officer of the court. Used for a variety of purposes, including the acquisition of jurisdiction over the property seized and the securing of property that may be used to satisfy a debt.
Property	Assets defined in the broadest legal sense. Property includes the unrealized receivables of a cash basis taxpayer, but not services rendered.
Exempt	Employees who are not covered by the Fair Labor Standards Act are exempt. Exempt employees are not eligible for overtime pay.
Homestead exemption	Homestead exemption is a legal regime designed to protect the value of the homes of residents from property taxes, creditors, and circumstances arising from the death of the homeowner spouse.
Homestead	A homestead is the one primary residence of a person, and no other exemption can be claimed on any other property anywhere, even outside the boundaries of the jurisdiction where the exemption is claimed.
Partnership interest	A partners share of the profits and losses of a limited partnership and the right to receive payments on partnership assets is a partnership interest.
Dissolution	Dissolution is the process of admitting or removing a partner in a partnership.
Authority	Authority in agency law, refers to an agent's ability to affect his principal's legal relations with third parties. Also used to refer to an actor's legal power or ability to do

something. In addition, sometimes used to refer to a statute, case, or other legal source that justifies a particular result.

Business philosophy	A business philosophy is any of a range of approaches to accounting, marketing, public relations, operations, training, labor relations, executive time management, investment, and/or corporate governance claimed to improve business performance in some measurable or otherwise provable way.
Controlling	A management function that involves determining whether or not an organization is progressing toward its goals and objectives, and taking corrective action if it is not is called controlling.
Agent	A person who makes economic decisions for another economic actor. A hired manager operates as an agent for a firm's owner.
Bankruptcy	Bankruptcy is a legally declared inability or impairment of ability of an individual or organization to pay their creditors.
Conflict resolution	Conflict resolution is the process of resolving a dispute or a conflict. Successful conflict resolution occurs by providing each side's needs, and adequately addressing their interests so that they are each satisfied with the outcome. Conflict resolution aims to end conflicts before they start or lead to physical fighting.
Termination	The ending of a corporation that occurs only after the winding-up of the corporation's affairs, the liquidation of its assets, and the distribution of the proceeds to the claimants are referred to as a termination.
Winding up	In partnership and corporation law, the orderly liquidation of the business's assets is called winding up.
Certificate of limited partnership	Certificate of limited partnership refers to a document that must be filed with a secretary of state to create a limited partnership.
A share	In finance the term A share has two distinct meanings, both relating to securities. The first is a designation for a 'class' of common or preferred stock. A share of common or preferred stock typically has enhanced voting rights or other benefits compared to the other forms of shares that may have been created. The equity structure, or how many types of shares are offered, is determined by the corporate charter.
Complexity	The technical sophistication of the product and hence the amount of understanding required to use it is referred to as complexity. It is the opposite of simplicity.
Stock exchange	A stock exchange is a corporation or mutual organization which provides facilities for stock brokers and traders, to trade company stocks and other securities.
Master limited partnership	A partnership that looks much like a corporation in that it acts like a corporation and is traded on the stock exchanges like a corporation, but is taxed like a partnership and thus avoids the corporate income tax is a master limited partnership.
Stock	In financial terminology, stock is the capital raized by a corporation, through the issuance and sale of shares.
Openness	Openness refers to the extent to which an economy is open, often measured by the ratio of its trade to GDP.
Limited liability partnership	Limited liability partnership refers to a form of business organization allowed by many of the states, where partners have a form of limited liability, similar to that of the shareholders of a corporation.
Regulation	Regulation refers to restrictions state and federal laws place on business with regard to the

conduct of its activities.

Domestic corporation	A corporation in the state in which it was formed is a domestic corporation.
Domestic	From or in one's own country. A domestic producer is one that produces inside the home country. A domestic price is the price inside the home country. Opposite of 'foreign' or 'world.'.
Foreign corporation	Foreign corporation refers to a corporation incorporated in one state doing business in another state. A corporation doing business in a jurisdiction in which it was not formed.
Alien corporation	A corporation incorporated in one country that is doing business in another country is called alien corporation.
Shareholder	A shareholder is an individual or company (including a corporation) that legally owns one or more shares of stock in a joined stock company.
Publicly held corporation	Publicly held corporation refers to a corporation that may have thousands of stockholders and whose stock is regularly traded on a national securities market.
Closely held corporation	Closely held corporation refers to a corporation where stock ownership is not widely dispersed. Rather, a few shareholders are in control of corporate policy and are in a position to benefit personally from that policy.
Security	Security refers to a claim on the borrower future income that is sold by the borrower to the lender. A security is a type of transferable interest representing financial value.
Incorporation	Incorporation is the forming of a new corporation. The corporation may be a business, a non-profit organization or even a government of a new city or town.
Charter	Charter refers to an instrument or authority from the sovereign power bestowing the right or power to do business under the corporate form of organization. Also, the organic law of a city or town, and representing a portion of the statute law of the state.
Deception	According to the Federal Trade Commission, a misrepresentation, omission, or practice that is likely to mislead the consumer acting reasonably in the circumstances to the consumer's detriment is referred to as deception.
Perpetuity	A perpetuity is an annuity in which the periodic payments begin on a fixed date and continue indefinitely. Fixed coupon payments on permanently invested (irredeemable) sums of money are prime examples of perpetuities. Scholarships paid perpetually from an endowment fit the definition of perpetuity.
Attest	To bear witness to is called attest. To affirm, certify by oath or signature. It is an official act establishing authenticity.
Articles of incorporation	Items on an application filed with a state agency for the formation of a corporation that contain such information as the corporation's name, its purpose, its location, its expected life, provisions for its capital stock, and a list of the members of its board of directors are referred to as articles of incorporation.
Principal	In agency law, one under whose direction an agent acts and for whose benefit that agent acts is a principal.
Capital stock	The total amount of physical capital that has been accumulated, usually in a country is capital stock. Also refers to the total issued capital of a firm, including ordinary and preferred shares.
Par value	The central value of a pegged exchange rate, around which the actual rate is permitted to fluctuate within set bounds is a par value.

Preemptive right	Preemptive right refers to a shareholder's option to purchase new issuances of shares in proportion to the shareholder's current ownership of the corporation.
Stockholder	A stockholder is an individual or company (including a corporation) that legally owns one or more shares of stock in a joined stock company. The shareholders are the owners of a corporation. Companies listed at the stock market strive to enhance shareholder value.
Right of first refusal	In corporation law, a share transfer restriction granting a corporation or its shareholders an option to match the offer that a selling shareholder receives for their share is a right of first refusal.
Bylaw	In corporation law, a document that supplements the articles of incorporation and contains less important rights, powers, and responsibilities of a corporation and its shareholders, officers, and directors is referred to as a bylaw.
Organizational meeting	A meeting that must be held by the initial directors of the corporation after the articles of incorporation are filed is referred to as organizational meeting.
Economy	The income, expenditures, and resources that affect the cost of running a business and household are called an economy.
Gain	In finance, gain is a profit or an increase in value of an investment such as a stock or bond. Gain is calculated by fair market value or the proceeds from the sale of the investment minus the sum of the purchase price and all costs associated with it.
Lender	Suppliers and financial institutions that lend money to companies is referred to as a lender.
Piercing the corporate veil	Holding a shareholder responsible for acts of a corporation due to a shareholder's domination and improper use of the corporation is referred to as piercing the corporate veil.
Pension	A pension is a steady income given to a person (usually after retirement). Pensions are typically payments made in the form of a guaranteed annuity to a retired or disabled employee.
Holding	The holding is a court's determination of a matter of law based on the issue presented in the particular case. In other words: under this law, with these facts, this result.
Board of directors	The group of individuals elected by the stockholders of a corporation to oversee its operations is a board of directors.
Purchase order	A form on which items or services needed by a business firm are specified and then communicated to the vendor is a purchase order.
Private placement	Private placement refers to the sale of securities directly to a financial institution by a corporation. This eliminates the middleman and reduces the cost of issue to the corporation.
Legal entity	A legal entity is a legal construct through which the law allows a group of natural persons to act as if it were an individual for certain purposes. The most common purposes are lawsuits, property ownership, and contracts.
Corporate tax	Corporate tax refers to a direct tax levied by various jurisdictions on the profits made by companies or associations. As a general principle, this varies substantially between jurisdictions.
Dividend	Amount of corporate profits paid out for each share of stock is referred to as dividend.
Loyalty	Marketers tend to define customer loyalty as making repeat purchases. Some argue that it should be defined attitudinally as a strongly positive feeling about the brand.
Employee stock ownership plan	Employee Stock Ownership Plan is a qualified employee-benefit plan in which employees are entitled and encouraged to invest in shares of the company's stock and often at a favorable price. The employer's contributions are tax deductible for the employer and tax deferred for

Go to **Cram101.com** for the Practice Tests for this Chapter.

the employee.

Securities and exchange commission	Securities and exchange commission refers to U.S. government agency that determines the financial statements that public companies must provide to stockholders and the measurement rules that they must use in producing those statements.
Annual report	An annual report is prepared by corporate management that presents financial information including financial statements, footnotes, and the management discussion and analysis.
Nonresident alien	Nonresident alien refers to an individual who is neither a citizen nor a resident of the United States. Citizenship is determined under the immigration and naturalization laws of the United States.
Common stock	Common stock refers to the basic, normal, voting stock issued by a corporation; called residual equity because it ranks after preferred stock for dividend and liquidation distributions.
Liquidation	Liquidation refers to a process whereby the assets of a business are converted to money. The conversion may be coerced by a legal process to pay off the debt of the business, or to satisfy any other business obligation that the business has not voluntarily satisfied.
Succession planning	Succession planning refers to the identification and tracking of high-potential employees capable of filling higher-level managerial positions.
Pension fund	Amounts of money put aside by corporations, nonprofit organizations, or unions to cover part of the financial needs of members when they retire is a pension fund.
Subsidiary	A company that is controlled by another company or corporation is a subsidiary.
Long run	In economic models, the long run time frame assumes no fixed factors of production. Firms can enter or leave the marketplace, and the cost (and availability) of land, labor, raw materials, and capital goods can be assumed to vary.
Small business	Small business refers to a business that is independently owned and operated, is not dominant in its field of operation, and meets certain standards of size in terms of employees or annual receipts.
Production	The creation of finished goods and services using the factors of production: land, labor, capital, entrepreneurship, and knowledge.
Operating agreement	Operating agreement refers to an agreement entered into among members that governs the affairs and business of the LLC and the relations among members, managers, and the LLC.
Forming	The first stage of team development, where the team is formed and the objectives for the team are set is referred to as forming.
Articles of Organization	The formal documents that must be filed at the secretary of state's office of the state of organization of an LLC to form the LLC are called Articles of Organization.
Draft	A signed, written order by which one party instructs another party to pay a specified sum to a third party, at sight or at a specific date is a draft.
Continuity	A media scheduling strategy where a continuous pattern of advertising is used over the time span of the advertising campaign is continuity.
Appeal	Appeal refers to the act of asking an appellate court to overturn a decision after the trial court's final judgment has been entered.
Net profit	Net profit is an accounting term which is commonly used in business. It is equal to the gross revenue for a given time period minus associated expenses.
Distribution	Distribution in economics, the manner in which total output and income is distributed among

individuals or factors.

Customs	Customs is an authority or agency in a country responsible for collecting customs duties and for controlling the flow of people, animals and goods (including personal effects and hazardous items) in and out of the country.
Target audience	That group that composes the present and potential prospects for a product or service is called the target audience.

60

Go to **Cram101.com** for the Practice Tests for this Chapter.

61

Franchising	Franchising is a method of doing business wherein a franchisor licenses trademarks and tried and proven methods of doing business to a franchisee in exchange for a recurring payment, and usually a percentage piece of gross sales or gross profits as well as the annual fees. The term " franchising " is used to describe a wide variety of business systems which may or may not fall into the legal definition provided above.
Franchise	A contractual right to sell certain products or services, use certain trademarks, or perform activities in a geographical region is called a franchise.
Regulation	Regulation refers to restrictions state and federal laws place on business with regard to the conduct of its activities.
Federal trade commission	The commission of five members established by the Federal Trade Commission Act of 1914 to investigate unfair competitive practices of firms, to hold hearings on the complaints of such practices, and to issue cease-and-desist orders when firms were found guilty of unfair practices.
Contract	A contract is a "promise" or an "agreement" that is enforced or recognized by the law. In the civil law, a contract is considered to be part of the general law of obligations.
Service	Service refers to a "non tangible product" that is not embodied in a physical good and that typically effects some change in another product, person, or institution. Contrasts with good.
Economy	The income, expenditures, and resources that affect the cost of running a business and household are called an economy.
Franchisor	A company that develops a product concept and sells others the rights to make and sell the products is referred to as a franchisor.
Marketing	Promoting and selling products or services to customers, or prospective customers, is referred to as marketing.
Trend	Trend refers to the long-term movement of an economic variable, such as its average rate of increase or decrease over enough years to encompass several business cycles.
Retail sale	The sale of goods and services to consumers for their own use is a retail sale.
Industry	A group of firms that produce identical or similar products is an industry. It is also used specifically to refer to an area of economic production focused on manufacturing which involves large amounts of capital investment before any profit can be realized, also called "heavy industry".
Distribution	Distribution in economics, the manner in which total output and income is distributed among individuals or factors.
Management	Management characterizes the process of leading and directing all or part of an organization, often a business, through the deployment and manipulation of resources. Early twentieth-century management writer Mary Parker Follett defined management as "the art of getting things done through people."
Accounting	A system that collects and processes financial information about an organization and reports that information to decision makers is referred to as accounting.
Parent company	Parent company refers to the entity that has a controlling influence over another company. It may have its own operations, or it may have been set up solely for the purpose of owning the Subject Company.
Trade name	A commercial legal name under which a company does business is referred to as the trade name.
Royalties	Remuneration paid to the owners of technology, patents, or trade names for the use of same

Go to **Cram101.com** for the Practice Tests for this Chapter.

name are called royalties.

Insurance	Insurance refers to a system by which individuals can reduce their exposure to risk of large losses by spreading the risks among a large number of persons.
Policy	Similar to a script in that a policy can be a less than completely rational decision-making method. Involves the use of a pre-existing set of decision steps for any problem that presents itself.
Independent business	In business, an independent business as a term of distinction generally refers to privately-owned companies (as opposed to those companies owned publicly through a distribution of shares on the market).
Product line	A group of products that are physically similar or are intended for a similar market are called the product line.
Advertising	Advertising refers to paid, nonpersonal communication through various media by organizations and individuals who are in some way identified in the advertising message.
Toyota	Toyota is a Japanese multinational corporation that manufactures automobiles, trucks and buses. Toyota is the world's second largest automaker by sales. Toyota also provides financial services through its subsidiary, Toyota Financial Services, and participates in other lines of business.
Brand	A name, symbol, or design that identifies the goods or services of one seller or group of sellers and distinguishes them from the goods and services of competitors is a brand.
Licensing	Licensing is a form of strategic alliance which involves the sale of a right to use certain proprietary knowledge (so called intellectual property) in a defined way.
Trademark	A distinctive word, name, symbol, device, or combination thereof, which enables consumers to identify favored products or services and which may find protection under state or federal law is a trademark.
Marketing strategy	Marketing strategy refers to the means by which a marketing goal is to be achieved, usually characterized by a specified target market and a marketing program to reach it.
Quality control	The measurement of products and services against set standards is referred to as quality control.
Control process	A process involving gathering processed data, analyzing processed data, and using this information to make adjustments to the process is a control process.
Comprehensive	A comprehensive refers to a layout accurate in size, color, scheme, and other necessary details to show how a final ad will look. For presentation only, never for reproduction.
Operation	A standardized method or technique that is performed repetitively, often on different materials resulting in different finished goods is called an operation.
License	A license in the sphere of Intellectual Property Rights (IPR) is a document, contract or agreement giving permission or the 'right' to a legally-definable entity to do something (such as manufacture a product or to use a service), or to apply something (such as a trademark), with the objective of achieving commercial gain.
Firm	An organization that employs resources to produce a good or service for profit and owns and operates one or more plants is referred to as a firm.
Aid	Assistance provided by countries and by international institutions such as the World Bank to developing countries in the form of monetary grants, loans at low interest rates, in kind, or a combination of these is called aid. Aid can also refer to assistance of any type rendered to benefit some group or individual.

Partnership	In the common law, a partnership is a type of business entity in which partners share with each other the profits or losses of the business undertaking in which they have all invested.
Trust	An arrangement in which shareholders of independent firms agree to give up their stock in exchange for trust certificates that entitle them to a share of the trust's common profits.
Long run	In economic models, the long run time frame assumes no fixed factors of production. Firms can enter or leave the marketplace, and the cost (and availability) of land, labor, raw materials, and capital goods can be assumed to vary.
Small business	Small business refers to a business that is independently owned and operated, is not dominant in its field of operation, and meets certain standards of size in terms of employees or annual receipts.
Mistake	In contract law a mistake is incorrect understanding by one or more parties to a contract and may be used as grounds to invalidate the agreement. Common law has identified three different types of mistake in contract: unilateral mistake, mutual mistake, and common mistake.
Margin	A deposit by a buyer in stocks with a seller or a stockbroker, as security to cover fluctuations in the market in reference to stocks that the buyer has purchased but for which he has not paid is a margin. Commodities are also traded on margin.
Trial	An examination before a competent tribunal, according to the law of the land, of the facts or law put in issue in a cause, for the purpose of determining such issue is a trial. When the court hears and determines any issue of fact or law for the purpose of determining the rights of the parties, it may be considered a trial.
Learning curve	Learning curve is a function that measures how labor-hours per unit decline as units of production increase because workers are learning and becoming better at their jobs.
Customer service	The ability of logistics management to satisfy users in terms of time, dependability, communication, and convenience is called the customer service.
Domestic	From or in one's own country. A domestic producer is one that produces inside the home country. A domestic price is the price inside the home country. Opposite of 'foreign' or 'world.'.
Capital	Capital generally refers to financial wealth, especially that used to start or maintain a business. In classical economics, capital is one of four factors of production, the others being land and labor and entrepreneurship.
Great Depression	The period of severe economic contraction and high unemployment that began in 1929 and continued throughout the 1930s is referred to as the Great Depression.
Depression	Depression refers to a prolonged period characterized by high unemployment, low output and investment, depressed business confidence, falling prices, and widespread business failures. A milder form of business downturn is a recession.
American Dream	The American Dream is the belief held by many in the United States of America that through hard work, courage, and determination one can achieve a better life for oneself, usually through financial prosperity.
Evaluation	The consumer's appraisal of the product or brand on important attributes is called evaluation.
Raw material	Raw material refers to a good that has not been transformed by production; a primary product.
Consultant	A professional that provides expert advice in a particular field or area in which customers occassionaly require this type of knowledge is a consultant.
Purchasing	Purchasing refers to the function in a firm that searches for quality material resources,

Go to **Cram101.com** for the Practice Tests for this Chapter.

finds the best suppliers, and negotiates the best price for goods and services.

Consideration	Consideration in contract law, a basic requirement for an enforceable agreement under traditional contract principles, defined in this text as legal value, bargained for and given in exchange for an act or promise. In corporation law, cash or property contributed to a corporation in exchange for shares, or a promise to contribute such cash or property.
Business plan	A detailed written statement that describes the nature of the business, the target market, the advantages the business will have in relation to competition, and the resources and qualifications of the owner is referred to as a business plan.
Inventory management	The planning, coordinating, and controlling activities related to the flow of inventory into, through, and out of an organization is referred to as inventory management.
Inventory	Tangible property held for sale in the normal course of business or used in producing goods or services for sale is an inventory.
Frequency	Frequency refers to the speed of the up and down movements of a fluctuating economic variable; that is, the number of times per unit of time that the variable completes a cycle of up and down movement.
Promotion	Promotion refers to all the techniques sellers use to motivate people to buy products or services. An attempt by marketers to inform people about products and to persuade them to participate in an exchange.
Privilege	Generally, a legal right to engage in conduct that would otherwise result in legal liability is a privilege. Privileges are commonly classified as absolute or conditional. Occasionally, privilege is also used to denote a legal right to refrain from particular behavior.
Compliance	A type of influence process where a receiver accepts the position advocated by a source to obtain favorable outcomes or to avoid punishment is the compliance.
Advertising campaign	A comprehensive advertising plan that consists of a series of messages in a variety of media that center on a single theme or idea is referred to as an advertising campaign.
Contribution	In business organization law, the cash or property contributed to a business by its owners is referred to as contribution.
Fixed asset	Fixed asset, also known as property, plant, and equipment (PP&E), is a term used in accountancy for assets and property which cannot easily be converted into cash. This can be compared with current assets such as cash or bank accounts, which are described as liquid assets. In most cases, only tangible assets are referred to as fixed.
Mortgage	Mortgage refers to a note payable issued for property, such as a house, usually repaid in equal installments consisting of part principle and part interest, over a specified period.
Lease	A contract for the possession and use of land or other property, including goods, on one side, and a recompense of rent or other income on the other is the lease.
Asset	An item of property, such as land, capital, money, a share in ownership, or a claim on others for future payment, such as a bond or a bank deposit is an asset.
Credit	Credit refers to a recording as positive in the balance of payments, any transaction that gives rise to a payment into the country, such as an export, the sale of an asset, or borrowing from abroad.
Administration	Administration refers to the management and direction of the affairs of governments and institutions; a collective term for all policymaking officials of a government; the execution and implementation of public policy.
Lender	Suppliers and financial institutions that lend money to companies is referred to as a lender.

Go to **Cram101.com** for the Practice Tests for this Chapter.

Fund	Independent accounting entity with a self-balancing set of accounts segregated for the purposes of carrying on specific activities is referred to as a fund.
Working capital	The dollar difference between total current assets and total current liabilities is called working capital.
Failure rate	Failure rate is the frequency with an engineered system or component fails, expressed for example in failures per hour. Failure rate is usually time dependent. In the special case when the likelihood of failure remains constant as time passes, failure rate is simply the inverse of the mean time to failure, expressed for example in hours per failure.
Fixture	Fixture refers to a thing that was originally personal property and that has been actually or constructively affixed to the soil itself or to some structure legally a part of the land.
Option	A contract that gives the purchaser the option to buy or sell the underlying financial instrument at a specified price, called the exercise price or strike price, within a specific period of time.
Market	A market is, as defined in economics, a social arrangement that allows buyers and sellers to discover information and carry out a voluntary exchange of goods or services.
Buying power	The dollar amount available to purchase securities on margin is buying power. The amount is calculated by adding the cash held in the brokerage accounts and the amount that could be spent if securities were fully margined to their limit. If an investor uses their buying power, they are purchasing securities on credit.
Quantity discounts	Quantity discounts refer to reductions in unit costs for a larger order.
Quantity discount	A quantity discount is a price reduction given for a large order.
Discount	The difference between the face value of a bond and its selling price, when a bond is sold for less than its face value it's referred to as a discount.
Economies of scale	In economics, returns to scale and economies of scale are related terms that describe what happens as the scale of production increases. They are different terms and not to be used interchangeably.
Zoning ordinances	Local laws that are adopted by municipalities and local governments to regulate land use within their boundaries are zoning ordinances. Zoning ordinances are adopted and enforced to protect the health, safety, morals, and general welfare of the community.
Ordinance	Ordinance refers to a legislative enactment of a county or an incorporated city or town. A law made by a non-sovereign body such as a city council or a colony.
Zoning	Government restrictions on the use of private property in order to ensure the orderly growth and development of a community and to protect the health, safety, and welfare of citizens is called zoning.
Demographic	A demographic is a term used in marketing and broadcasting, to describe a demographic grouping or a market segment.
Exclusive distribution	Distribution that sends products to only one retail outlet in a given geographic area is an exclusive distribution.
Profit	Profit refers to the return to the resource entrepreneurial ability; total revenue minus total cost.
Grant	Grant refers to an intergovernmental transfer of funds . Since the New Deal, state and local governments have become increasingly dependent upon federal grants for an almost infinite

Go to **Cram101.com** for the Practice Tests for this Chapter.

variety of programs.

Appeal	Appeal refers to the act of asking an appellate court to overturn a decision after the trial court's final judgment has been entered.
Franchise agreement	An arrangement whereby someone with a good idea for a business sells the rights to use the business name and sell a product or service to others in a given territory is a franchise agreement.
Fair dealing	Fair dealing is a doctrine of limitations and exceptions to copyright which is found in many of the common law jurisdictions of the Commonwealth of Nations.
Enterprise	Enterprise refers to another name for a business organization. Other similar terms are business firm, sometimes simply business, sometimes simply firm, as well as company, and entity.
Covenant of good faith and fair dealing	Under this implied covenant, the parties to a contract not only are held to the express terms of the contract but also are required to act in 'good faith' and deal fairly in all respects in obtaining the objective of the contract is referred to as covenant of good faith and fair dealing.
Covenant	A covenant is a signed written agreement between two or more parties. Also referred to as a contract.
Entrepreneur	The owner/operator. The person who organizes, manages, and assumes the risks of a firm, taking a new idea or a new product and turning it into a successful business is an entrepreneur.
Committee	A long-lasting, sometimes permanent team in the organization structure created to deal with tasks that recur regularly is the committee.
American Bar Association	The American Bar Association is a voluntary bar association of lawyers and law students, which is not specific to any jurisdiction in the United States. The most important activities are the setting of academic standards for law schools, and the formulation of model legal codes.
Drawback	Drawback refers to rebate of import duties when the imported good is re-exported or used as input to the production of an exported good.
Profit sharing	A compenzation plan in which payments are based on a measure of organization performance and do not become part of the employees' base salary is profit sharing.
Revenue	Revenue is a U.S. business term for the amount of money that a company receives from its activities, mostly from sales of products and/or services to customers.
A share	In finance the term A share has two distinct meanings, both relating to securities. The first is a designation for a 'class' of common or preferred stock. A share of common or preferred stock typically has enhanced voting rights or other benefits compared to the other forms of shares that may have been created. The equity structure, or how many types of shares are offered, is determined by the corporate charter.
Capital requirement	The capital requirement is a bank regulation, which sets a framework on how banks and depository institutions must handle their capital. The categorization of assets and capital is highly standardized so that it can be risk weighted.
Investment	Investment refers to spending for the production and accumulation of capital and additions to inventories. In a financial sense, buying an asset with the expectation of making a return.
Commerce	Commerce is the exchange of something of value between two entities. It is the central mechanism from which capitalism is derived.

Go to **Cram101.com** for the Practice Tests for this Chapter.

Go to **Cram101.com** for the Practice Tests for this Chapter.
And, **NEVER** highlight a book again!

Preparation	Preparation refers to usually the first stage in the creative process. It includes education and formal training.
Total cost	The sum of fixed cost and variable cost is referred to as total cost.
Normal profit	Normal profit refers to the payment made by a firm to obtain and retain entrepreneurial ability; the minimum income entrepreneurial ability must receive to induce it to perform entrepreneurial functions for a firm.
Profit margin	Profit margin is a measure of profitability. It is calculated using a formula and written as a percentage or a number. Profit margin = Net income before tax and interest / Revenue.
Expense	In accounting, an expense represents an event in which an asset is used up or a liability is incurred. In terms of the accounting equation, expenses reduce owners' equity.
Antitrust	Government intervention to alter market structure or prevent abuse of market power is called antitrust.
Supply	Supply is the aggregate amount of any material good that can be called into being at a certain price point; it comprises one half of the equation of supply and demand. In classical economic theory, a curve representing supply is one of the factors that produce price.
Standardization	Standardization, in the context related to technologies and industries, is the process of establishing a technical standard among competing entities in a market, where this will bring benefits without hurting competition.
Disclosure	Disclosure means the giving out of information, either voluntarily or to be in compliance with legal regulations or workplace rules.
Arbitration	Arbitration is a form of mediation or conciliation, where the mediating party is given power by the disputant parties to settle the dispute by making a finding. In practice arbitration is generally used as a substitute for judicial systems, particularly when the judicial processes are viewed as too slow, expensive or biased. Arbitration is also used by communities which lack formal law, as a substitute for formal law.
Deception	According to the Federal Trade Commission, a misrepresentation, omission, or practice that is likely to mislead the consumer acting reasonably in the circumstances to the consumer's detriment is referred to as deception.
Disclosure statement	A statement that is presented to the Court and must contain adequate information about the proposed plan of reorganization that is supplied to the creditors and equity holders is called disclosure statement.
Personnel	A collective term for all of the employees of an organization. Personnel is also commonly used to refer to the personnel management function or the organizational unit responsible for administering personnel programs.
Bankruptcy	Bankruptcy is a legally declared inability or impairment of ability of an individual or organization to pay their creditors.
Utility	Utility refers to the want-satisfying power of a good or service; the satisfaction or pleasure a consumer obtains from the consumption of a good or service.
Estate	An estate is the totality of the legal rights, interests, entitlements and obligations attaching to property. In the context of wills and probate, it refers to the totality of the property which the deceased owned or in which some interest was held.
Logo	Logo refers to device or other brand name that cannot be spoken.
Service mark	A mark that distinguishes the services rather than the product of the holder from those of its competitors is a service mark.

Copyright	The legal right to the proceeds from and control over the use of a created product, such a written work, audio, video, film, or software is a copyright. This right generally extends over the life of the author plus fifty years.
Patent	The legal right to the proceeds from and control over the use of an invented product or process, granted for a fixed period of time, usually 20 years. Patent is one form of intellectual property that is subject of the TRIPS agreement.
Financial statement	Financial statement refers to a summary of all the transactions that have occurred over a particular period.
Fraud	Tax fraud falls into two categories: civil and criminal. Under civil fraud, the IRS may impose as a penalty of an amount equal to as much as 75 percent of the underpayment.
Interest	In finance and economics, interest is the price paid by a borrower for the use of a lender's money. In other words, interest is the amount of paid to "rent" money for a period of time.
Market research	Market research is the process of systematic gathering, recording and analyzing of data about customers, competitors and the market. Market research can help create a business plan, launch a new product or service, fine tune existing products and services, expand into new markets etc. It can be used to determine which portion of the population will purchase the product/service, based on variables like age, gender, location and income level. It can be found out what market characteristics your target market has.
Market opportunities	Market opportunities refer to areas where a company believes there are favorable demand trends, needs, and/or wants that are not being satisfied, and where it can compete effectively.
Trade show	A type of exhibition or forum where manufacturers can display their products to current as well as prospective buyers is referred to as trade show.
Rate of return	A rate of return is a comparison of the money earned (or lost) on an investment to the amount of money invested.
Screening	Screening in economics refers to a strategy of combating adverse selection, one of the potential decision-making complications in cases of asymmetric information.
Litigation	The process of bringing, maintaining, and defending a lawsuit is litigation.
Turnover	Turnover in a financial context refers to the rate at which a provider of goods cycles through its average inventory. Turnover in a human resources context refers to the characteristic of a given company or industry, relative to rate at which an employer gains and loses staff.
Investment banker	Investment banker refers to a financial organization that specializes in selling primary offerings of securities. Investment bankers can also perform other financial functions, such as advising clients, negotiating mergers and takeovers, and selling secondary offerings.
Statutory law	State and federal constitutions, legislative enactments, treaties, and ordinances, in other words, written laws are referred to as statutory law.
Termination	The ending of a corporation that occurs only after the winding-up of the corporation's affairs, the liquidation of its assets, and the distribution of the proceeds to the claimants are referred to as a termination.
Export	In economics, an export is any good or commodity, shipped or otherwise transported out of a country, province, town to another part of the world in a legitimate fashion, typically for use in trade or sale.
Red tape	Red tape is a derisive term for excessive regulations or rigid conformity to formal rules that are considered redundant or bureaucratic and hinders or prevents action or decision-

Go to **Cram101.com** for the Practice Tests for this Chapter.

making.

Market share	That fraction of an industry's output accounted for by an individual firm or group of firms is called market share.
Global advertising	Global advertising refers to the use of the same basic advertising message in all international markets.
Budget	Budget refers to an account, usually for a year, of the planned expenditures and the expected receipts of an entity. For a government, the receipts are tax revenues.
Innovation	Innovation refers to the first commercially successful introduction of a new product, the use of a new method of production, or the creation of a new form of business organization.
Premium	Premium refers to the fee charged by an insurance company for an insurance policy. The rate of losses must be relatively predictable: In order to set the premium (prices) insurers must be able to estimate them accurately.
Free enterprise	Free enterprise refers to a system in which economic agents are free to own property and engage in commercial transactions.
Goodwill	Goodwill is an important accounting concept that describes the value of a business entity not directly attributable to its tangible assets and liabilities.
Complaint	The pleading in a civil case in which the plaintiff states his claim and requests relief is called complaint. In the common law, it is a formal legal document that sets out the basic facts and legal reasons that the filing party (the plaintiffs) believes are sufficient to support a claim against another person, persons, entity or entities (the defendants) that entitles the plaintiff(s) to a remedy (either money damages or injunctive relief).
Buyer	A buyer refers to a role in the buying center with formal authority and responsibility to select the supplier and negotiate the terms of the contract.
Service business	A business firm that provides services to consumers, such as accounting and legal services, is referred to as a service business.
Market niche	A market niche or niche market is a focused, targetable portion of a market. By definition, then, a business that focuses on a niche market is addressing a need for a product or service that is not being addressed by mainstream providers.
Niche	In industry, a niche is a situation or an activity perfectly suited to a person. A niche can imply a working position or an area suited to a person who occupies it. Basically, a job where a person is able to succeed and thrive.
Downsizing	The process of eliminating managerial and non-managerial positions are called downsizing.
Globalization	The increasing world-wide integration of markets for goods, services and capital that attracted special attention in the late 1990s is called globalization.
Entrepreneurship	The assembling of resources to produce new or improved products and technologies is referred to as entrepreneurship.
Coupon	In finance, a coupon is "attached" to a bond, either physically (as with old bonds) or electronically. Each coupon represents a predetermined payment promized to the bond-holder in return for his or her loan of money to the bond-issuer. .
Negotiation	Negotiation is the process whereby interested parties resolve disputes, agree upon courses of action, bargain for individual or collective advantage, and/or attempt to craft outcomes which serve their mutual interests.
Arthur Andersen	Arthur Andersen was once one of the Big Five accounting firms, performing auditing, tax, and consulting services for large corporations. In 2002 the firm voluntarily surrendered its

Go to **Cram101.com** for the Practice Tests for this Chapter.

licenses to practice as Certified Public Accountants in the U.S. pending the result of prosecution by the U.S. Department of Justice over the firm's handling of the auditing of Enron.

Primary market	The market for the raising of new funds as opposed to the trading of securities already in existence is called primary market.
Mobil	Mobil is a major oil company which merged with the Exxon Corporation in 1999. Today Mobil continues as a major brand name within the combined company.
Conversion	Conversion refers to any distinct act of dominion wrongfully exerted over another's personal property in denial of or inconsistent with his rights therein. That tort committed by a person who deals with chattels not belonging to him in a manner that is inconsistent with the ownership of the lawful owner.
Gain	In finance, gain is a profit or an increase in value of an investment such as a stock or bond. Gain is calculated by fair market value or the proceeds from the sale of the investment minus the sum of the purchase price and all costs associated with it.
Targeting	In advertizing, targeting is to select a demographic or other group of people to advertise to, and create advertisements appropriately.
Complementary products	Products that use similar technologies and can coexist in a family of products are called complementary products. They tend to be purchased jointly and whose demands therefore are related.
Pizza Hut	Pizza Hut is the world's largest pizza restaurant chain with nearly 34,000 restaurants, delivery-carry out units, and kiosks in 100 countries
Texaco	Texaco is the name of an American oil company that was merged into Chevron Corporation in 2001. For many years, Texaco was the only company selling gasoline in all 50 states, but this is no longer true.
Piggyback franchising	A variation of franchising in which stores operated by one chain sell the products or services of another franchized firm is piggyback franchising.
Brainstorming	Brainstorming refers to a technique designed to overcome our natural tendency to evaluate and criticize ideas and thereby reduce the creative output of those ideas. People are encouraged to produce ideas/options without criticizing, often at a very fast pace to minimize our natural tendency to criticize.
Big Business	Big business is usually used as a pejorative reference to the significant economic and political power which large and powerful corporations (especially multinational corporations), are capable of wielding.
Wall Street Journal	Dow Jones & Company was founded in 1882 by reporters Charles Dow, Edward Jones and Charles Bergstresser. Jones converted the small Customers' Afternoon Letter into The Wall Street Journal, first published in 1889, and began delivery of the Dow Jones News Service via telegraph. The Journal featured the Jones 'Average', the first of several indexes of stock and bond prices on the New York Stock Exchange.
Journal	Book of original entry, in which transactions are recorded in a general ledger system, is referred to as a journal.
Personal finance	Personal finance is the application of the principles of financial economics to an individual's (or a family's) financial decisions.

Buyout	A buyout is an investment transaction by which the entire or a controlling part of the stock of a company is sold. A firm buysout the stake of the company to strengthen its influence on the company's decision making body. A buyout can take the forms of a leveraged buyout or a management buyout.
Negotiation	Negotiation is the process whereby interested parties resolve disputes, agree upon courses of action, bargain for individual or collective advantage, and/or attempt to craft outcomes which serve their mutual interests.
Entrepreneur	The owner/operator. The person who organizes, manages, and assumes the risks of a firm, taking a new idea or a new product and turning it into a successful business is an entrepreneur.
Market	A market is, as defined in economics, a social arrangement that allows buyers and sellers to discover information and carry out a voluntary exchange of goods or services.
Evaluation	The consumer's appraisal of the product or brand on important attributes is called evaluation.
Purchasing	Purchasing refers to the function in a firm that searches for quality material resources, finds the best suppliers, and negotiates the best price for goods and services.
Financial statement	Financial statement refers to a summary of all the transactions that have occurred over a particular period.
Business opportunity	A business opportunity involves the sale or lease of any product, service, equipment, etc. that will enable the purchaser-licensee to begin a business
Dividend	Amount of corporate profits paid out for each share of stock is referred to as dividend.
Vendor	A person who sells property to a vendee is a vendor. The words vendor and vendee are more commonly applied to the seller and purchaser of real estate, and the words seller and buyer are more commonly applied to the seller and purchaser of personal property.
Policy	Similar to a script in that a policy can be a less than completely rational decision-making method. Involves the use of a pre-existing set of decision steps for any problem that presents itself.
Consultant	A professional that provides expert advice in a particular field or area in which customers occassionaly require this type of knowledge is a consultant.
Investment	Investment refers to spending for the production and accumulation of capital and additions to inventories. In a financial sense, buying an asset with the expectation of making a return.
Revenue	Revenue is a U.S. business term for the amount of money that a company receives from its activities, mostly from sales of products and/or services to customers.
Expense	In accounting, an expense represents an event in which an asset is used up or a liability is incurred. In terms of the accounting equation, expenses reduce owners' equity.
Option	A contract that gives the purchaser the option to buy or sell the underlying financial instrument at a specified price, called the exercise price or strike price, within a specific period of time.
Entrepreneurship	The assembling of resources to produce new or improved products and technologies is referred to as entrepreneurship.
Profit	Profit refers to the return to the resource entrepreneurial ability; total revenue minus total cost.
Buyer	A buyer refers to a role in the buying center with formal authority and responsibility to select the supplier and negotiate the terms of the contract.

Go to **Cram101.com** for the Practice Tests for this Chapter.

Service	Service refers to a "non tangible product" that is not embodied in a physical good and that typically effects some change in another product, person, or institution. Contrasts with good.
Supply	Supply is the aggregate amount of any material good that can be called into being at a certain price point; it comprises one half of the equation of supply and demand. In classical economic theory, a curve representing supply is one of the factors that produce price.
Production	The creation of finished goods and services using the factors of production: land, labor, capital, entrepreneurship, and knowledge.
Operation	A standardized method or technique that is performed repetitively, often on different materials resulting in different finished goods is called an operation.
Trial	An examination before a competent tribunal, according to the law of the land, of the facts or law put in issue in a cause, for the purpose of determining such issue is a trial. When the court hears and determines any issue of fact or law for the purpose of determining the rights of the parties, it may be considered a trial.
Replacement cost	The current purchase price of replacing a property damaged or lost with similar property is the replacement cost.
Trade credit	Trade credit refers to an amount that is loaned to an exporter to be repaid when the exports are paid for by the foreign importer.
Inventory	Tangible property held for sale in the normal course of business or used in producing goods or services for sale is an inventory.
Credit	Credit refers to a recording as positive in the balance of payments, any transaction that gives rise to a payment into the country, such as an export, the sale of an asset, or borrowing from abroad.
Balance	In banking and accountancy, the outstanding balance is the amount of money owned, (or due), that remains in a deposit account (or a loan account) at a given date, after all past remittances, payments and withdrawal have been accounted for. It can be positive (then, in the balance sheet of a firm, it is an asset) or negative (a liability).
Leverage	Leverage is using given resources in such a way that the potential positive or negative outcome is magnified. In finance, this generally refers to borrowing.
Lender	Suppliers and financial institutions that lend money to companies is referred to as a lender.
Consideration	Consideration in contract law, a basic requirement for an enforceable agreement under traditional contract principles, defined in this text as legal value, bargained for and given in exchange for an act or promise. In corporation law, cash or property contributed to a corporation in exchange for shares, or a promise to contribute such cash or property.
Business plan	A detailed written statement that describes the nature of the business, the target market, the advantages the business will have in relation to competition, and the resources and qualifications of the owner is referred to as a business plan.
Creditor	A person to whom a debt or legal obligation is owed, and who has the right to enforce payment of that debt or obligation is referred to as creditor.
Building code	A building code is a set of rules that specify the minimum acceptable level of safety for constructed objects such as buildings and nonbuilding structures. Their main purpose is to protect public health, safety and general welfare as they relate to the construction and occupancy of buildings and structures.
Lease	A contract for the possession and use of land or other property, including goods, on one side, and a recompense of rent or other income on the other is the lease.

Go to **Cram101.com** for the Practice Tests for this Chapter.

Management	Management characterizes the process of leading and directing all or part of an organization, often a business, through the deployment and manipulation of resources. Early twentieth-century management writer Mary Parker Follett defined management as "the art of getting things done through people."
Termination	The ending of a corporation that occurs only after the winding-up of the corporation's affairs, the liquidation of its assets, and the distribution of the proceeds to the claimants are referred to as a termination.
Demographic	A demographic is a term used in marketing and broadcasting, to describe a demographic grouping or a market segment.
Trend	Trend refers to the long-term movement of an economic variable, such as its average rate of increase or decrease over enough years to encompass several business cycles.
Competitor	Other organizations in the same industry or type of business that provide a good or service to the same set of customers is referred to as a competitor.
Operating expense	In throughput accounting, the cost accounting aspect of Theory of Constraints (TOC), operating expense is the money spent turning inventory into throughput. In TOC, operating expense is limited to costs that vary strictly with the quantity produced, like raw materials and purchased components.
Innovation	Innovation refers to the first commercially successful introduction of a new product, the use of a new method of production, or the creation of a new form of business organization.
Precedent	A previously decided court decision that is recognized as authority for the disposition of future decisions is a precedent.
Balance sheet	A statement of the assets, liabilities, and net worth of a firm or individual at some given time often at the end of its "fiscal year," is referred to as a balance sheet.
Mistake	In contract law a mistake is incorrect understanding by one or more parties to a contract and may be used as grounds to invalidate the agreement. Common law has identified three different types of mistake in contract: unilateral mistake, mutual mistake, and common mistake.
Market value	Market value refers to the price of an asset agreed on between a willing buyer and a willing seller; the price an asset could demand if it is sold on the open market.
Inflation	An increase in the overall price level of an economy, usually as measured by the CPI or by the implicit price deflator is called inflation.
Real value	Real value is the value of anything expressed in money of the day with the effects of inflation removed.
Asset	An item of property, such as land, capital, money, a share in ownership, or a claim on others for future payment, such as a bond or a bank deposit is an asset.
Accounts receivable	Accounts receivable is one of a series of accounting transactions dealing with the billing of customers which owe money to a person, company or organization for goods and services that have been provided to the customer. This is typically done in a one person organization by writing an invoice and mailing or delivering it to each customer.
Face value	The nominal or par value of an instrument as expressed on its face is referred to as the face value.
Stock	In financial terminology, stock is the capital raized by a corporation, through the issuance and sale of shares.
Acquisition	A company's purchase of the property and obligations of another company is an acquisition.
Interest	In finance and economics, interest is the price paid by a borrower for the use of a lender's

	money. In other words, interest is the amount of paid to "rent" money for a period of time.
Trade association	An industry trade group or trade association is generally a public relations organization founded and funded by corporations that operate in a specific industry. Its purpose is generally to promote that industry through PR activities such as advertizing, education, political donations, political pressure, publishing, and astroturfing.
Industry	A group of firms that produce identical or similar products is an industry. It is also used specifically to refer to an area of economic production focused on manufacturing which involves large amounts of capital investment before any profit can be realized, also called "heavy industry".
Staffing	Staffing refers to a management function that includes hiring, motivating, and retaining the best people available to accomplish the company's objectives.
Due diligence	Due diligence is the effort made by an ordinarily prudent or reasonable party to avoid harm to another party or himself. Failure to make this effort is considered negligence. Failure to make this effort is considered negligence.
Better Business Bureau	An organization established and funded by businesses that operates primarily at the local level to monitor activities of companies and promote fair advertising and selling practices is a better business bureau.
Business broker	A business broker is a person or firm engaged in the business of enabling other businesses, including internet businesses and websites, to get sold.
Insurance	Insurance refers to a system by which individuals can reduce their exposure to risk of large losses by spreading the risks among a large number of persons.
Broker	In commerce, a broker is a party that mediates between a buyer and a seller. A broker who also acts as a seller or as a buyer becomes a principal party to the deal.
Agent	A person who makes economic decisions for another economic actor. A hired manager operates as an agent for a firm's owner.
Cash flow	In finance, cash flow refers to the amounts of cash being received and spent by a business during a defined period of time, sometimes tied to a specific project. Most of the time they are being used to determine gaps in the liquid position of a company.
Fund	Independent accounting entity with a self-balancing set of accounts segregated for the purposes of carrying on specific activities is referred to as a fund.
Interest payment	The payment to holders of bonds payable, calculated by multiplying the stated rate on the face of the bond by the par, or face, value of the bond. If bonds are issued at a discount or premium, the interest payment does not equal the interest expense.
Balloon payment	Large final payment due at the maturity of a debt that otherwise requires systematic smaller payments over the term of the loan prior to maturity is a balloon payment.
Principal	In agency law, one under whose direction an agent acts and for whose benefit that agent acts is a principal.
Channel	Channel, in communications (sometimes called communications channel), refers to the medium used to convey information from a sender (or transmitter) to a receiver.
Contract	A contract is a "promise" or an "agreement" that is enforced or recognized by the law. In the civil law, a contract is considered to be part of the general law of obligations.
Legal offer	An offer that shows objective intent to enter into the contract, is definite, and is communicated to the offeree is a legal offer.
Closing	The finalization of a real estate sales transaction that passes title to the property from

Go to **Cram101.com** for the Practice Tests for this Chapter.

the seller to the buyer is referred to as a closing. Closing is a sales term which refers to the process of making a sale. It refers to reaching the final step, which may be an exchange of money or acquiring a signature.

Property	Assets defined in the broadest legal sense. Property includes the unrealized receivables of a cash basis taxpayer, but not services rendered.
Liability	A liability is a present obligation of the enterprise arizing from past events, the settlement of which is expected to result in an outflow from the enterprise of resources embodying economic benefits.
Warranty	An obligation of a company to replace defective goods or correct any deficiencies in performance or quality of a product is called a warranty.
Bulk transfer	A bulk transfer, such as is governed by Article Six of the Uniform Commercial Code, usually refers to a series of contracts for transferring the ownership of a business which has a physical inventory of merchandise and fixed capital
Closing date	Date when all advertising material must be submitted to a publication is referred to as the closing date.
Escrow	Escrow is a legal arrangement whereby an asset (often money, but sometimes other property such as art, a deed of title, website, or software source code) is delivered to a third party to be held in trust pending a contingency or the fulfillment of a condition or conditions in a contract.
Stakeholder	A stakeholder is an individual or group with a vested interest in or expectation for organizational performance. Usually stakeholders can either have an effect on or are affected by an organization.
Commerce	Commerce is the exchange of something of value between two entities. It is the central mechanism from which capitalism is derived.
Budget	Budget refers to an account, usually for a year, of the planned expenditures and the expected receipts of an entity. For a government, the receipts are tax revenues.
Firm	An organization that employs resources to produce a good or service for profit and owns and operates one or more plants is referred to as a firm.
Book value	The book value of an asset or group of assets is sometimes the price at which they were originally acquired, in many cases equal to purchase price.
Fixture	Fixture refers to a thing that was originally personal property and that has been actually or constructively affixed to the soil itself or to some structure legally a part of the land.
Aging the accounts receivable	Aging the accounts receivable refers to the analysis of customer credit balances by the length of time they have been unpaid. This technique is used to estimate the proportion of accounts that will be ultimately collected.
Intangible assets	Assets that have special rights but not physical substance are referred to as intangible assets.
Intangible asset	An intangible assets is defined as an asset that is not physical in nature. The most common types are trade secrets (e.g., customer lists and know-how), copyrights, patents, trademarks, and goodwill.
Tangible asset	Assets that have physical substance that cannot easily be converted into cash are referd to as a tangible asset.
Tangible	Having a physical existence is referred to as the tangible. Personal property other than real estate, such as cars, boats, stocks, or other assets.

Downsizing	The process of eliminating managerial and non-managerial positions are called downsizing.
Marketing	Promoting and selling products or services to customers, or prospective customers, is referred to as marketing.
Specialist	A specialist is a trader who makes a market in one or several stocks and holds the limit order book for those stocks.
Debt service	The payments made by a borrower on their debt, usually including both interest payments and partial repayment of principal, are called debt service.
Zoning	Government restrictions on the use of private property in order to ensure the orderly growth and development of a community and to protect the health, safety, and welfare of citizens is called zoning.
Sales forecast	Sales forecast refers to the maximum total sales of a product that a firm expects to sell during a specified time period under specified environmental conditions and its own marketing efforts.
Marketing Plan	Marketing plan refers to a road map for the marketing activities of an organization for a specified future period of time, such as one year or five years.
Product line	A group of products that are physically similar or are intended for a similar market are called the product line.
Lien	In its most extensive meaning, it is a charge on property for the payment or discharge of a debt or duty is referred to as lien.
Assignment	A transfer of property or some right or interest is referred to as assignment.
Covenant	A covenant is a signed written agreement between two or more parties. Also referred to as a contract.
Good title	Good title refers to title that is free from any encumbrances or other defects that are not disclosed but would affect the value of the property.
Uniform Commercial Code	Uniform commercial code refers to a comprehensive commercial law adopted by every state in the United States; it covers sales laws and other commercial laws.
Compliance	A type of influence process where a receiver accepts the position advocated by a source to obtain favorable outcomes or to avoid punishment is the compliance.
Possession	Possession refers to respecting real property, exclusive dominion and control such as owners of like property usually exercise over it. Manual control of personal property either as owner or as one having a qualified right in it.
Lessor	The person who transfers the right of possession and use of goods under the lease is referred to as lessor.
Restrictive covenant	A restrictive covenant is a legal obligation imposed in a deed by the seller upon the buyer of real estate to do or not to do something.
Product liability	Part of tort law that holds businesses liable for harm that results from the production, design, sale, or use of products they market is referred to as product liability.
Contribution	In business organization law, the cash or property contributed to a business by its owners is referred to as contribution.
Pension fund	Amounts of money put aside by corporations, nonprofit organizations, or unions to cover part of the financial needs of members when they retire is a pension fund.
Pension	A pension is a steady income given to a person (usually after retirement). Pensions are typically payments made in the form of a guaranteed annuity to a retired or disabled

employee.

Accounting	A system that collects and processes financial information about an organization and reports that information to decision makers is referred to as accounting.
Sales tax	A sales tax is a tax on consumption. It is normally a certain percentage that is added onto the price of a good or service that is purchased.
Income statement	Income statement refers to a financial statement that presents the revenues and expenses and resulting net income or net loss of a company for a specific period of time.
Creative accounting	Creative accounting refers to an accounting practice that may or may not follow the letter of the rules of standard accounting practices but certainly deviate from the spirit of those rules. They are characterized by excessive complication and the use of novel ways of characterizing income, assets or liabilities.
Small business	Small business refers to a business that is independently owned and operated, is not dominant in its field of operation, and meets certain standards of size in terms of employees or annual receipts.
Fringe benefits	The rewards other than wages that employees receive from their employers and that include pensions, medical and dental insurance, paid vacations, and sick leaves are referred to as fringe benefits.
Fringe benefit	Benefits such as sick-leave pay, vacation pay, pension plans, and health plans that represent additional compenzation to employees beyond base wages is a fringe benefit.
Cash flow forecast	Forecast that predicts the cash inflows and outflows in future periods is a cash flow forecast.It is a company's projected cash receipts and disbursements over a set time horizon.
Valuation	In finance, valuation is the process of estimating the market value of a financial asset or liability. They can be done on assets (for example, investments in marketable securities such as stocks, options, business enterprises, or intangible assets such as patents and trademarks) or on liabilities (e.g., Bonds issued by a company).
Goodwill	Goodwill is an important accounting concept that describes the value of a business entity not directly attributable to its tangible assets and liabilities.
Net worth	Net worth is the total assets minus total liabilities of an individual or company
Commodity	Could refer to any good, but in trade a commodity is usually a raw material or primary product that enters into international trade, such as metals or basic agricultural products.
Marketing strategy	Marketing strategy refers to the means by which a marketing goal is to be achieved, usually characterized by a specified target market and a marketing program to reach it.
Authority	Authority in agency law, refers to an agent's ability to affect his principal's legal relations with third parties. Also used to refer to an actor's legal power or ability to do something. In addition, sometimes used to refer to a statute, case, or other legal source that justifies a particular result.
Invoice	The itemized bill for a transaction, stating the nature of the transaction and its cost. In international trade, the invoice price is often the preferred basis for levying an ad valorem tariff.
Current liability	Current liability refers to a debt that can reasonably be expected to be paid from existing current assets or through the creation of other current liabilities, within one year or the operating cycle, whichever is longer.
Finished goods	Completed products awaiting sale are called finished goods. An item considered a finished good in a supplying plant might be considered a component or raw material in a receiving

Go to **Cram101.com** for the Practice Tests for this Chapter.
And, **NEVER** highlight a book again!

plant.

Current asset	A current asset is an asset on the balance sheet which is expected to be sold or otherwise used up in the near future, usually within one year.
Raw material	Raw material refers to a good that has not been transformed by production; a primary product.
Fixed asset	Fixed asset, also known as property, plant, and equipment (PP&E), is a term used in accountancy for assets and property which cannot easily be converted into cash. This can be compared with current assets such as cash or bank accounts, which are described as liquid assets. In most cases, only tangible assets are referred to as fixed.
Mortgage	Mortgage refers to a note payable issued for property, such as a house, usually repaid in equal installments consisting of part principle and part interest, over a specified period.
Equity	Equity is the name given to the set of legal principles, in countries following the English common law tradition, which supplement strict rules of law where their application would operate harshly, so as to achieve what is sometimes referred to as "natural justice."
Estate	An estate is the totality of the legal rights, interests, entitlements and obligations attaching to property. In the context of wills and probate, it refers to the totality of the property which the deceased owned or in which some interest was held.
Physical asset	A physical asset is an item of economic value that has a tangible or material existence. A physical asset usually refers to cash, equipment, inventory and properties owned by a business.
Depreciation	Depreciation is an accounting and finance term for the method of attributing the cost of an asset across the useful life of the asset. Depreciation is a reduction in the value of a currency in floating exchange rate.
Allowance	Reduction in the selling price of goods extended to the buyer because the goods are defective or of lower quality than the buyer ordered and to encourage a buyer to keep merchandise that would otherwise be returned is the allowance.
Yield	The interest rate that equates a future value or an annuity to a given present value is a yield.
Opportunity cost	The cost of something in terms of opportunity foregone. The opportunity cost to a country of producing a unit more of a good, such as for export or to replace an import, is the quantity of some other good that could have been produced instead.
Inflation premium	Inflation premium refers to a premium to compensate the investor for the eroding effect of inflation on the value of the dollar. The inflation premium ensures that you do not lose the purchasing power of your investment over time.
Premium	Premium refers to the fee charged by an insurance company for an insurance policy. The rate of losses must be relatively predictable: In order to set the premium (prices) insurers must be able to estimate them accurately.
Bond	Bond refers to a debt instrument, issued by a borrower and promising a specified stream of payments to the purchaser, usually regular interest payments plus a final repayment of principal.
Rate of return	A rate of return is a comparison of the money earned (or lost) on an investment to the amount of money invested.
Net earnings	Another name for net income is net earnings. That part of a company's profits remaining after all expenses and taxes have been paid and out of which dividends may be paid.
Capital asset	In accounting, a capital asset is an asset that is recorded as property that creates more

property, e.g. a factory that creates shoes, or a forest that yields a quantity of wood.

Capital	Capital generally refers to financial wealth, especially that used to start or maintain a business. In classical economics, capital is one of four factors of production, the others being land and labor and entrepreneurship.
Net profit	Net profit is an accounting term which is commonly used in business. It is equal to the gross revenue for a given time period minus associated expenses.
Pro forma income	Pro forma income refers to a measure of income that usually excludes items that a company thinks are unusual or nonrecurring; forecast income.
Pro forma income statement	A projection of anticipated sales, expenses, and income is called pro forma income statement. If the projections predict a downturn in profitability, you can make operational changes such as increasing prices or decreasing costs before these projections become reality.
Weighted average	The weighted average unit cost of the goods available for sale for both cost of goods sold and ending inventory.
Perceived risk	The anxieties felt because the consumer cannot anticipate the outcomes of a purchase but believes that there may be negative consequences is called a perceived risk.
Present value	The value today of a stream of payments and/or receipts over time in the future and/or the past, converted to the present using an interest rate. If X_t is the amount in period t and r the interest rate, then present value at time $t=0$ is $V = ?T / t$.
Sweepstakes	Sales promotions consisting of a game of chance requiring no analytical or creative effort by the consumer is a sweepstakes.
Sweepstake	A sweepstake is technically a lottery in which the prize is financed through the tickets sold. In the United States the word has become associated with promotions where prizes are given away for free.
Time value of money	Time value of money is the concept that the value of money varies depending on the timing of the cash flows, given any interest rate greater than zero.
Value of money	Value of money refers to the quantity of goods and services for which a unit of money can be exchanged; the purchasing power of a unit of money; the reciprocal of the price level.
Discount	The difference between the face value of a bond and its selling price, when a bond is sold for less than its face value it's referred to as a discount.
Net present value	Net present value is a standard method in finance of capital budgeting – the planning of long-term investments. Using this method a potential investment project should be undertaken if the present value of all cash inflows minus the present value of all cash outflows (which equals the net present value) is greater than zero.
Earnings per share	Earnings per share refers to annual profit of the corporation divided by the number of shares outstanding.
Preferred stock	Stock that has specified rights over common stock is a preferred stock.
Stock dividend	Stock dividend refers to pro rata distributions of stock or stock rights on common stock. They are usually issued in proportion to shares owned.
Common stock	Common stock refers to the basic, normal, voting stock issued by a corporation; called residual equity because it ranks after preferred stock for dividend and liquidation distributions.
P/E ratio	In finance, the P/E ratio of a stock is used to measure how cheap or expensive share prices are. It is probably the single most consistent red flag to excessive optimism and over-investment.

Drawback	Drawback refers to rebate of import duties when the imported good is re-exported or used as input to the production of an exported good.
Enterprise	Enterprise refers to another name for a business organization. Other similar terms are business firm, sometimes simply business, sometimes simply firm, as well as company, and entity.
Preparation	Preparation refers to usually the first stage in the creative process. It includes education and formal training.
Strike	The withholding of labor services by an organized group of workers is referred to as a strike.
Exit strategy	In entrepreneurship and strategic management an exit strategy is a way to terminate either ones ownership of a company or the operation of some part of the company.
Capital gain	Capital gain refers to the gain in value that the owner of an asset experiences when the price of the asset rises, including when the currency in which the asset is denominated appreciates.
Gain	In finance, gain is a profit or an increase in value of an investment such as a stock or bond. Gain is calculated by fair market value or the proceeds from the sale of the investment minus the sum of the purchase price and all costs associated with it.
Limited partner	An owner of a limited partnership who has no right to manage the business but who possesses liability limited to his capital contribution to the business is referred to as limited partner.
General partner	An owner who has unlimited liability and is active in managing the firm is a general partner. The individual or firm that organizes and manages the limited partnership. For example a hedge fund.
Partnership agreement	A document that defines the specific terms of a partnership or business relationship, such as how much work each partner will do and how the profits are divided is a partnership agreement.
Partnership	In the common law, a partnership is a type of business entity in which partners share with each other the profits or losses of the business undertaking in which they have all invested.
Corporation	A legal entity chartered by a state or the Federal government that is distinct and separate from the individuals who own it is a corporation. This separation gives the corporation unique powers which other legal entities lack.
Leveraged buyout	An attempt by employees, management, or a group of investors to purchase an organization primarily through borrowing is a leveraged buyout.
Remainder	A remainder in property law is a future interest created in a transferee that is capable of becoming possessory upon the natural termination of a prior estate created by the same instrument.
Employee stock ownership plan	Employee Stock Ownership Plan is a qualified employee-benefit plan in which employees are entitled and encouraged to invest in shares of the company's stock and often at a favorable price. The employer's contributions are tax deductible for the employer and tax deferred for the employee.
Trust	An arrangement in which shareholders of independent firms agree to give up their stock in exchange for trust certificates that entitle them to a share of the trust's common profits.
Collateral	Property that is pledged to the lender to guarantee payment in the event that the borrower is unable to make debt payments is called collateral.

Go to **Cram101.com** for the Practice Tests for this Chapter.

Shares	Shares refer to an equity security, representing a shareholder's ownership of a corporation. Shares are one of a finite number of equal portions in the capital of a company, entitling the owner to a proportion of distributed, non-reinvested profits known as dividends and to a portion of the value of the company in case of liquidation.
Shareholder	A shareholder is an individual or company (including a corporation) that legally owns one or more shares of stock in a joined stock company.
Appeal	Appeal refers to the act of asking an appellate court to overturn a decision after the trial court's final judgment has been entered.
Economy	The income, expenditures, and resources that affect the cost of running a business and household are called an economy.
Enabling	Enabling refers to giving workers the education and tools they need to assume their new decision-making powers.
Business risk	The risk related to the inability of the firm to hold its competitive position and maintain stability and growth in earnings is business risk.
Concession	A concession is a business operated under a contract or license associated with a degree of exclusivity in exploiting a business within a certain geographical area. For example, sports arenas or public parks may have concession stands; and public services such as water supply may be operated as concessions.
Exchange	The trade of things of value between buyer and seller so that each is better off after the trade is called the exchange.
Accounts payable	A written record of all vendors to whom the business firm owes money is referred to as accounts payable.
Bankruptcy	Bankruptcy is a legally declared inability or impairment of ability of an individual or organization to pay their creditors.
Utility	Utility refers to the want-satisfying power of a good or service; the satisfaction or pleasure a consumer obtains from the consumption of a good or service.
Payables	Obligations to make future economic sacrifices, usually cash payments, are referred to as payables. Same as current liabilities.
Internal Revenue Service	In 1862, during the Civil War, President Lincoln and Congress created the office of Commissioner of Internal Revenue and enacted an income tax to pay war expenses. The position of Commissioner still exists today. The Commissioner is the head of the Internal Revenue Service.
Liquidation	Liquidation refers to a process whereby the assets of a business are converted to money. The conversion may be coerced by a legal process to pay off the debt of the business, or to satisfy any other business obligation that the business has not voluntarily satisfied.
Limited partnership	A partnership in which some of the partners are limited partners. At least one of the partners in a limited partnership must be a general partner.
Restructuring	Restructuring is the corporate management term for the act of partially dismantling and reorganizing a company for the purpose of making it more efficient and therefore more profitable.
Forming	The first stage of team development, where the team is formed and the objectives for the team are set is referred to as forming.
Cooperative	A business owned and controlled by the people who use it, producers, consumers, or workers with similar needs who pool their resources for mutual gain is called cooperative.

Go to **Cram101.com** for the Practice Tests for this Chapter.

Brief	Brief refers to a statement of a party's case or legal arguments, usually prepared by an attorney. Also used to make legal arguments before appellate courts.

Business plan	A detailed written statement that describes the nature of the business, the target market, the advantages the business will have in relation to competition, and the resources and qualifications of the owner is referred to as a business plan.
Credit	Credit refers to a recording as positive in the balance of payments, any transaction that gives rise to a payment into the country, such as an export, the sale of an asset, or borrowing from abroad.
Lender	Suppliers and financial institutions that lend money to companies is referred to as a lender.
Entrepreneur	The owner/operator. The person who organizes, manages, and assumes the risks of a firm, taking a new idea or a new product and turning it into a successful business is an entrepreneur.
Insurance	Insurance refers to a system by which individuals can reduce their exposure to risk of large losses by spreading the risks among a large number of persons.
Business opportunity	A business opportunity involves the sale or lease of any product, service, equipment, etc. that will enable the purchaser-licensee to begin a business
Mission statement	Mission statement refers to an outline of the fundamental purposes of an organization.
Target market	One or more specific groups of potential consumers toward which an organization directs its marketing program are a target market.
Budget	Budget refers to an account, usually for a year, of the planned expenditures and the expected receipts of an entity. For a government, the receipts are tax revenues.
Market	A market is, as defined in economics, a social arrangement that allows buyers and sellers to discover information and carry out a voluntary exchange of goods or services.
Industry	A group of firms that produce identical or similar products is an industry. It is also used specifically to refer to an area of economic production focused on manufacturing which involves large amounts of capital investment before any profit can be realized, also called "heavy industry".
Small business	Small business refers to a business that is independently owned and operated, is not dominant in its field of operation, and meets certain standards of size in terms of employees or annual receipts.
Firm	An organization that employs resources to produce a good or service for profit and owns and operates one or more plants is referred to as a firm.
Venture capital firm	A financial intermediary that pools the resources of its partners and uses the funds to help entrepreneurs start up new businesses is referred to as a venture capital firm.
Creditworthiness	Creditworthiness indicates whether a borrower has in the past made loan payments when due.
Venture capital	Venture capital is capital provided by outside investors for financing of new, growing or struggling businesses. Venture capital investments generally are high risk investments but offer the potential for above average returns.
Capital	Capital generally refers to financial wealth, especially that used to start or maintain a business. In classical economics, capital is one of four factors of production, the others being land and labor and entrepreneurship.
Fund	Independent accounting entity with a self-balancing set of accounts segregated for the purposes of carrying on specific activities is referred to as a fund.
Operation	A standardized method or technique that is performed repetitively, often on different materials resulting in different finished goods is called an operation.

Go to **Cram101.com** for the Practice Tests for this Chapter.

Investment	Investment refers to spending for the production and accumulation of capital and additions to inventories. In a financial sense, buying an asset with the expectation of making a return.
Driving force	The key external pressure that will shape the future for an organization is a driving force. The driving force in an industry are the main underlying causes of changing industry and competitive conditions.
Financial institution	A financial institution acts as an agent that provides financial services for its clients. Financial institutions generally fall under financial regulation from a government authority.
Trend	Trend refers to the long-term movement of an economic variable, such as its average rate of increase or decrease over enough years to encompass several business cycles.
Federal Reserve	The Federal Reserve System was created via the Federal Reserve Act of December 23rd, 1913. All national banks were required to join the system and other banks could join. The Reserve Banks opened for business on November 16th, 1914. Federal Reserve Notes were created as part of the legislation, to provide an elastic supply of currency.
Economy	The income, expenditures, and resources that affect the cost of running a business and household are called an economy.
Wage	The payment for the service of a unit of labor, per unit time. In trade theory, it is the only payment to labor, usually unskilled labor. In empirical work, wage data may exclude other compenzation, which must be added to get the total cost of employment.
Service	Service refers to a "non tangible product" that is not embodied in a physical good and that typically effects some change in another product, person, or institution. Contrasts with good.
Strategic management	A philosophy of management that links strategic planning with dayto-day decision making. Strategic management seeks a fit between an organization's external and internal environments.
Foundation	A Foundation is a type of philanthropic organization set up by either individuals or institutions as a legal entity (either as a corporation or trust) with the purpose of distributing grants to support causes in line with the goals of the foundation.
Management	Management characterizes the process of leading and directing all or part of an organization, often a business, through the deployment and manipulation of resources. Early twentieth-century management writer Mary Parker Follett defined management as "the art of getting things done through people."
Devise	In a will, a gift of real property is called a devise.
Product line	A group of products that are physically similar or are intended for a similar market are called the product line.
Product life cycle	Product life cycle refers to a series of phases in a product's sales and cash flows over time; these phases, in order of occurrence, are introductory, growth, maturity, and decline.
Competitor	Other organizations in the same industry or type of business that provide a good or service to the same set of customers is referred to as a competitor.
Productivity	Productivity refers to the total output of goods and services in a given period of time divided by work hours.
Advertising	Advertising refers to paid, nonpersonal communication through various media by organizations and individuals who are in some way identified in the advertising message.
Gain	In finance, gain is a profit or an increase in value of an investment such as a stock or bond. Gain is calculated by fair market value or the proceeds from the sale of the investment

109

minus the sum of the purchase price and all costs associated with it.

Tangible	Having a physical existence is referred to as the tangible. Personal property other than real estate, such as cars, boats, stocks, or other assets.
Technology	The body of knowledge and techniques that can be used to combine economic resources to produce goods and services is called technology.
Gap	In December of 1995, Gap became the first major North American retailer to accept independent monitoring of the working conditions in a contract factory producing its garments. Gap is the largest specialty retailer in the United States.
Forming	The first stage of team development, where the team is formed and the objectives for the team are set is referred to as forming.
Patent	The legal right to the proceeds from and control over the use of an invented product or process, granted for a fixed period of time, usually 20 years. Patent is one form of intellectual property that is subject of the TRIPS agreement.
Marketing strategy	Marketing strategy refers to the means by which a marketing goal is to be achieved, usually characterized by a specified target market and a marketing program to reach it.
Marketing	Promoting and selling products or services to customers, or prospective customers, is referred to as marketing.
Profit	Profit refers to the return to the resource entrepreneurial ability; total revenue minus total cost.
Raw material	Raw material refers to a good that has not been transformed by production; a primary product.
Production	The creation of finished goods and services using the factors of production: land, labor, capital, entrepreneurship, and knowledge.
Supply	Supply is the aggregate amount of any material good that can be called into being at a certain price point; it comprises one half of the equation of supply and demand. In classical economic theory, a curve representing supply is one of the factors that produce price.
Proprietary	Proprietary indicates that a party, or proprietor, exercises private ownership, control or use over an item of property, usually to the exclusion of other parties. Where a party, holds or claims proprietary interests in relation to certain types of property (eg. a creative literary work, or software), that property may also be the subject of intellectual property law (eg. copyright or patents).
Mistake	In contract law a mistake is incorrect understanding by one or more parties to a contract and may be used as grounds to invalidate the agreement. Common law has identified three different types of mistake in contract: unilateral mistake, mutual mistake, and common mistake.
Target audience	That group that composes the present and potential prospects for a product or service is called the target audience.
Market niche	A market niche or niche market is a focused, targetable portion of a market. By definition, then, a business that focuses on a niche market is addressing a need for a product or service that is not being addressed by mainstream providers.
Niche	In industry, a niche is a situation or an activity perfectly suited to a person. A niche can imply a working position or an area suited to a person who occupies it. Basically, a job where a person is able to succeed and thrive.
Interest	In finance and economics, interest is the price paid by a borrower for the use of a lender's money. In other words, interest is the amount of paid to "rent" money for a period of time.
Prototype	A prototype is built to test the function of a new design before starting production of a

product.

Brand	A name, symbol, or design that identifies the goods or services of one seller or group of sellers and distinguishes them from the goods and services of competitors is a brand.
Initial public offering	Firms in the process of becoming publicly traded companies will issue shares of stock using an initial public offering, which is merely the process of selling stock for the first time to interested investors.
Bankruptcy	Bankruptcy is a legally declared inability or impairment of ability of an individual or organization to pay their creditors.
Market research	Market research is the process of systematic gathering, recording and analyzing of data about customers, competitors and the market. Market research can help create a business plan, launch a new product or service, fine tune existing products and services, expand into new markets etc. It can be used to determine which portion of the population will purchase the product/service, based on variables like age, gender, location and income level. It can be found out what market characteristics your target market has.
Price point	A price point is a price for which demand is relatively high.
Points	Loan origination fees that may be deductible as interest by a buyer of property. A seller of property who pays points reduces the selling price by the amount of the points paid for the buyer.
Credibility	The extent to which a source is perceived as having knowledge, skill, or experience relevant to a communication topic and can be trusted to give an unbiased opinion or present objective information on the issue is called credibility.
Demographic	A demographic is a term used in marketing and broadcasting, to describe a demographic grouping or a market segment.
Business model	A business model is the instrument by which a business intends to generate revenue and profits. It is a summary of how a company means to serve its employees and customers, and involves both strategy (what an business intends to do) as well as an implementation.
Prototyping	An iterative approach to design in which a series of mock-ups or models are developed until the customer and the designer come to agreement as to the final design is called prototyping.
Banner ad	A banner ad is a form of advertising on the World Wide Web. This form of online advertising entails embedding an advertisement into a web page.
Advertising campaign	A comprehensive advertising plan that consists of a series of messages in a variety of media that center on a single theme or idea is referred to as an advertising campaign.
Promotion	Promotion refers to all the techniques sellers use to motivate people to buy products or services. An attempt by marketers to inform people about products and to persuade them to participate in an exchange.
Competitor analysis	Competitor analysis in marketing and strategic management is an assessment of the strengths and weaknesses of current and potential competitors.
Market share	That fraction of an industry's output accounted for by an individual firm or group of firms is called market share.
Shares	Shares refer to an equity security, representing a shareholder's ownership of a corporation. Shares are one of a finite number of equal portions in the capital of a company, entitling the owner to a proportion of distributed, non-reinvested profits known as dividends and to a portion of the value of the company in case of liquidation.
Trade	An industry trade group or trade association is generally a public relations organization

association	founded and funded by corporations that operate in a specific industry. Its purpose is generally to promote that industry through PR activities such as advertizing, education, political donations, political pressure, publishing, and astroturfing.
Journal	Book of original entry, in which transactions are recorded in a general ledger system, is referred to as a journal.
Targeting	In advertizing, targeting is to select a demographic or other group of people to advertise to, and create advertisements appropriately.
Management team	A management team is directly responsible for managing the day-to-day operations (and profitability) of a company.
Stock option	A stock option is a specific type of option that uses the stock itself as an underlying instrument to determine the option's pay-off and therefore its value.
Incentive	An incentive is any factor (financial or non-financial) that provides a motive for a particular course of action, or counts as a reason for preferring one choice to the alternatives.
Option	A contract that gives the purchaser the option to buy or sell the underlying financial instrument at a specified price, called the exercise price or strike price, within a specific period of time.
Stock	In financial terminology, stock is the capital raized by a corporation, through the issuance and sale of shares.
Contract	A contract is a "promise" or an "agreement" that is enforced or recognized by the law. In the civil law, a contract is considered to be part of the general law of obligations.
Financial statement	Financial statement refers to a summary of all the transactions that have occurred over a particular period.
Certified Public Accountant	Certified Public Accountant refers to an individual in the United States who have passed the Uniform Certified Public Accountant Examination and have met additional state education and experience requirements for certification as a Certified Public Accountant.
Capital expenditures	Major investments in long-term assets such as land, buildings, equipment, or research and development are referred to as capital expenditures.
Capital expenditure	A substantial expenditure that is used by a company to acquire or upgrade physical assets such as equipment, property, industrial buildings, including those which improve the quality and life of an asset is referred to as a capital expenditure.
Income statement	Income statement refers to a financial statement that presents the revenues and expenses and resulting net income or net loss of a company for a specific period of time.
Balance sheet	A statement of the assets, liabilities, and net worth of a firm or individual at some given time often at the end of its "fiscal year," is referred to as a balance sheet.
Cash budget	A projection of anticipated cash flows, usually over a one to two year period is called a cash budget.
Balance	In banking and accountancy, the outstanding balance is the amount of money owned, (or due), that remains in a deposit account (or a loan account) at a given date, after all past remittances, payments and withdrawal have been accounted for. It can be positive (then, in the balance sheet of a firm, it is an asset) or negative (a liability).
Cash flow statement	A cash flow statement is a financial report that shows incoming and outgoing money during a particular period (often monthly or quarterly). The statement shows how changes in balance sheet and income accounts affected cash and cash equivalents and breaks the analysis down

according to operating, investing, and financing activities.

Cash flow	In finance, cash flow refers to the amounts of cash being received and spent by a business during a defined period of time, sometimes tied to a specific project. Most of the time they are being used to determine gaps in the liquid position of a company.
Financial analysis	Financial analysis is the analysis of the accounts and the economic prospects of a firm.
Consultant	A professional that provides expert advice in a particular field or area in which customers occassionaly require this type of knowledge is a consultant.
Aptitude	An aptitude is an innate inborn ability to do a certain kind of work. Aptitudes may be physical or mental. Many of them have been identified and are testable.
Ratio analysis	Ratio analysis refers to an analytical tool designed to identify significant relationships; measures the proportional relationship between two financial statement amounts.
Accounts receivable	Accounts receivable is one of a series of accounting transactions dealing with the billing of customers which owe money to a person, company or organization for goods and services that have been provided to the customer. This is typically done in a one person organization by writing an invoice and mailing or delivering it to each customer.
Cost of goods sold	In accounting, the cost of goods sold describes the direct expenses incurred in producing a particular good for sale, including the actual cost of materials that comprise the good, and direct labor expense in putting the good in salable condition.
Operating expense	In throughput accounting, the cost accounting aspect of Theory of Constraints (TOC), operating expense is the money spent turning inventory into throughput. In TOC, operating expense is limited to costs that vary strictly with the quantity produced, like raw materials and purchased components.
Inventory	Tangible property held for sale in the normal course of business or used in producing goods or services for sale is an inventory.
Expense	In accounting, an expense represents an event in which an asset is used up or a liability is incurred. In terms of the accounting equation, expenses reduce owners' equity.
Working capital	The dollar difference between total current assets and total current liabilities is called working capital.
Vendor	A person who sells property to a vendee is a vendor. The words vendor and vendee are more commonly applied to the seller and purchaser of real estate, and the words seller and buyer are more commonly applied to the seller and purchaser of personal property.
Exit strategy	In entrepreneurship and strategic management an exit strategy is a way to terminate either ones ownership of a company or the operation of some part of the company.
Rate of return	A rate of return is a comparison of the money earned (or lost) on an investment to the amount of money invested.
Consideration	Consideration in contract law, a basic requirement for an enforceable agreement under traditional contract principles, defined in this text as legal value, bargained for and given in exchange for an act or promise. In corporation law, cash or property contributed to a corporation in exchange for shares, or a promise to contribute such cash or property.
Applicant	In many tribunal and administrative law suits, the person who initiates the claim is called the applicant.
Yield	The interest rate that equates a future value or an annuity to a given present value is a yield.

Go to **Cram101.com** for the Practice Tests for this Chapter.

Evaluation	The consumer's appraisal of the product or brand on important attributes is called evaluation.
Equity investment	Equity investment generally refers to the buying and holding of shares of stock on a stock market by individuals and funds in anticipation of income from dividends and capital gain as the value of the stock rises.
Equity	Equity is the name given to the set of legal principles, in countries following the English common law tradition, which supplement strict rules of law where their application would operate harshly, so as to achieve what is sometimes referred to as "natural justice."
Clutter	The nonprogram material that appears in a broadcast environment, including commercials, promotional messages for shows, public service announcements, and the like is called clutter.
Personal finance	Personal finance is the application of the principles of financial economics to an individual's (or a family's) financial decisions.
Jargon	Jargon is terminology, much like slang, that relates to a specific activity, profession, or group. It develops as a kind of shorthand, to express ideas that are frequently discussed between members of a group, and can also have the effect of distinguishing those belonging to a group from those who are not.
Industry attractiveness	Industry attractiveness refers to the relative industry profitability outlook for an industry in relation to the expected average profitability of all industry.
Payback	A value that indicates the time period required to recoup an initial investment is a payback. The payback does not include the time-value-of-money concept.
Aid	Assistance provided by countries and by international institutions such as the World Bank to developing countries in the form of monetary grants, loans at low interest rates, in kind, or a combination of these is called aid. Aid can also refer to assistance of any type rendered to benefit some group or individual.
Proactive	To be proactive is to act before a situation becomes a source of confrontation or crisis. It is the opposite of "retroactive," which refers to actions taken after an event.
Collateral	Property that is pledged to the lender to guarantee payment in the event that the borrower is unable to make debt payments is called collateral.
Liquidity	Liquidity refers to the capacity to turn assets into cash, or the amount of assets in a portfolio that have that capacity.
Security	Security refers to a claim on the borrower future income that is sold by the borrower to the lender. A security is a type of transferable interest representing financial value.
Pledge	In law a pledge (also pawn) is a bailment of personal property as a security for some debt or engagement.
Asset	An item of property, such as land, capital, money, a share in ownership, or a claim on others for future payment, such as a bond or a bank deposit is an asset.
Default	In finance, default occurs when a debtor has not met its legal obligations according to the debt contract, e.g. it has not made a scheduled payment, or violated a covenant (condition) of the debt contract.
Unsecured loan	A loan that's not backed by any specific assets is an unsecured loan. The risk of repossession does not exist. This doesn't mean that the lender cannot take legal action in order to recover his money. However, such a legal process would be significantly longer and more expensive than with secured loans.
Intel	Intel Corporation, founded in 1968 and based in Santa Clara, California, USA, is the world's

largest semiconductor company. Intel is best known for its PC microprocessors, where it maintains roughly 80% market share.

Inflation rate	The percentage increase in the price level per year is an inflation rate. Alternatively, the inflation rate is the rate of decrease in the purchasing power of money.
Interest rate	The rate of return on bonds, loans, or deposits. When one speaks of 'the' interest rate, it is usually in a model where there is only one.
Inflation	An increase in the overall price level of an economy, usually as measured by the CPI or by the implicit price deflator is called inflation.
Corporation	A legal entity chartered by a state or the Federal government that is distinct and separate from the individuals who own it is a corporation. This separation gives the corporation unique powers which other legal entities lack.
Royalties	Remuneration paid to the owners of technology, patents, or trade names for the use of same name are called royalties.
Domestic	From or in one's own country. A domestic producer is one that produces inside the home country. A domestic price is the price inside the home country. Opposite of 'foreign' or 'world.'.
Policy	Similar to a script in that a policy can be a less than completely rational decision-making method. Involves the use of a pre-existing set of decision steps for any problem that presents itself.
Estate	An estate is the totality of the legal rights, interests, entitlements and obligations attaching to property. In the context of wills and probate, it refers to the totality of the property which the deceased owned or in which some interest was held.
Brainstorming	Brainstorming refers to a technique designed to overcome our natural tendency to evaluate and criticize ideas and thereby reduce the creative output of those ideas. People are encouraged to produce ideas/options without criticizing, often at a very fast pace to minimize our natural tendency to criticize.
Business Week	Business Week is a business magazine published by McGraw-Hill. It was first published in 1929 under the direction of Malcolm Muir, who was serving as president of the McGraw-Hill Publishing company at the time. It is considered to be the standard both in industry and among students.
Comprehensive	A comprehensive refers to a layout accurate in size, color, scheme, and other necessary details to show how a final ad will look. For presentation only, never for reproduction.
Forbes	David Churbuck founded online Forbes in 1996. The site drew attention when it uncovered Stephen Glass' journalistic fraud in The New Republic in 1998, a scoop that gave credibility to internet journalism.

Marketing strategy	Marketing strategy refers to the means by which a marketing goal is to be achieved, usually characterized by a specified target market and a marketing program to reach it.
Small business	Small business refers to a business that is independently owned and operated, is not dominant in its field of operation, and meets certain standards of size in terms of employees or annual receipts.
Marketing	Promoting and selling products or services to customers, or prospective customers, is referred to as marketing.
Entrepreneur	The owner/operator. The person who organizes, manages, and assumes the risks of a firm, taking a new idea or a new product and turning it into a successful business is an entrepreneur.
Promotion	Promotion refers to all the techniques sellers use to motivate people to buy products or services. An attempt by marketers to inform people about products and to persuade them to participate in an exchange.
Business plan	A detailed written statement that describes the nature of the business, the target market, the advantages the business will have in relation to competition, and the resources and qualifications of the owner is referred to as a business plan.
Financial plan	The financial plan section of a business plan consists of three financial statements (the income statement, the cash flow projection, and the balance sheet) and a brief analysis of these three statements.
Marketing Plan	Marketing plan refers to a road map for the marketing activities of an organization for a specified future period of time, such as one year or five years.
Service	Service refers to a "non tangible product" that is not embodied in a physical good and that typically effects some change in another product, person, or institution. Contrasts with good.
Competitor	Other organizations in the same industry or type of business that provide a good or service to the same set of customers is referred to as a competitor.
Production	The creation of finished goods and services using the factors of production: land, labor, capital, entrepreneurship, and knowledge.
Operation	A standardized method or technique that is performed repetitively, often on different materials resulting in different finished goods is called an operation.
Market	A market is, as defined in economics, a social arrangement that allows buyers and sellers to discover information and carry out a voluntary exchange of goods or services.
Budget	Budget refers to an account, usually for a year, of the planned expenditures and the expected receipts of an entity. For a government, the receipts are tax revenues.
Distribution	Distribution in economics, the manner in which total output and income is distributed among individuals or factors.
Industry	A group of firms that produce identical or similar products is an industry. It is also used specifically to refer to an area of economic production focused on manufacturing which involves large amounts of capital investment before any profit can be realized, also called "heavy industry".
Venue	A requirement distinct from jurisdiction that the court be geographically situated so that it is the most appropriate and convenient court to try the case is the venue.
Stock	In financial terminology, stock is the capital raized by a corporation, through the issuance and sale of shares.

Safeway	On April 18, 2005, Safeway began a 100 million dollar brand re-positioning campaign labeled "Ingredients for life". This was done in an attempt to differentiate itself from its competitors, and to increase brand involvement. Steve Burd described it as "branding the shopping experience".
Product line	A group of products that are physically similar or are intended for a similar market are called the product line.
Technology	The body of knowledge and techniques that can be used to combine economic resources to produce goods and services is called technology.
Brand	A name, symbol, or design that identifies the goods or services of one seller or group of sellers and distinguishes them from the goods and services of competitors is a brand.
Competitive market	A market in which no buyer or seller has market power is called a competitive market.
Investment	Investment refers to spending for the production and accumulation of capital and additions to inventories. In a financial sense, buying an asset with the expectation of making a return.
Foundation	A Foundation is a type of philanthropic organization set up by either individuals or institutions as a legal entity (either as a corporation or trust) with the purpose of distributing grants to support causes in line with the goals of the foundation.
Target market	One or more specific groups of potential consumers toward which an organization directs its marketing program are a target market.
Market research	Market research is the process of systematic gathering, recording and analyzing of data about customers, competitors and the market. Market research can help create a business plan, launch a new product or service, fine tune existing products and services, expand into new markets etc. It can be used to determine which portion of the population will purchase the product/service, based on variables like age, gender, location and income level. It can be found out what market characteristics your target market has.
Competitive advantage	A business is said to have a competitive advantage when its unique strengths, often based on cost, quality, time, and innovation, offer consumers a greater percieved value and there by differtiating it from its competitors.
DuPont	DuPont was the inventor of CFCs (along with General Motors) and the largest producer of these ozone depleting chemicals (used primarily in aerosol sprays and refrigerants) in the world, with a 25% market share in the late 1980s.
Gain	In finance, gain is a profit or an increase in value of an investment such as a stock or bond. Gain is calculated by fair market value or the proceeds from the sale of the investment minus the sum of the purchase price and all costs associated with it.
Firm	An organization that employs resources to produce a good or service for profit and owns and operates one or more plants is referred to as a firm.
Preference	The act of a debtor in paying or securing one or more of his creditors in a manner more favorable to them than to other creditors or to the exclusion of such other creditors is a preference. In the absence of statute, a preference is perfectly good, but to be legal it must be bona fide, and not a mere subterfuge of the debtor to secure a future benefit to himself or to prevent the application of his property to his debts.
Appeal	Appeal refers to the act of asking an appellate court to overturn a decision after the trial court's final judgment has been entered.
Layout	Layout refers to the physical arrangement of the various parts of an advertisement including the headline, subheads, illustrations, body copy, and any identifying marks.

Demographic	A demographic is a term used in marketing and broadcasting, to describe a demographic grouping or a market segment.
Trend	Trend refers to the long-term movement of an economic variable, such as its average rate of increase or decrease over enough years to encompass several business cycles.
Family business	A family business is a company owned, controlled, and operated by members of one or several families. Many companies that are now publicly held were founded as family businesses. Many family businesses have non-family members as employees, but, particularly in smaller companies, the top positions are often allocated to family members.
Advertising	Advertising refers to paid, nonpersonal communication through various media by organizations and individuals who are in some way identified in the advertising message.
Bankruptcy	Bankruptcy is a legally declared inability or impairment of ability of an individual or organization to pay their creditors.
Fund	Independent accounting entity with a self-balancing set of accounts segregated for the purposes of carrying on specific activities is referred to as a fund.
Mistake	In contract law a mistake is incorrect understanding by one or more parties to a contract and may be used as grounds to invalidate the agreement. Common law has identified three different types of mistake in contract: unilateral mistake, mutual mistake, and common mistake.
Margin	A deposit by a buyer in stocks with a seller or a stockbroker, as security to cover fluctuations in the market in reference to stocks that the buyer has purchased but for which he has not paid is a margin. Commodities are also traded on margin.
Market opportunities	Market opportunities refer to areas where a company believes there are favorable demand trends, needs, and/or wants that are not being satisfied, and where it can compete effectively.
Data mining	The extraction of hidden predictive information from large databases is referred to as data mining.
Customer loyalty	Marketers tend to define customer loyalty as making repeat purchases. Some argue that it should be defined attitudinally as a strongly positive feeling about the brand.
Profit margin	Profit margin is a measure of profitability. It is calculated using a formula and written as a percentage or a number. Profit margin = Net income before tax and interest / Revenue.
Profit	Profit refers to the return to the resource entrepreneurial ability; total revenue minus total cost.
Customer retention	Customer retention refers to the percentage of customers who return to a service provider or continue to purchase a manufactured product.
Purchasing	Purchasing refers to the function in a firm that searches for quality material resources, finds the best suppliers, and negotiates the best price for goods and services.
Discount	The difference between the face value of a bond and its selling price, when a bond is sold for less than its face value it's referred to as a discount.
Buyer	A buyer refers to a role in the buying center with formal authority and responsibility to select the supplier and negotiate the terms of the contract.
Coupon	In finance, a coupon is "attached" to a bond, either physically (as with old bonds) or electronically. Each coupon represents a predetermined payment promized to the bond-holder in return for his or her loan of money to the bond-issuer. .
Basket	A basket is an economic term for a group of several securities created for the purpose of simultaneous buying or selling. Baskets are frequently used for program trading.

Bottom line	The bottom line is net income on the last line of a income statement.
Artificial intelligence	Computers or computer enhaned machines that can be programmed to think, learn, and make decisions in a manner similar to people is is the subject of artificial intelligence.
Voucher	A voucher is an internally generated document that includes spaces for recording transaction data and designated authorizations.
Market share	That fraction of an industry's output accounted for by an individual firm or group of firms is called market share.
Complaint	The pleading in a civil case in which the plaintiff states his claim and requests relief is called complaint. In the common law, it is a formal legal document that sets out the basic facts and legal reasons that the filing party (the plaintiffs) believes are sufficient to support a claim against another person, persons, entity or entities (the defendants) that entitles the plaintiff(s) to a remedy (either money damages or injunctive relief).
Business strategy	Business strategy, which refers to the aggregated operational strategies of single business firm or that of an SBU in a diversified corporation refers to the way in which a firm competes in its chosen arenas.
Boston Consulting Group	The Boston Consulting Group is a management consulting firm founded by Harvard Business School alum Bruce Henderson in 1963. In 1965 Bruce Henderson thought that to survive, much less grow, in a competitive landscape occupied by hundreds of larger and better-known consulting firms, a distinctive identity was needed, and pioneered "Business Strategy" as a special area of expertise.
Expense	In accounting, an expense represents an event in which an asset is used up or a liability is incurred. In terms of the accounting equation, expenses reduce owners' equity.
Business opportunity	A business opportunity involves the sale or lease of any product, service, equipment, etc. that will enable the purchaser-licensee to begin a business
Customer service	The ability of logistics management to satisfy users in terms of time, dependability, communication, and convenience is called the customer service.
Trust	An arrangement in which shareholders of independent firms agree to give up their stock in exchange for trust certificates that entitle them to a share of the trust's common profits.
Customer satisfaction	Customer satisfaction is a business term which is used to capture the idea of measuring how satisfied an enterprise's customers are with the organization's efforts in a marketplace.
Customer orientation	Customer orientation is a set of beliefs/ strategy that customer needs and satisfaction are the priority of an organization. It focuses on dynamic interactions between the organization and customers as well as competitors in the market and its internal stakeholders.
Allocate	Allocate refers to the assignment of income for various tax purposes. A multistate corporation's nonbusiness income usually is distributed to the state where the nonbusiness assets are located; it is not apportioned with the rest of the entity's income.
Credit	Credit refers to a recording as positive in the balance of payments, any transaction that gives rise to a payment into the country, such as an export, the sale of an asset, or borrowing from abroad.
Personal selling	Personal selling is interpersonal communication, often face to face, between a sales representative and an individual or group, usually with the objective of making a sale.
Company culture	Company culture is the term given to the values and practices shared by the employees of a firm.
Continuous	The constant effort to eliminate waste, reduce response time, simplify the design of both

Go to **Cram101.com** for the Practice Tests for this Chapter.

improvement	products and processes, and improve quality and customer service is referred to as continuous improvement.
DMAIC	An acronym for the five phases of a Six Sigma project, DMAIC is the most common application of the Six Sigma methodology employed when an existing process needs to be improved.
Wholesale	According to the United Nations Statistics Division Wholesale is the resale of new and used goods to retailers, to industrial, commercial, institutional or professional users, or to other wholesalers, or involves acting as an agent or broker in buying merchandise for, or selling merchandise, to such persons or companies.
Rate of return	A rate of return is a comparison of the money earned (or lost) on an investment to the amount of money invested.
Quality improvement	Quality is inversely proportional to variability thus quality Improvement is the reduction of variability in products and processes.
Tangibles	Dimension of service quality-appearance of physical facilities, equipment, personnel, and communication materials are called tangibles.
Tangible	Having a physical existence is referred to as the tangible. Personal property other than real estate, such as cars, boats, stocks, or other assets.
Empathy	Empathy refers to dimension of service quality-caring individualized attention provided to customers.
Teamwork	That which occurs when group members work together in ways that utilize their skills well to accomplish a purpose is called teamwork.
Contract	A contract is a "promise" or an "agreement" that is enforced or recognized by the law. In the civil law, a contract is considered to be part of the general law of obligations.
Authority	Authority in agency law, refers to an agent's ability to affect his principal's legal relations with third parties. Also used to refer to an actor's legal power or ability to do something. In addition, sometimes used to refer to a statute, case, or other legal source that justifies a particular result.
Exchange	The trade of things of value between buyer and seller so that each is better off after the trade is called the exchange.
Agent	A person who makes economic decisions for another economic actor. A hired manager operates as an agent for a firm's owner.
Goodwill	Goodwill is an important accounting concept that describes the value of a business entity not directly attributable to its tangible assets and liabilities.
Innovation	Innovation refers to the first commercially successful introduction of a new product, the use of a new method of production, or the creation of a new form of business organization.
Revenue	Revenue is a U.S. business term for the amount of money that a company receives from its activities, mostly from sales of products and/or services to customers.
Research and development	The use of resources for the deliberate discovery of new information and ways of doing things, together with the application of that information in inventing new products or processes is referred to as research and development.
Commodity	Could refer to any good, but in trade a commodity is usually a raw material or primary product that enters into international trade, such as metals or basic agricultural products.
Mission statement	Mission statement refers to an outline of the fundamental purposes of an organization.

131

Core	A core is the set of feasible allocations in an economy that cannot be improved upon by subset of the set of the economy's consumers (a coalition). In construction, when the force in an element is within a certain center section, the core, the element will only be under compression.
Management team	A management team is directly responsible for managing the day-to-day operations (and profitability) of a company.
Management	Management characterizes the process of leading and directing all or part of an organization, often a business, through the deployment and manipulation of resources. Early twentieth-century management writer Mary Parker Follett defined management as "the art of getting things done through people."
Enterprise	Enterprise refers to another name for a business organization. Other similar terms are business firm, sometimes simply business, sometimes simply firm, as well as company, and entity.
Holder	A person in possession of a document of title or an instrument payable or indorsed to him, his order, or to bearer is a holder.
Retail company	Retail company refers to a merchandizing company that buys goods, adds value, and sells the goods to consumers.
Level of service	The degree of service provided to the customer by self, limited, and full-service retailers is referred to as the level of service.
Manufacturing	Production of goods primarily by the application of labor and capital to raw materials and other intermediate inputs, in contrast to agriculture, mining, forestry, fishing, and services a manufacturing.
Focus group	A small group of people who meet under the direction of a discussion leader to communicate their opinions about an organization, its products, or other given issues is a focus group.
Starbucks	Although it has endured much criticism for its purported monopoly on the global coffee-bean market, Starbucks purchases only 3% of the coffee beans grown worldwide. In 2000 the company introduced a line of fair trade products and now offers three options for socially conscious coffee drinkers. According to Starbucks, they purchased 4.8 million pounds of Certified Fair Trade coffee in fiscal year 2004 and 11.5 million pounds in 2005.
Corporation	A legal entity chartered by a state or the Federal government that is distinct and separate from the individuals who own it is a corporation. This separation gives the corporation unique powers which other legal entities lack.
Complexity	The technical sophistication of the product and hence the amount of understanding required to use it is referred to as complexity. It is the opposite of simplicity.
Flowchart	A flowchart is a schematic display of a process. Commonly used to help visualize the content better, or to find flaws in the process.
Variable	A variable is something measured by a number; it is used to analyze what happens to other things when the size of that number changes.
Motivation and productivity	The stage of group development in which members cooperate, help each other, and work toward accomplishing tasks is motivation and productivity.
Productivity	Productivity refers to the total output of goods and services in a given period of time divided by work hours.
Labor	People's physical and mental talents and efforts that are used to help produce goods and services are called labor.

Go to **Cram101.com** for the Practice Tests for this Chapter.

Household	An economic unit that provides the economy with resources and uses the income received to purchase goods and services that satisfy economic wants is called household.
Niche	In industry, a niche is a situation or an activity perfectly suited to a person. A niche can imply a working position or an area suited to a person who occupies it. Basically, a job where a person is able to succeed and thrive.
Cash flow	In finance, cash flow refers to the amounts of cash being received and spent by a business during a defined period of time, sometimes tied to a specific project. Most of the time they are being used to determine gaps in the liquid position of a company.
Home Shopping Network	The Home Shopping Network is a mostly 24-hour shopping network that is seen on cable, satellite, and some terrestrial channels in the United States. It expanded into the first national shopping network three years later on July 1, 1985, It pioneered the concept of the viewer shopping for items in the comfort of their own home.
Inventory	Tangible property held for sale in the normal course of business or used in producing goods or services for sale is an inventory.
Scope	Scope of a project is the sum total of all projects products and their requirements or features.
Security	Security refers to a claim on the borrower future income that is sold by the borrower to the lender. A security is a type of transferable interest representing financial value.
Retail sale	The sale of goods and services to consumers for their own use is a retail sale.
Core competency	A company's core competency are things that a firm can (alsosns) do well and that meet the following three conditions. 1. It provides customer benefits, 2. It is hard for competitors to imitate, and 3. it can be leveraged widely to many products and market. A core competency can take various forms, including technical/subject matter knowhow, a reliable process, and/or close relationships with customers and suppliers. It may also include product development or culture such as employee dedication. Modern business theories suggest that most activities that are not part of a company's core competency should be outsourced.
Advertisement	Advertisement is the promotion of goods, services, companies and ideas, usually by an identified sponsor. Marketers see advertising as part of an overall promotional strategy.
Target audience	That group that composes the present and potential prospects for a product or service is called the target audience.
Users	Users refer to people in the organization who actually use the product or service purchased by the buying center.
Marketing mix	The marketing mix approach to marketing is a model of crafting and implementing marketing strategies. It stresses the "mixing" or blending of various factors in such a way that both organizational and consumer (target markets) objectives are attained.
Inventory control	Inventory control, in the field of loss prevention, are systems designed to introduce technical barriers to shoplifting.
Introductory stage	The first stage of the product life cycle in which sales grow slowly and profit is minimal is the introductory stage.
Growth stage	The second stage of the product life cycle characterized by rapid increases in sales and by the appearance of competitors is referred to as the growth stage.
Peak	Peak refers to the point in the business cycle when an economic expansion reaches its highest point before turning down. Contrasts with trough.
Maturity	Maturity refers to the final payment date of a loan or other financial instrument, after

Go to **Cram101.com** for the Practice Tests for this Chapter.

which point no further interest or principal need be paid.

Product life cycle	Product life cycle refers to a series of phases in a product's sales and cash flows over time; these phases, in order of occurrence, are introductory, growth, maturity, and decline.
Product innovation	The development and sale of a new or improved product is a product innovation. Production of a new product on a commercial basis.
Decline stage	The fourth and last stage of the product life cycle when sales and profits begin to drop is called the decline stage.
Place utility	Adding value to products by having them where people want them is called place utility.
Utility	Utility refers to the want-satisfying power of a good or service; the satisfaction or pleasure a consumer obtains from the consumption of a good or service.
Marketing channel	Individuals and firms involved in the process of making a product or service available for use or consumption by consumers or industrial users is a marketing channel.
Channel	Channel, in communications (sometimes called communications channel), refers to the medium used to convey information from a sender (or transmitter) to a receiver.
Intermediaries	Intermediaries specialize in information either to bring together two parties to a transaction or to buy in order to sell again.
Channel of distribution	A whole set of marketing intermediaries, such as wholesalers and retailers, who join together to transport and store goods in their path from producers to consumers is referred to as channel of distribution.
Industrial goods	Components produced for use in the production of other products are called industrial goods.
Consumer good	Products and services that are ultimately consumed rather than used in the production of another good are a consumer good.
Distribution channel	A distribution channel is a chain of intermediaries, each passing a product down the chain to the next organization, before it finally reaches the consumer or end-user.
Nonprice competition	Competition based on distinguishing one's product by means of product differentiation and then advertising the distinguished product to consumers is referred to as nonprice competition.
Warranty	An obligation of a company to replace defective goods or correct any deficiencies in performance or quality of a product is called a warranty.
Trial	An examination before a competent tribunal, according to the law of the land, of the facts or law put in issue in a cause, for the purpose of determining such issue is a trial. When the court hears and determines any issue of fact or law for the purpose of determining the rights of the parties, it may be considered a trial.
American Management Association	American Management Association International is the world's largest membership-based management development and executive training organization. Their products include instructor led seminars, workshops, conferences, customized corporate programs, online learning, books, newsletters, research surveys and reports.
Primary product	A good that has not been processed and is therefore in its natural state, specifically products of agriculture, forestry, fishing, and mining is referred to as primary product.
Forbes	David Churbuck founded online Forbes in 1996. The site drew attention when it uncovered Stephen Glass' journalistic fraud in The New Republic in 1998, a scoop that gave credibility to internet journalism.
Brand awareness	How quickly or easily a given brand name comes to mind when a product category is mentioned

is brand awareness.

Wall Street Journal	Dow Jones & Company was founded in 1882 by reporters Charles Dow, Edward Jones and Charles Bergstresser. Jones converted the small Customers' Afternoon Letter into The Wall Street Journal, first published in 1889, and began delivery of the Dow Jones News Service via telegraph. The Journal featured the Jones 'Average', the first of several indexes of stock and bond prices on the New York Stock Exchange.
Journal	Book of original entry, in which transactions are recorded in a general ledger system, is referred to as a journal.

138

Go to **Cram101.com** for the Practice Tests for this Chapter.

Financial statement	Financial statement refers to a summary of all the transactions that have occurred over a particular period.
Small business	Small business refers to a business that is independently owned and operated, is not dominant in its field of operation, and meets certain standards of size in terms of employees or annual receipts.
Ratio analysis	Ratio analysis refers to an analytical tool designed to identify significant relationships; measures the proportional relationship between two financial statement amounts.
Financial plan	The financial plan section of a business plan consists of three financial statements (the income statement, the cash flow projection, and the balance sheet) and a brief analysis of these three statements.
Lender	Suppliers and financial institutions that lend money to companies is referred to as a lender.
Entrepreneur	The owner/operator. The person who organizes, manages, and assumes the risks of a firm, taking a new idea or a new product and turning it into a successful business is an entrepreneur.
Statement of cash flow	Reports inflows and outflows of cash during the accounting period in the categories of operating, investing, and financing is a statement of cash flow.
Financial report	Financial report refers to a written statement-also called an accountant's certificate, accountant's opinion, or audit report-prepared by an independent accountant or auditor after an audit.
Income statement	Income statement refers to a financial statement that presents the revenues and expenses and resulting net income or net loss of a company for a specific period of time.
Balance sheet	A statement of the assets, liabilities, and net worth of a firm or individual at some given time often at the end of its "fiscal year," is referred to as a balance sheet.
Cash flow	In finance, cash flow refers to the amounts of cash being received and spent by a business during a defined period of time, sometimes tied to a specific project. Most of the time they are being used to determine gaps in the liquid position of a company.
Balance	In banking and accountancy, the outstanding balance is the amount of money owned, (or due), that remains in a deposit account (or a loan account) at a given date, after all past remittances, payments and withdrawal have been accounted for. It can be positive (then, in the balance sheet of a firm, it is an asset) or negative (a liability).
Firm	An organization that employs resources to produce a good or service for profit and owns and operates one or more plants is referred to as a firm.
Creditor	A person to whom a debt or legal obligation is owed, and who has the right to enforce payment of that debt or obligation is referred to as creditor.
Asset	An item of property, such as land, capital, money, a share in ownership, or a claim on others for future payment, such as a bond or a bank deposit is an asset.
Market value	Market value refers to the price of an asset agreed on between a willing buyer and a willing seller; the price an asset could demand if it is sold on the open market.
Net worth	Net worth is the total assets minus total liabilities of an individual or company
Equity	Equity is the name given to the set of legal principles, in countries following the English common law tradition, which supplement strict rules of law where their application would operate harshly, so as to achieve what is sometimes referred to as "natural justice."
Market	A market is, as defined in economics, a social arrangement that allows buyers and sellers to discover information and carry out a voluntary exchange of goods or services.

Accounts receivable	Accounts receivable is one of a series of accounting transactions dealing with the billing of customers which owe money to a person, company or organization for goods and services that have been provided to the customer. This is typically done in a one person organization by writing an invoice and mailing or delivering it to each customer.
Operating cycle	Operating cycle refers to the time it takes for a company to purchase goods or services from suppliers, sell those goods and services to customers, and collect cash from customers.
Current asset	A current asset is an asset on the balance sheet which is expected to be sold or otherwise used up in the near future, usually within one year.
Fixed asset	Fixed asset, also known as property, plant, and equipment (PP&E), is a term used in accountancy for assets and property which cannot easily be converted into cash. This can be compared with current assets such as cash or bank accounts, which are described as liquid assets. In most cases, only tangible assets are referred to as fixed.
Inventory	Tangible property held for sale in the normal course of business or used in producing goods or services for sale is an inventory.
Intangible assets	Assets that have special rights but not physical substance are referred to as intangible assets.
Intangible asset	An intangible assets is defined as an asset that is not physical in nature. The most common types are trade secrets (e.g., customer lists and know-how), copyrights, patents, trademarks, and goodwill.
Copyright	The legal right to the proceeds from and control over the use of a created product, such a written work, audio, video, film, or software is a copyright. This right generally extends over the life of the author plus fifty years.
Goodwill	Goodwill is an important accounting concept that describes the value of a business entity not directly attributable to its tangible assets and liabilities.
Tangible	Having a physical existence is referred to as the tangible. Personal property other than real estate, such as cars, boats, stocks, or other assets.
Patent	The legal right to the proceeds from and control over the use of an invented product or process, granted for a fixed period of time, usually 20 years. Patent is one form of intellectual property that is subject of the TRIPS agreement.
Wage	The payment for the service of a unit of labor, per unit time. In trade theory, it is the only payment to labor, usually unskilled labor. In empirical work, wage data may exclude other compenzation, which must be added to get the total cost of employment.
Current liability	Current liability refers to a debt that can reasonably be expected to be paid from existing current assets or through the creation of other current liabilities, within one year or the operating cycle, whichever is longer.
Accrued interest	In finance, accrued interest is the interest that has accumulated since the principal investment, or since the previous interest payment if there has been one already. For a financial instrument such as a bond, interest is calculated and paid in set intervals.
Business plan	A detailed written statement that describes the nature of the business, the target market, the advantages the business will have in relation to competition, and the resources and qualifications of the owner is referred to as a business plan.
Liability	A liability is a present obligation of the enterprise arizing from past events, the settlement of which is expected to result in an outflow from the enterprise of resources embodying economic benefits.
Marketing	Promoting and selling products or services to customers, or prospective customers, is

143

referred to as marketing.

Allowance	Reduction in the selling price of goods extended to the buyer because the goods are defective or of lower quality than the buyer ordered and to encourage a buyer to keep merchandise that would otherwise be returned is the allowance.
Interest	In finance and economics, interest is the price paid by a borrower for the use of a lender's money. In other words, interest is the amount of paid to "rent" money for a period of time.
Capital contribution	Capital contribution refers to various means by which a shareholder makes additional funds available to the corporation, sometimes without the receipt of additional stock.
Contribution	In business organization law, the cash or property contributed to a business by its owners is referred to as contribution.
Net income	Net income is equal to the income that a firm has after subtracting costs and expenses from the total revenue. Expenses will typically include tax expense.
Revenue	Revenue is a U.S. business term for the amount of money that a company receives from its activities, mostly from sales of products and/or services to customers.
Expense	In accounting, an expense represents an event in which an asset is used up or a liability is incurred. In terms of the accounting equation, expenses reduce owners' equity.
Capital	Capital generally refers to financial wealth, especially that used to start or maintain a business. In classical economics, capital is one of four factors of production, the others being land and labor and entrepreneurship.
Profit and loss statement	Profit and loss statement refers to another term for the income statement.
Profit	Profit refers to the return to the resource entrepreneurial ability; total revenue minus total cost.
Bottom line	The bottom line is net income on the last line of a income statement.
Investment	Investment refers to spending for the production and accumulation of capital and additions to inventories. In a financial sense, buying an asset with the expectation of making a return.
Net sales	Gross sales less sales returns and allowances and sales discounts are referred to as net sales.
Cost of goods sold	In accounting, the cost of goods sold describes the direct expenses incurred in producing a particular good for sale, including the actual cost of materials that comprise the good, and direct labor expense in putting the good in salable condition.
Total cost	The sum of fixed cost and variable cost is referred to as total cost.
Beginning inventory	Goods on hand at the beginning of the inventory period are referred to as beginning inventory.
Ending inventory	Inventory on hand at the end of the accounting period, shown on the balance sheet in the current assets section is called ending inventory.
Service	Service refers to a "non tangible product" that is not embodied in a physical good and that typically effects some change in another product, person, or institution. Contrasts with good.
Gross profit	Net sales less cost of goods sold is called gross profit.
Net loss	Net loss refers to the amount by which expenses exceed revenues. The difference between income received and expenses, when expenses are greater.

Gross profit margin	Gross Profit Margin equals Gross Profit divided by Revenue, expressed as a percentage. The percentage represents the amount of each dollar of Revenue that results in Gross Profit.
Profit margin	Profit margin is a measure of profitability. It is calculated using a formula and written as a percentage or a number. Profit margin = Net income before tax and interest / Revenue.
Margin	A deposit by a buyer in stocks with a seller or a stockbroker, as security to cover fluctuations in the market in reference to stocks that the buyer has purchased but for which he has not paid is a margin. Commodities are also traded on margin.
Manufacturing	Production of goods primarily by the application of labor and capital to raw materials and other intermediate inputs, in contrast to agriculture, mining, forestry, fishing, and services a manufacturing.
Purchasing	Purchasing refers to the function in a firm that searches for quality material resources, finds the best suppliers, and negotiates the best price for goods and services.
Industry	A group of firms that produce identical or similar products is an industry. It is also used specifically to refer to an area of economic production focused on manufacturing which involves large amounts of capital investment before any profit can be realized, also called "heavy industry".
Operating expense	In throughput accounting, the cost accounting aspect of Theory of Constraints (TOC), operating expense is the money spent turning inventory into throughput. In TOC, operating expense is limited to costs that vary strictly with the quantity produced, like raw materials and purchased components.
Distribution	Distribution in economics, the manner in which total output and income is distributed among individuals or factors.
Indirect cost	Indirect cost refers to a cost that cannot be traced to a particular department.
Fund	Independent accounting entity with a self-balancing set of accounts segregated for the purposes of carrying on specific activities is referred to as a fund.
Working capital	The dollar difference between total current assets and total current liabilities is called working capital.
Total revenue	Total revenue refers to the total number of dollars received by a firm from the sale of a product; equal to the total expenditures for the product produced by the firm; equal to the quantity sold multiplied by the price at which it is sold.
Operation	A standardized method or technique that is performed repetitively, often on different materials resulting in different finished goods is called an operation.
Depreciation	Depreciation is an accounting and finance term for the method of attributing the cost of an asset across the useful life of the asset. Depreciation is a reduction in the value of a currency in floating exchange rate.
Brand	A name, symbol, or design that identifies the goods or services of one seller or group of sellers and distinguishes them from the goods and services of competitors is a brand.
Enterprise	Enterprise refers to another name for a business organization. Other similar terms are business firm, sometimes simply business, sometimes simply firm, as well as company, and entity.
Cash discount	Cash discount refers to a discount offered on merchandise sold to encourage prompt payment; offered by sellers of merchandise and represents sales discounts to the seller when they are used and purchase discounts to the purchaser of the merchandise.
Discount	The difference between the face value of a bond and its selling price, when a bond is sold

for less than its face value it's referred to as a discount.

Credit	Credit refers to a recording as positive in the balance of payments, any transaction that gives rise to a payment into the country, such as an export, the sale of an asset, or borrowing from abroad.
Grant	Grant refers to an intergovernmental transfer of funds . Since the New Deal, state and local governments have become increasingly dependent upon federal grants for an almost infinite variety of programs.
Sales forecast	Sales forecast refers to the maximum total sales of a product that a firm expects to sell during a specified time period under specified environmental conditions and its own marketing efforts.
Option	A contract that gives the purchaser the option to buy or sell the underlying financial instrument at a specified price, called the exercise price or strike price, within a specific period of time.
Entrepreneurship	The assembling of resources to produce new or improved products and technologies is referred to as entrepreneurship.
Pro forma income	Pro forma income refers to a measure of income that usually excludes items that a company thinks are unusual or nonrecurring; forecast income.
Pro forma income statement	A projection of anticipated sales, expenses, and income is called pro forma income statement. If the projections predict a downturn in profitability, you can make operational changes such as increasing prices or decreasing costs before these projections become reality.
Net profit	Net profit is an accounting term which is commonly used in business. It is equal to the gross revenue for a given time period minus associated expenses.
Fixture	Fixture refers to a thing that was originally personal property and that has been actually or constructively affixed to the soil itself or to some structure legally a part of the land.
Financial control	A process in which a firm periodically compares its actual revenues, costs, and expenses with its projected ones is called financial control.
Financial accounting	Financial accounting is the branch of accountancy concerned with the preparation of financial statements for external decision makers, such as stockholders, suppliers, banks and government agencies. The fundamental need for financial accounting is to reduce principal-agent problem by measuring and monitoring agents' performance.
Accounting	A system that collects and processes financial information about an organization and reports that information to decision makers is referred to as accounting.
Vendor	A person who sells property to a vendee is a vendor. The words vendor and vendee are more commonly applied to the seller and purchaser of real estate, and the words seller and buyer are more commonly applied to the seller and purchaser of personal property.
Productivity	Productivity refers to the total output of goods and services in a given period of time divided by work hours.
Financial analysis	Financial analysis is the analysis of the accounts and the economic prospects of a firm.
Financial ratio	A financial ratio is a ratio of two numbers of reported levels or flows of a company. It may be two financial flows categories divided by each other (profit margin, profit/revenue). It may be a level divided by a financial flow (price/earnings). It may be a flow divided by a level (return on equity or earnings/equity). The numerator or denominator may itself be a ratio (PEG ratio).

Sales tax	A sales tax is a tax on consumption. It is normally a certain percentage that is added onto the price of a good or service that is purchased.
Chapter 11 bankruptcy	Chapter 11 bankruptcy governs the process of reorganization under the bankruptcy laws of the United States. It is an attempt to stay in business while a bankruptcy court supervises the "reorganization" of the company's contractual and debt obligations.
Bankruptcy	Bankruptcy is a legally declared inability or impairment of ability of an individual or organization to pay their creditors.
Staffing	Staffing refers to a management function that includes hiring, motivating, and retaining the best people available to accomplish the company's objectives.
Analyst	Analyst refers to a person or tool with a primary function of information analysis, generally with a more limited, practical and short term set of goals than a researcher.
Operating results	Operating results refers to measures that are important to monitoring and tracking the effectiveness of a company's operations.
Ledger	Ledger refers to a specialized accounting book in which information from accounting journals is accumulated into specific categories and posted so that managers can find all the information about one account in the same place.
Standing	Standing refers to the legal requirement that anyone seeking to challenge a particular action in court must demonstrate that such action substantially affects his legitimate interests before he will be entitled to bring suit.
Liquidity ratio	A financial ratio that indicates the organization's ability to meet its current debt obligations is referred to as liquidity ratio.
Liquidity	Liquidity refers to the capacity to turn assets into cash, or the amount of assets in a portfolio that have that capacity.
Business opportunity	A business opportunity involves the sale or lease of any product, service, equipment, etc. that will enable the purchaser-licensee to begin a business
Current ratio	The current ratio is a comparison of a firm's current assets to its current liabilities. The current ratio is an indication of a firm's market liquidity and ability to meet short-term debt obligations.
Quick ratio	The Acid-test or quick ratio measures the ability of a company to use its "near cash" or quick assets to immediately extinguish its current liabilities. Quick assets include those current assets that presumably can be quickly converted to cash at close to their book values.
Solvency	The ability of a company to pay interest as it comes due and to repay the face value of debt at maturity is called solvency.
Marketable securities	Marketable securities refer to securities that are readily traded in the secondary securities market.
Business cycle	Business cycle refers to the pattern followed by macroeconommic variables, such as GDP and unemployment that rise and fall irregularly over time, relative to trend.
Security	Security refers to a claim on the borrower future income that is sold by the borrower to the lender. A security is a type of transferable interest representing financial value.
Accrual	An accrual is an accounting event in which the transaction is recognized when the action takes place, instead of when cash is disbursed or received.
Book value	The book value of an asset or group of assets is sometimes the price at which they were originally acquired, in many cases equal to purchase price.

Go to **Cram101.com** for the Practice Tests for this Chapter.

Quick asset	An asset that can be converted to cash in a short period of time is a quick asset.
Leverage ratio	Leverage ratio refers to a bank's capital divided by its assets.
Leverage	Leverage is using given resources in such a way that the potential positive or negative outcome is magnified. In finance, this generally refers to borrowing.
Financial risk	The risk related to the inability of the firm to meet its debt obligations as they come due is called financial risk.
Downturn	A decline in a stock market or economic cycle is a downturn.
Debt ratio	Debt ratio refers to the calculation of the total liabilities divided by the total liabilities plus capital. This results in the measurment of the debt level of the business (leverage).
Bond	Bond refers to a debt instrument, issued by a borrower and promising a specified stream of payments to the purchaser, usually regular interest payments plus a final repayment of principal.
Default	In finance, default occurs when a debtor has not met its legal obligations according to the debt contract, e.g. it has not made a scheduled payment, or violated a covenant (condition) of the debt contract.
Liquidation	Liquidation refers to a process whereby the assets of a business are converted to money. The conversion may be coerced by a legal process to pay off the debt of the business, or to satisfy any other business obligation that the business has not voluntarily satisfied.
Retained earnings	Cumulative earnings of a company that are not distributed to the owners and are reinvested in the business are called retained earnings.
Earned surplus	Earned surplus also called retained earnings, is the accumulated profit of a company after the payment of dividends and may or may not be reivested in the business.
Capital stock	The total amount of physical capital that has been accumulated, usually in a country is capital stock. Also refers to the total issued capital of a firm, including ordinary and preferred shares.
Stock	In financial terminology, stock is the capital raized by a corporation, through the issuance and sale of shares.
Times interest earned ratio	A measure of a company's solvency, calculated by dividing income before interest expense and taxes by interest expense is a times interest earned ratio.
Times interest earned	Times interest earned refers to net income before interest and taxes, divided by interest expense; describes a company's ability to make interest payments on its debt.
Interest payment	The payment to holders of bonds payable, calculated by multiplying the stated rate on the face of the bond by the par, or face, value of the bond. If bonds are issued at a discount or premium, the interest payment does not equal the interest expense.
Earnings before interest and taxes	Income from operations before subtracting interest expense and income taxes is an earnings before interest and taxes.
Interest expense	The cost a business incurs to borrow money. With respect to bonds payable, the interest expense is calculated by multiplying the market rate of interest by the carrying value of the bonds on the date of the payment.
Management	Management characterizes the process of leading and directing all or part of an organization, often a business, through the deployment and manipulation of resources. Early twentieth-century management writer Mary Parker Follett defined management as "the art of getting

things done through people."

Credit risk	The risk of loss due to a counterparty defaulting on a contract, or more generally the risk of loss due to some "credit event" is called credit risk.
Customer service	The ability of logistics management to satisfy users in terms of time, dependability, communication, and convenience is called the customer service.
Research and development	The use of resources for the deliberate discovery of new information and ways of doing things, together with the application of that information in inventing new products or processes is referred to as research and development.
Capital expenditures	Major investments in long-term assets such as land, buildings, equipment, or research and development are referred to as capital expenditures.
Capital expenditure	A substantial expenditure that is used by a company to acquire or upgrade physical assets such as equipment, property, industrial buildings, including those which improve the quality and life of an asset is referred to as a capital expenditure.
Acquisition	A company's purchase of the property and obligations of another company is an acquisition.
Line of credit	Line of credit refers to a given amount of unsecured short-term funds a bank will lend to a business, provided the funds are readily available.
Equity financing	Financing that consists of funds that are invested in exchange for ownership in the company is called equity financing.
Deductible	The dollar sum of costs that an insured individual must pay before the insurer begins to pay is called deductible.
Turnover	Turnover in a financial context refers to the rate at which a provider of goods cycles through its average inventory. Turnover in a human resources context refers to the characteristic of a given company or industry, relative to rate at which an employer gains and loses staff.
Inventory turnover ratio	Inventory turnover ratio refers to a ratio that measures the number of times on average the inventory sold during the period; computed by dividing cost of goods sold by the average inventory during the period.
Oversupply	Oversupply refers to a stock or supply of a given product or service that is greater than that which can be cleared under prevailing prices levels and market conditions.
Supply	Supply is the aggregate amount of any material good that can be called into being at a certain price point; it comprises one half of the equation of supply and demand. In classical economic theory, a curve representing supply is one of the factors that produce price.
Policy	Similar to a script in that a policy can be a less than completely rational decision-making method. Involves the use of a pre-existing set of decision steps for any problem that presents itself.
Accounts payable	A written record of all vendors to whom the business firm owes money is referred to as accounts payable.
Payables	Obligations to make future economic sacrifices, usually cash payments, are referred to as payables. Same as current liabilities.
Profitability ratios	Measures of the income or operating success of a company for a given period of time are called profitability ratios.
Profitability ratio	A financial ratio that describes the firm's profits is referred to as profitability ratio. It helps to explain the profitability of an entity during a defined period of time.

Rate of return on investment	The rate of return on investment refers to the benefits to an investor (the profit) relative to the cost of the initial investment.
Return on investment	Return on investment refers to the return a businessperson gets on the money he and other owners invest in the firm; for example, a business that earned $100 on a $1,000 investment would have a ROI of 10 percent: 100 divided by 1000.
Rate of return	A rate of return is a comparison of the money earned (or lost) on an investment to the amount of money invested.
Interest rate	The rate of return on bonds, loans, or deposits. When one speaks of 'the' interest rate, it is usually in a model where there is only one.
Controlling	A management function that involves determining whether or not an organization is progressing toward its goals and objectives, and taking corrective action if it is not is called controlling.
Normal value	Normal value refers to price charged for a product on the domestic market of the producer. Used to compare with export price in determining dumping.
Preparation	Preparation refers to usually the first stage in the creative process. It includes education and formal training.
Technology	The body of knowledge and techniques that can be used to combine economic resources to produce goods and services is called technology.
Wholesale	According to the United Nations Statistics Division Wholesale is the resale of new and used goods to retailers, to industrial, commercial, institutional or professional users, or to other wholesalers, or involves acting as an agent or broker in buying merchandise for, or selling merchandise, to such persons or companies.
Trade association	An industry trade group or trade association is generally a public relations organization founded and funded by corporations that operate in a specific industry. Its purpose is generally to promote that industry through PR activities such as advertizing, education, political donations, political pressure, publishing, and astroturfing.
Securities and exchange commission	Securities and exchange commission refers to U.S. government agency that determines the financial statements that public companies must provide to stockholders and the measurement rules that they must use in producing those statements.
Interstate commerce commission	A federal regulatory group created by Congress in 1887 to oversee and correct abuses in the railroad industry is an interstate commerce commission.
Commerce	Commerce is the exchange of something of value between two entities. It is the central mechanism from which capitalism is derived.
Exchange	The trade of things of value between buyer and seller so that each is better off after the trade is called the exchange.
Federal trade commission	The commission of five members established by the Federal Trade Commission Act of 1914 to investigate unfair competitive practices of firms, to hold hearings on the complaints of such practices, and to issue cease-and-desist orders when firms were found guilty of unfair practices.
Slump	A decline in performance, in a firm is a slump in sales or profits, or in a country is a slump in output or employment.
Average collection period	The average amount of time that a receivable is outstanding, calculated by dividing 365 days by the receivables turnover ratio is an average collection period.

Trade credit	Trade credit refers to an amount that is loaned to an exporter to be repaid when the exports are paid for by the foreign importer.
Inventory turns	In business management, inventory turns measures the number of times capital invested in goods to be sold turns over in a year.
Management team	A management team is directly responsible for managing the day-to-day operations (and profitability) of a company.
Labor	People's physical and mental talents and efforts that are used to help produce goods and services are called labor.
Personnel	A collective term for all of the employees of an organization. Personnel is also commonly used to refer to the personnel management function or the organizational unit responsible for administering personnel programs.
Competitor	Other organizations in the same industry or type of business that provide a good or service to the same set of customers is referred to as a competitor.
Financial institution	A financial institution acts as an agent that provides financial services for its clients. Financial institutions generally fall under financial regulation from a government authority.
Screening	Screening in economics refers to a strategy of combating adverse selection, one of the potential decision-making complications in cases of asymmetric information.
Breakeven point	Breakeven point refers to quantity of output sold at which total revenues equal total costs, that is where the economic profit is zero.
Variable	A variable is something measured by a number; it is used to analyze what happens to other things when the size of that number changes.
Variable cost	The portion of a firm or industry's cost that changes with output, in contrast to fixed cost is referred to as variable cost.
Fixed cost	The cost that a firm bears if it does not produce at all and that is independent of its output. The presence of a fixed cost tends to imply increasing returns to scale. Contrasts with variable cost.
Depreciation expense	Depreciation expense refers to the amount recognized as an expense in one period resulting from the periodic recognition of the used portion of the cost of a long-term tangible asset over its life.
Fixed expense	A fixed expense is an expense that remains constant as activity changes within the relevant range. Any costs not related directly to the production of your product or service.
Raw material	Raw material refers to a good that has not been transformed by production; a primary product.
Production	The creation of finished goods and services using the factors of production: land, labor, capital, entrepreneurship, and knowledge.
Budget	Budget refers to an account, usually for a year, of the planned expenditures and the expected receipts of an entity. For a government, the receipts are tax revenues.
Slope	The slope of a line in the plane containing the x and y axes is generally represented by the letter m, and is defined as the change in the y coordinate divided by the corresponding change in the x coordinate, between two distinct points on the line.
Accounting equation	Expression of the relationship between the assets and the claims on those assets is referred to as the accounting equation, specifically Assets = Liabilities + Owners' equity.
Trend	Trend refers to the long-term movement of an economic variable, such as its average rate of increase or decrease over enough years to encompass several business cycles.

Go to **Cram101.com** for the Practice Tests for this Chapter.

159

Brief	Brief refers to a statement of a party's case or legal arguments, usually prepared by an attorney. Also used to make legal arguments before appellate courts.
Financial management	The job of managing a firm's resources so it can meet its goals and objectives is called financial management.
Wall Street Journal	Dow Jones & Company was founded in 1882 by reporters Charles Dow, Edward Jones and Charles Bergstresser. Jones converted the small Customers' Afternoon Letter into The Wall Street Journal, first published in 1889, and began delivery of the Dow Jones News Service via telegraph. The Journal featured the Jones 'Average', the first of several indexes of stock and bond prices on the New York Stock Exchange.
Journal	Book of original entry, in which transactions are recorded in a general ledger system, is referred to as a journal.

Cash budget	A projection of anticipated cash flows, usually over a one to two year period is called a cash budget.
Budget	Budget refers to an account, usually for a year, of the planned expenditures and the expected receipts of an entity. For a government, the receipts are tax revenues.
Accounts receivable	Accounts receivable is one of a series of accounting transactions dealing with the billing of customers which owe money to a person, company or organization for goods and services that have been provided to the customer. This is typically done in a one person organization by writing an invoice and mailing or delivering it to each customer.
Accounts payable	A written record of all vendors to whom the business firm owes money is referred to as accounts payable.
Management	Management characterizes the process of leading and directing all or part of an organization, often a business, through the deployment and manipulation of resources. Early twentieth-century management writer Mary Parker Follett defined management as "the art of getting things done through people."
Inventory	Tangible property held for sale in the normal course of business or used in producing goods or services for sale is an inventory.
Bankruptcy	Bankruptcy is a legally declared inability or impairment of ability of an individual or organization to pay their creditors.
Asset	An item of property, such as land, capital, money, a share in ownership, or a claim on others for future payment, such as a bond or a bank deposit is an asset.
Firm	An organization that employs resources to produce a good or service for profit and owns and operates one or more plants is referred to as a firm.
Small business	Small business refers to a business that is independently owned and operated, is not dominant in its field of operation, and meets certain standards of size in terms of employees or annual receipts.
Balance sheet	A statement of the assets, liabilities, and net worth of a firm or individual at some given time often at the end of its "fiscal year," is referred to as a balance sheet.
Balance	In banking and accountancy, the outstanding balance is the amount of money owned, (or due), that remains in a deposit account (or a loan account) at a given date, after all past remittances, payments and withdrawal have been accounted for. It can be positive (then, in the balance sheet of a firm, it is an asset) or negative (a liability).
Gap	In December of 1995, Gap became the first major North American retailer to accept independent monitoring of the working conditions in a contract factory producing its garments. Gap is the largest specialty retailer in the United States.
Entrepreneur	The owner/operator. The person who organizes, manages, and assumes the risks of a firm, taking a new idea or a new product and turning it into a successful business is an entrepreneur.
Cash flow	In finance, cash flow refers to the amounts of cash being received and spent by a business during a defined period of time, sometimes tied to a specific project. Most of the time they are being used to determine gaps in the liquid position of a company.
Revenue	Revenue is a U.S. business term for the amount of money that a company receives from its activities, mostly from sales of products and/or services to customers.
Expense	In accounting, an expense represents an event in which an asset is used up or a liability is incurred. In terms of the accounting equation, expenses reduce owners' equity.

Income statement	Income statement refers to a financial statement that presents the revenues and expenses and resulting net income or net loss of a company for a specific period of time.
Profit	Profit refers to the return to the resource entrepreneurial ability; total revenue minus total cost.
Bottom line	The bottom line is net income on the last line of a income statement.
Medium of exchange	Medium of exchange refers to any item sellers generally accept and buyers generally use to pay for a good or service; money; a convenient means of exchanging goods and services without engaging in barter.
Exchange	The trade of things of value between buyer and seller so that each is better off after the trade is called the exchange.
Creditor	A person to whom a debt or legal obligation is owed, and who has the right to enforce payment of that debt or obligation is referred to as creditor.
Lender	Suppliers and financial institutions that lend money to companies is referred to as a lender.
Fast track	Fast track refers to a procedure adopted by the U.S. Congress, at the request of the President, committing it to consider trade agreements without amendment.
Supply	Supply is the aggregate amount of any material good that can be called into being at a certain price point; it comprises one half of the equation of supply and demand. In classical economic theory, a curve representing supply is one of the factors that produce price.
Equity	Equity is the name given to the set of legal principles, in countries following the English common law tradition, which supplement strict rules of law where their application would operate harshly, so as to achieve what is sometimes referred to as "natural justice."
Cash flow cycle	The pattern in which cash moves in and out of the firm is a cash flow cycle. The primary consideration in managing the cash flow cycle is to ensure that inflows and outflows of cash are properly synchronized for transaction purposes.
Stockbroker	A registered representative who works as a market intermediary to buy and sell securities for clients is a stockbroker.
Cash disbursement	Cash disbursement is a transaction that is posted to a cardholder's credit card account in which the cardholder receives cash at an ATM, or cash or travelers checks at a branch of a member financial institution or at a qualified and approved agent of a member financial institution.
Finished goods	Completed products awaiting sale are called finished goods. An item considered a finished good in a supplying plant might be considered a component or raw material in a receiving plant.
Cash outflow	Cash flowing out of the business from all sources over a period of time is cash outflow.
Cash inflow	Cash coming into the company as the result of a previous investment is a cash inflow.
Total revenue	Total revenue refers to the total number of dollars received by a firm from the sale of a product; equal to the total expenditures for the product produced by the firm; equal to the quantity sold multiplied by the price at which it is sold.
Net income	Net income is equal to the income that a firm has after subtracting costs and expenses from the total revenue. Expenses will typically include tax expense.
Liquidity	Liquidity refers to the capacity to turn assets into cash, or the amount of assets in a portfolio that have that capacity.
Production	The creation of finished goods and services using the factors of production: land, labor,

Go to **Cram101.com** for the Practice Tests for this Chapter.

Go to **Cram101.com** for the Practice Tests for this Chapter.
And, **NEVER** highlight a book again!

capital, entrepreneurship, and knowledge.

Credit	Credit refers to a recording as positive in the balance of payments, any transaction that gives rise to a payment into the country, such as an export, the sale of an asset, or borrowing from abroad.
Short run	Short run refers to a period of time that permits an increase or decrease in current production volume with existing capacity, but one that is too short to permit enlargement of that capacity itself (eg, the building of new plants, training of additional workers, etc.).
Variable	A variable is something measured by a number; it is used to analyze what happens to other things when the size of that number changes.
Planning horizon	The length of time it takes to conceive, develop, and complete a project and to recover the cost of the project on a discounted cash flow basis is referred to as planning horizon.
Consultant	A professional that provides expert advice in a particular field or area in which customers occassionaly require this type of knowledge is a consultant.
Accounting	A system that collects and processes financial information about an organization and reports that information to decision makers is referred to as accounting.
Bad debt expense	The expense associated with uncollectible accounts is bad debt expense. When it is a significant amount, the bad debt expense is estimated with the allowance method.
Depreciation	Depreciation is an accounting and finance term for the method of attributing the cost of an asset across the useful life of the asset. Depreciation is a reduction in the value of a currency in floating exchange rate.
Bad debt	In accounting and finance, bad debt is the portion of receivables that can no longer be collected, typically from accounts receivable or loans. Bad debt in accounting is considered an expense.
Corporation	A legal entity chartered by a state or the Federal government that is distinct and separate from the individuals who own it is a corporation. This separation gives the corporation unique powers which other legal entities lack.
Chapter 11 bankruptcy	Chapter 11 bankruptcy governs the process of reorganization under the bankruptcy laws of the United States. It is an attempt to stay in business while a bankruptcy court supervises the "reorganization" of the company's contractual and debt obligations.
Reorganization	Reorganization occurs, among other instances, when one corporation acquires another in a merger or acquisition, a single corporation divides into two or more entities, or a corporation makes a substantial change in its capital structure.
Mistake	In contract law a mistake is incorrect understanding by one or more parties to a contract and may be used as grounds to invalidate the agreement. Common law has identified three different types of mistake in contract: unilateral mistake, mutual mistake, and common mistake.
Sales forecast	Sales forecast refers to the maximum total sales of a product that a firm expects to sell during a specified time period under specified environmental conditions and its own marketing efforts.
Interest payment	The payment to holders of bonds payable, calculated by multiplying the stated rate on the face of the bond by the par, or face, value of the bond. If bonds are issued at a discount or premium, the interest payment does not equal the interest expense.
Interest	In finance and economics, interest is the price paid by a borrower for the use of a lender's money. In other words, interest is the amount of paid to "rent" money for a period of time.
Capital	Capital generally refers to financial wealth, especially that used to start or maintain a

Go to **Cram101.com** for the Practice Tests for this Chapter.

business. In classical economics, capital is one of four factors of production, the others being land and labor and entrepreneurship.

Interest income	Interest income refers to payments of income to those who supply the economy with capital.
Trade association	An industry trade group or trade association is generally a public relations organization founded and funded by corporations that operate in a specific industry. Its purpose is generally to promote that industry through PR activities such as advertizing, education, political donations, political pressure, publishing, and astroturfing.
Commerce	Commerce is the exchange of something of value between two entities. It is the central mechanism from which capitalism is derived.
Industry	A group of firms that produce identical or similar products is an industry. It is also used specifically to refer to an area of economic production focused on manufacturing which involves large amounts of capital investment before any profit can be realized, also called "heavy industry".
Marketing research	Marketing research refers to the analysis of markets to determine opportunities and challenges, and to find the information needed to make good decisions.
Marketing	Promoting and selling products or services to customers, or prospective customers, is referred to as marketing.
Market	A market is, as defined in economics, a social arrangement that allows buyers and sellers to discover information and carry out a voluntary exchange of goods or services.
Service	Service refers to a "non tangible product" that is not embodied in a physical good and that typically effects some change in another product, person, or institution. Contrasts with good.
Rental income	Rental income refers to the payments received by those who supply land to the economy.
Credit sale	A credit sale occurs when a customer does not pay cash at the time of the sale but instead agrees to pay later. The sale occurs now, with payment from the customer to follow at a later time.
Dividend	Amount of corporate profits paid out for each share of stock is referred to as dividend.
Tying	Tying is the practice of making the sale of one good (the tying good) to the de facto or de jure customer conditional on the purchase of a second distinctive good.
Exporter	A firm that sells its product in another country is an exporter.
Tactic	A short-term immediate decision that, in its totality, leads to the achievement of strategic goals is called a tactic.
Insurance	Insurance refers to a system by which individuals can reduce their exposure to risk of large losses by spreading the risks among a large number of persons.
Eximbank	An eximbank is the official export credit agency of the United States Government. It is an independent agency of the Executive Branch of The United States Governemnt established by the Congress of the United States in 1945 that finances or insures foreign purchases of U.S. goods for customers unable or unwilling to accept credit risk.
Export	In economics, an export is any good or commodity, shipped or otherwise transported out of a country, province, town to another part of the world in a legitimate fashion, typically for use in trade or sale.
Letter of credit	An instrument containing a request to pay to the bearer or person named money, or sell him or her some commodity on credit or give something of value and look to the drawer of the letter for recompense is called letter of credit.

Default	In finance, default occurs when a debtor has not met its legal obligations according to the debt contract, e.g. it has not made a scheduled payment, or violated a covenant (condition) of the debt contract.
Wall Street Journal	Dow Jones & Company was founded in 1882 by reporters Charles Dow, Edward Jones and Charles Bergstresser. Jones converted the small Customers' Afternoon Letter into The Wall Street Journal, first published in 1889, and began delivery of the Dow Jones News Service via telegraph. The Journal featured the Jones 'Average', the first of several indexes of stock and bond prices on the New York Stock Exchange.
Journal	Book of original entry, in which transactions are recorded in a general ledger system, is referred to as a journal.
Trend	Trend refers to the long-term movement of an economic variable, such as its average rate of increase or decrease over enough years to encompass several business cycles.
Fund	Independent accounting entity with a self-balancing set of accounts segregated for the purposes of carrying on specific activities is referred to as a fund.
Investment	Investment refers to spending for the production and accumulation of capital and additions to inventories. In a financial sense, buying an asset with the expectation of making a return.
Economic order quantity	Decision model that calculates the optimal quantity of inventory to order under a set of assumptions is called economic order quantity.
Cash discount	Cash discount refers to a discount offered on merchandise sold to encourage prompt payment; offered by sellers of merchandise and represents sales discounts to the seller when they are used and purchase discounts to the purchaser of the merchandise.
Discount	The difference between the face value of a bond and its selling price, when a bond is sold for less than its face value it's referred to as a discount.
Line of credit	Line of credit refers to a given amount of unsecured short-term funds a bank will lend to a business, provided the funds are readily available.
Payables	Obligations to make future economic sacrifices, usually cash payments, are referred to as payables. Same as current liabilities.
Chief financial officer	Chief financial officer refers to executive responsible for overseeing the financial operations of an organization.
Stock	In financial terminology, stock is the capital raized by a corporation, through the issuance and sale of shares.
Competitor	Other organizations in the same industry or type of business that provide a good or service to the same set of customers is referred to as a competitor.
Retail sale	The sale of goods and services to consumers for their own use is a retail sale.
Wholesale	According to the United Nations Statistics Division Wholesale is the resale of new and used goods to retailers, to industrial, commercial, institutional or professional users, or to other wholesalers, or involves acting as an agent or broker in buying merchandise for, or selling merchandise, to such persons or companies.
Policy	Similar to a script in that a policy can be a less than completely rational decision-making method. Involves the use of a pre-existing set of decision steps for any problem that presents itself.
Public relations firm	An organization that develops and implements programs to manage a company's publicity, image, and affairs with consumers and other relevant publics is referred to as a public relations firm.

Public relations	Public relations refers to the management function that evaluates public attitudes, changes policies and procedures in response to the public's requests, and executes a program of action and information to earn public understanding and acceptance.
Creditworthiness	Creditworthiness indicates whether a borrower has in the past made loan payments when due.
Securities and exchange commission	Securities and exchange commission refers to U.S. government agency that determines the financial statements that public companies must provide to stockholders and the measurement rules that they must use in producing those statements.
Stock exchange	A stock exchange is a corporation or mutual organization which provides facilities for stock brokers and traders, to trade company stocks and other securities.
Stock market	An organized marketplace in which common stocks are traded. In the United States, the largest stock market is the New York Stock Exchange, on which are traded the stocks of the largest U.S. companies.
Security	Security refers to a claim on the borrower future income that is sold by the borrower to the lender. A security is a type of transferable interest representing financial value.
NASDAQ	NASDAQ is an American electronic stock exchange. It was founded in 1971 by the National Association of Securities Dealers who divested it in a series of sales in 2000 and 2001.
Gain	In finance, gain is a profit or an increase in value of an investment such as a stock or bond. Gain is calculated by fair market value or the proceeds from the sale of the investment minus the sum of the purchase price and all costs associated with it.
Business plan	A detailed written statement that describes the nature of the business, the target market, the advantages the business will have in relation to competition, and the resources and qualifications of the owner is referred to as a business plan.
Contract	A contract is a "promise" or an "agreement" that is enforced or recognized by the law. In the civil law, a contract is considered to be part of the general law of obligations.
Writing off	Writing off refers to the allocation of the cost of an asset over several accounting periods. Also, to expense a cost, that is, put it on the income statement as an expense.
Invoice	The itemized bill for a transaction, stating the nature of the transaction and its cost. In international trade, the invoice price is often the preferred basis for levying an ad valorem tariff.
Purchase order	A form on which items or services needed by a business firm are specified and then communicated to the vendor is a purchase order.
Xerox	Xerox was founded in 1906 as "The Haloid Company" manufacturing photographic paper and equipment. The company came to prominence in 1959 with the introduction of the first plain paper photocopier using the process of xerography (electrophotography) developed by Chester Carlson, the Xerox 914.
Closing	The finalization of a real estate sales transaction that passes title to the property from the seller to the buyer is referred to as a closing. Closing is a sales term which refers to the process of making a sale. It refers to reaching the final step, which may be an exchange of money or acquiring a signature.
In transit	A state in which goods are in the possession of a bailee or carrier and not in the hands of the buyer, seller, lessee, or lessor is referred to as in transit.
Proactive	To be proactive is to act before a situation becomes a source of confrontation or crisis. It is the opposite of "retroactive," which refers to actions taken after an event.
Small claims	A court that hears civil cases involving small dollar amounts is called small claims court.

Go to **Cram101.com** for the Practice Tests for this Chapter.

173

court	
Option	A contract that gives the purchaser the option to buy or sell the underlying financial instrument at a specified price, called the exercise price or strike price, within a specific period of time.
Sweep account	An account that allows companies to maintain zero balances with all excess cash swept into an interest-earning account at the close of the business day is referred to as a sweep account.
Cash on delivery	Cash on delivery is a financial transaction where the payment of products and/or services received is done at the time of actual delivery rather than paid for in advance.
Vendor	A person who sells property to a vendee is a vendor. The words vendor and vendee are more commonly applied to the seller and purchaser of real estate, and the words seller and buyer are more commonly applied to the seller and purchaser of personal property.
Controlling	A management function that involves determining whether or not an organization is progressing toward its goals and objectives, and taking corrective action if it is not is called controlling.
Trade credit	Trade credit refers to an amount that is loaned to an exporter to be repaid when the exports are paid for by the foreign importer.
Grant	Grant refers to an intergovernmental transfer of funds . Since the New Deal, state and local governments have become increasingly dependent upon federal grants for an almost infinite variety of programs.
Freelance	A freelance worker is a self-employed person working in a profession or trade in which full-time employment is also common.
Premium	Premium refers to the fee charged by an insurance company for an insurance policy. The rate of losses must be relatively predictable: In order to set the premium (prices) insurers must be able to estimate them accurately.
Manufacturing	Production of goods primarily by the application of labor and capital to raw materials and other intermediate inputs, in contrast to agriculture, mining, forestry, fishing, and services a manufacturing.
Fixed cost	The cost that a firm bears if it does not produce at all and that is independent of its output. The presence of a fixed cost tends to imply increasing returns to scale. Contrasts with variable cost.
Scope	Scope of a project is the sum total of all projects products and their requirements or features.
Evaluation	The consumer's appraisal of the product or brand on important attributes is called evaluation.
Operation	A standardized method or technique that is performed repetitively, often on different materials resulting in different finished goods is called an operation.
Recession	A significant decline in economic activity. In the U.S., recession is approximately defined as two successive quarters of falling GDP, as judged by NBER.
Barter	Barter is a type of trade where goods or services are exchanged for a certain amount of other goods or services; no money is involved in the transaction.
Trademark	A distinctive word, name, symbol, device, or combination thereof, which enables consumers to identify favored products or services and which may find protection under state or federal law is a trademark.
Buyer	A buyer refers to a role in the buying center with formal authority and responsibility to

Go to **Cram101.com** for the Practice Tests for this Chapter.

select the supplier and negotiate the terms of the contract.

Overhead cost	An expenses of operating a business over and above the direct costs of producing a product is an overhead cost. They can include utilities (eg, electricity, telephone), advertizing and marketing, and any other costs not billed directly to the client or included in the price of the product.
Lease	A contract for the possession and use of land or other property, including goods, on one side, and a recompense of rent or other income on the other is the lease.
Operating lease	Operating lease refers to a contractual arrangement giving the lessee temporary use of the property with continued ownership of the property by the lessor. Accounted for as a rental.
Capital lease	A type of lease whose characteristics make it similar to a debt-financed purchase and that is consequently accounted for in that fashion is called capital lease. A capital lease is usually used to finance equipment for the major part of its useful life, and there is a reasonable assurance that the lessee will obtain ownership of the equipment by the end of the lease term.
Common mistake	A common mistake is where both parties hold the same mistaken belief of the facts.
Advertising	Advertising refers to paid, nonpersonal communication through various media by organizations and individuals who are in some way identified in the advertising message.
Slowdown	A slowdown is an industrial action in which employees perform their duties but seek to reduce productivity or efficiency in their performance of these duties. A slowdown may be used as either a prelude or an alternative to a strike, as it is seen as less disruptive as well as less risky and costly for workers and their union.
Customer service	The ability of logistics management to satisfy users in terms of time, dependability, communication, and convenience is called the customer service.
Purchasing	Purchasing refers to the function in a firm that searches for quality material resources, finds the best suppliers, and negotiates the best price for goods and services.
Startup	Any new company can be considered a startup, but the description is usually applied to aggressive young companies that are actively courting private financing from venture capitalists, including wealthy individuals and investment companies.
Broker	In commerce, a broker is a party that mediates between a buyer and a seller. A broker who also acts as a seller or as a buyer becomes a principal party to the deal.
Operating expense	In throughput accounting, the cost accounting aspect of Theory of Constraints (TOC), operating expense is the money spent turning inventory into throughput. In TOC, operating expense is limited to costs that vary strictly with the quantity produced, like raw materials and purchased components.
Audit	An examination of the financial reports to ensure that they represent what they claim and conform with generally accepted accounting principles is referred to as audit.
Specialist	A specialist is a trader who makes a market in one or several stocks and holds the limit order book for those stocks.
Control system	A control system is a device or set of devices that manage the behavior of other devices. Some devices or systems are not controllable.A control system is an interconnection of components connected or related in such a manner as to command, direct, or regulate itself or another system.
Bank statement	Monthly report from a bank that shows deposits recorded, checks cleared, other debits and credits, and a running bank balance is referred to as a bank statement.

Go to **Cram101.com** for the Practice Tests for this Chapter.

Merchant	Under the Uniform Commercial Code, one who regularly deals in goods of the kind sold in the contract at issue, or holds himself out as having special knowledge or skill relevant to such goods, or who makes the sale through an agent who regularly deals in such goods or claims such knowledge or skill is referred to as merchant.
Fraud	Tax fraud falls into two categories: civil and criminal. Under civil fraud, the IRS may impose as a penalty of an amount equal to as much as 75 percent of the underpayment.
Free On Board	Free On Board is an Incoterm. It means that the seller pays for transportation of the goods to the port of shipment, plus loading costs. The buyer pays freight, insurance, unloading costs and transportation from the port of destination to his factory. The passing of risks occurs when the goods pass the ship's rail at the port of shipment.
Yield	The interest rate that equates a future value or an annuity to a given present value is a yield.
Brokerage firm	A company that conducts various aspects of securities trading, analysis and advisory services is a brokerage firm.
Interest expense	The cost a business incurs to borrow money. With respect to bonds payable, the interest expense is calculated by multiplying the market rate of interest by the carrying value of the bonds on the date of the payment.
Leverage	Leverage is using given resources in such a way that the potential positive or negative outcome is magnified. In finance, this generally refers to borrowing.
Rate of return	A rate of return is a comparison of the money earned (or lost) on an investment to the amount of money invested.
Internal control	Internal control refers to the plan of organization and all the related methods and measures adopted within a business to safeguard its assets and enhance the accuracy and reliability of its accounting records.
Application service provider	An application service provider is a business that provides computer-based services to customers over a network.
Core business	The core business of an organization is an idealized construct intended to express that organization's "main" or "essential" activity.
Technology	The body of knowledge and techniques that can be used to combine economic resources to produce goods and services is called technology.
Core	A core is the set of feasible allocations in an economy that cannot be improved upon by subset of the set of the economy's consumers (a coalition). In construction, when the force in an element is within a certain center section, the core, the element will only be under compression.
Brief	Brief refers to a statement of a party's case or legal arguments, usually prepared by an attorney. Also used to make legal arguments before appellate courts.
Forbes	David Churbuck founded online Forbes in 1996. The site drew attention when it uncovered Stephen Glass' journalistic fraud in The New Republic in 1998, a scoop that gave credibility to internet journalism.
Business model	A business model is the instrument by which a business intends to generate revenue and profits. It is a summary of how a company means to serve its employees and customers, and involves both strategy (what an business intends to do) as well as an implementation.

Firm	An organization that employs resources to produce a good or service for profit and owns and operates one or more plants is referred to as a firm.
Service	Service refers to a "non tangible product" that is not embodied in a physical good and that typically effects some change in another product, person, or institution. Contrasts with good.
Revenue	Revenue is a U.S. business term for the amount of money that a company receives from its activities, mostly from sales of products and/or services to customers.
Entrepreneur	The owner/operator. The person who organizes, manages, and assumes the risks of a firm, taking a new idea or a new product and turning it into a successful business is an entrepreneur.
Profit margin	Profit margin is a measure of profitability. It is calculated using a formula and written as a percentage or a number. Profit margin = Net income before tax and interest / Revenue.
Profit	Profit refers to the return to the resource entrepreneurial ability; total revenue minus total cost.
Margin	A deposit by a buyer in stocks with a seller or a stockbroker, as security to cover fluctuations in the market in reference to stocks that the buyer has purchased but for which he has not paid is a margin. Commodities are also traded on margin.
Market	A market is, as defined in economics, a social arrangement that allows buyers and sellers to discover information and carry out a voluntary exchange of goods or services.
Price floor	Price floor refers to a government-imposed lower limit on the price that may be charged for a product. If that limit is binding, it implies a situation of excess supply, which the government may need to purchase to keep price from falling below the floor.
Total cost	The sum of fixed cost and variable cost is referred to as total cost.
Market research	Market research is the process of systematic gathering, recording and analyzing of data about customers, competitors and the market. Market research can help create a business plan, launch a new product or service, fine tune existing products and services, expand into new markets etc. It can be used to determine which portion of the population will purchase the product/service, based on variables like age, gender, location and income level. It can be found out what market characteristics your target market has.
Price ceiling	Price ceiling refers to a government-imposed upper limit on the price that may be charged for a product. If that limit is binding, it implies a situation of excess demand and shortage.
Operation	A standardized method or technique that is performed repetitively, often on different materials resulting in different finished goods is called an operation.
Policy	Similar to a script in that a policy can be a less than completely rational decision-making method. Involves the use of a pre-existing set of decision steps for any problem that presents itself.
Business marketing	Business marketing is the practice of organizations, including commercial businesses, governments and institutions, facilitating the sale of their products or services to other companies or organizations that in turn resell them, use them as components in products or services they offer, or use them to support their operations.
Marketing strategy	Marketing strategy refers to the means by which a marketing goal is to be achieved, usually characterized by a specified target market and a marketing program to reach it.
Small business	Small business refers to a business that is independently owned and operated, is not dominant in its field of operation, and meets certain standards of size in terms of employees or annual receipts.

Go to **Cram101.com** for the Practice Tests for this Chapter.

181

Marketing	Promoting and selling products or services to customers, or prospective customers, is referred to as marketing.
Consultant	A professional that provides expert advice in a particular field or area in which customers occassionaly require this type of knowledge is a consultant.
Advertising	Advertising refers to paid, nonpersonal communication through various media by organizations and individuals who are in some way identified in the advertising message.
Industry	A group of firms that produce identical or similar products is an industry. It is also used specifically to refer to an area of economic production focused on manufacturing which involves large amounts of capital investment before any profit can be realized, also called "heavy industry".
Raw material	Raw material refers to a good that has not been transformed by production; a primary product.
Wall Street Journal	Dow Jones & Company was founded in 1882 by reporters Charles Dow, Edward Jones and Charles Bergstresser. Jones converted the small Customers' Afternoon Letter into The Wall Street Journal, first published in 1889, and began delivery of the Dow Jones News Service via telegraph. The Journal featured the Jones 'Average', the first of several indexes of stock and bond prices on the New York Stock Exchange.
Journal	Book of original entry, in which transactions are recorded in a general ledger system, is referred to as a journal.
Forbes	David Churbuck founded online Forbes in 1996. The site drew attention when it uncovered Stephen Glass' journalistic fraud in The New Republic in 1998, a scoop that gave credibility to internet journalism.
Credibility	The extent to which a source is perceived as having knowledge, skill, or experience relevant to a communication topic and can be trusted to give an unbiased opinion or present objective information on the issue is called credibility.
Technology	The body of knowledge and techniques that can be used to combine economic resources to produce goods and services is called technology.
Premium	Premium refers to the fee charged by an insurance company for an insurance policy. The rate of losses must be relatively predictable: In order to set the premium (prices) insurers must be able to estimate them accurately.
Inflation	An increase in the overall price level of an economy, usually as measured by the CPI or by the implicit price deflator is called inflation.
Pricing strategy	The process in which the price of a product can be determined and is decided upon is a pricing strategy.
Tactic	A short-term immediate decision that, in its totality, leads to the achievement of strategic goals is called a tactic.
Option	A contract that gives the purchaser the option to buy or sell the underlying financial instrument at a specified price, called the exercise price or strike price, within a specific period of time.
Marketing Plan	Marketing plan refers to a road map for the marketing activities of an organization for a specified future period of time, such as one year or five years.
Precedent	A previously decided court decision that is recognized as authority for the disposition of future decisions is a precedent.
Market share	That fraction of an industry's output accounted for by an individual firm or group of firms is called market share.

Go to **Cram101.com** for the Practice Tests for this Chapter.

Competitor	Other organizations in the same industry or type of business that provide a good or service to the same set of customers is referred to as a competitor.
Promotion	Promotion refers to all the techniques sellers use to motivate people to buy products or services. An attempt by marketers to inform people about products and to persuade them to participate in an exchange.
Mistake	In contract law a mistake is incorrect understanding by one or more parties to a contract and may be used as grounds to invalidate the agreement. Common law has identified three different types of mistake in contract: unilateral mistake, mutual mistake, and common mistake.
Underpricing	When new or additional shares of stock are to be sold, investment bankers will generally set the price at slightly below the current market value to ensure a receptive market for the securities, we have underpricing.
Demand curve	Demand curve refers to the graph of quantity demanded as a function of price, normally downward sloping, straight or curved, and drawn with quantity on the horizontal axis and price on the vertical axis.
Competitive market	A market in which no buyer or seller has market power is called a competitive market.
Distribution	Distribution in economics, the manner in which total output and income is distributed among individuals or factors.
Gain	In finance, gain is a profit or an increase in value of an investment such as a stock or bond. Gain is calculated by fair market value or the proceeds from the sale of the investment minus the sum of the purchase price and all costs associated with it.
Penetration pricing	Setting a low initial price for a new product in order to penetrate the market deeply and gain a large and broad market share is referred to as penetration pricing.
Discount	The difference between the face value of a bond and its selling price, when a bond is sold for less than its face value it's referred to as a discount.
Brand loyalty	The degree to which customers are satisfied, like the brand, and are committed to further purchase is referred to as brand loyalty.
Loyalty	Marketers tend to define customer loyalty as making repeat purchases. Some argue that it should be defined attitudinally as a strongly positive feeling about the brand.
Brand	A name, symbol, or design that identifies the goods or services of one seller or group of sellers and distinguishes them from the goods and services of competitors is a brand.
Penetration strategy	Strategy in which a product is priced low to attract many customers and discourage competition is referred to as penetration strategy.
Product development	In business and engineering, new product development is the complete process of bringing a new product to market. There are two parallel aspects to this process : one involves product engineering ; the other marketing analysis. Marketers see new product development as the first stage in product life cycle management, engineers as part of Product Lifecycle Management.
Expense	In accounting, an expense represents an event in which an asset is used up or a liability is incurred. In terms of the accounting equation, expenses reduce owners' equity.
Unit cost	Unit cost refers to cost computed by dividing some amount of total costs by the related number of units. Also called average cost.
Appeal	Appeal refers to the act of asking an appellate court to overturn a decision after the trial court's final judgment has been entered.

Go to **Cram101.com** for the Practice Tests for this Chapter.

Price lining	Setting the price of line products at a limited number of different specific pricing points is referred to as price lining.
Price line	A straight line representing the combinations of variables, usually two goods that cost the same at some given prices. The slope of a price line measures relative prices, and changes in prices.
Stock	In financial terminology, stock is the capital raized by a corporation, through the issuance and sale of shares.
Markup	Markup is a term used in marketing to indicate how much the price of a product is above the cost of producing and distributing the product.
Price war	Price war refers to successive and continued decreases in the prices charged by firms in an oligopolistic industry. Each firm lowers its price below rivals' prices, hoping to increase its sales and revenues at its rivals' expense.
Michael Dell	Michael Dell is the founder of Dell, Inc., the world's largest computer manufacturer which revolutionized the home computer industry.
Zone pricing	Zone pricing is where prices increase as shipping distances increase. This is sometimes done by drawing concentric circles on a map with the plant or warehouse at the center and each circle defining the boundary of a price zone.
Postal Service	The postal service was created in Philadelphia under Benjamin Franklin on July 26, 1775 by decree of the Second Continental Congress. Based on a clause in the United States Constitution empowering Congress "To establish Post Offices and post Roads."
Price discrimination	Price discrimination refers to the sale by a firm to buyers at two different prices. When this occurs internationally and the lower price is charged for export, it is regarded as dumping.
Clayton act	The Clayton act is a federal antitrust act of 1914 that strengthened the Sherman Act by making it illegal for firms to engage in certain specified practices.
Delivered pricing	A pricing method where the price the seller quotes includes all transportation costs is called delivered pricing.
Uniform delivered pricing	Uniform delivered pricing refers to the price the seller quotes including all transportation costs.
Supply	Supply is the aggregate amount of any material good that can be called into being at a certain price point; it comprises one half of the equation of supply and demand. In classical economic theory, a curve representing supply is one of the factors that produce price.
Price gouging	Price gouging is a reference to a seller's asking a price that is much higher than what is seen as 'fair' under the circumstances.
Seasonal discount	A price reduction given to buyers who purchase goods or services out of season is a seasonal discount.
Grant	Grant refers to an intergovernmental transfer of funds . Since the New Deal, state and local governments have become increasingly dependent upon federal grants for an almost infinite variety of programs.
Suggested Retail Price	The Suggested Retail Price of a product is the price the manufacturer recommends that the retailer sell it for. This helps to standardize prices among locations.
Wholesale	According to the United Nations Statistics Division Wholesale is the resale of new and used goods to retailers, to industrial, commercial, institutional or professional users, or to

	other wholesalers, or involves acting as an agent or broker in buying merchandise for, or selling merchandise, to such persons or companies.
Invoice	The itemized bill for a transaction, stating the nature of the transaction and its cost. In international trade, the invoice price is often the preferred basis for levying an ad valorem tariff.
Cost structure	The relative proportion of an organization's fixed, variable, and mixed costs is referred to as cost structure.
Consideration	Consideration in contract law, a basic requirement for an enforceable agreement under traditional contract principles, defined in this text as legal value, bargained for and given in exchange for an act or promise. In corporation law, cash or property contributed to a corporation in exchange for shares, or a promise to contribute such cash or property.
Sherman Antitrust Act	The Sherman Antitrust Act, formally known as the Act of July 2, 1890 was the first United States federal government action to limit monopolies.
Antitrust	Government intervention to alter market structure or prevent abuse of market power is called antitrust.
Competitive advantage	A business is said to have a competitive advantage when its unique strengths, often based on cost, quality, time, and innovation, offer consumers a greater percieved value and there by diffetiating it from its competitors.
Variable	A variable is something measured by a number; it is used to analyze what happens to other things when the size of that number changes.
Customer service	The ability of logistics management to satisfy users in terms of time, dependability, communication, and convenience is called the customer service.
Credit	Credit refers to a recording as positive in the balance of payments, any transaction that gives rise to a payment into the country, such as an export, the sale of an asset, or borrowing from abroad.
Points	Loan origination fees that may be deductible as interest by a buyer of property. A seller of property who pays points reduces the selling price by the amount of the points paid for the buyer.
Price competition	Price competition is where a company tries to distinguish its product or service from competing products on the basis of low price.
Nonprice competition	Competition based on distinguishing one's product by means of product differentiation and then advertising the distinguished product to consumers is referred to as nonprice competition.
Manufacturing	Production of goods primarily by the application of labor and capital to raw materials and other intermediate inputs, in contrast to agriculture, mining, forestry, fishing, and services a manufacturing.
Retailing	All activities involved in selling, renting, and providing goods and services to ultimate consumers for personal, family, or household use is referred to as retailing.
Customer loyalty	Marketers tend to define customer loyalty as making repeat purchases. Some argue that it should be defined attitudinally as a strongly positive feeling about the brand.
Financial plan	The financial plan section of a business plan consists of three financial statements (the income statement, the cash flow projection, and the balance sheet) and a brief analysis of these three statements.
Operating	In throughput accounting, the cost accounting aspect of Theory of Constraints (TOC),

Go to **Cram101.com** for the Practice Tests for this Chapter.

expense	operating expense is the money spent turning inventory into throughput. In TOC, operating expense is limited to costs that vary strictly with the quantity produced, like raw materials and purchased components.
Depreciation	Depreciation is an accounting and finance term for the method of attributing the cost of an asset across the useful life of the asset. Depreciation is a reduction in the value of a currency in floating exchange rate.
Net sales	Gross sales less sales returns and allowances and sales discounts are referred to as net sales.
Utility	Utility refers to the want-satisfying power of a good or service; the satisfaction or pleasure a consumer obtains from the consumption of a good or service.
Advertisement	Advertisement is the promotion of goods, services, companies and ideas, usually by an identified sponsor. Marketers see advertising as part of an overall promotional strategy.
Selling and administrative costs	Selling and administrative costs refer to costs that cannot be directly traced to products that are recognized as expenses in the period in which they are incurred. Examples include advertizing expense and rent expense.
Administrative cost	An administrative cost is all executive, organizational, and clerical costs associated with the general management of an organization rather than with manufacturing, marketing, or selling
Factory overhead	Manufacturing costs that are not raw material or direct labor costs are factory overhead. Variable factory overhead is usually distinguished from factory overhead.
Direct labor	The earnings of employees who work directly on the products being manufactured are direct labor.
Labor	People's physical and mental talents and efforts that are used to help produce goods and services are called labor.
Cost accounting	Cost accounting measures and reports financial and nonfinancial information relating to the cost of acquiring or consuming resources in an organization. It provides information for both management accounting and financial accounting.
Accounting	A system that collects and processes financial information about an organization and reports that information to decision makers is referred to as accounting.
Absorption costing	Method of inventory costing in which all variable manufacturing costs and all fixed manufacturing costs are included. Often called "full absorption costing " since all costs are fully absorbed.
Overhead cost	An expenses of operating a business over and above the direct costs of producing a product is an overhead cost. They can include utilities (eg, electricity, telephone), advertizing and marketing, and any other costs not billed directly to the client or included in the price of the product.
Absorption	Total demand for goods and services by all residents of a country is absorption. The term was introduced as part of the Absorption Approach.
Financial statement	Financial statement refers to a summary of all the transactions that have occurred over a particular period.
Financial analysis	Financial analysis is the analysis of the accounts and the economic prospects of a firm.
Annual report	An annual report is prepared by corporate management that presents financial information including financial statements, footnotes, and the management discussion and analysis.

Go to **Cram101.com** for the Practice Tests for this Chapter.

Insurance	Insurance refers to a system by which individuals can reduce their exposure to risk of large losses by spreading the risks among a large number of persons.
Variable cost	The portion of a firm or industry's cost that changes with output, in contrast to fixed cost is referred to as variable cost.
Fixed cost	The cost that a firm bears if it does not produce at all and that is independent of its output. The presence of a fixed cost tends to imply increasing returns to scale. Contrasts with variable cost.
Production	The creation of finished goods and services using the factors of production: land, labor, capital, entrepreneurship, and knowledge.
Yield	The interest rate that equates a future value or an annuity to a given present value is a yield.
Income statement	Income statement refers to a financial statement that presents the revenues and expenses and resulting net income or net loss of a company for a specific period of time.
Allocate	Allocate refers to the assignment of income for various tax purposes. A multistate corporation's nonbusiness income usually is distributed to the state where the nonbusiness assets are located; it is not apportioned with the rest of the entity's income.
Fixed expense	A fixed expense is an expense that remains constant as activity changes within the relevant range. Any costs not related directly to the production of your product or service.
Contribution margin	A company's contribution margin can be expressed as the percentage of each sale that remains after the variable costs are subtracted. In simplest terms, the contribution margin is total revenue minus total variable cost.
Total revenue	Total revenue refers to the total number of dollars received by a firm from the sale of a product; equal to the total expenditures for the product produced by the firm; equal to the quantity sold multiplied by the price at which it is sold.
Contribution	In business organization law, the cash or property contributed to a business by its owners is referred to as contribution.
Short run	Short run refers to a period of time that permits an increase or decrease in current production volume with existing capacity, but one that is too short to permit enlargement of that capacity itself (eg, the building of new plants, training of additional workers, etc.).
Allowance	Reduction in the selling price of goods extended to the buyer because the goods are defective or of lower quality than the buyer ordered and to encourage a buyer to keep merchandise that would otherwise be returned is the allowance.
Merchant	Under the Uniform Commercial Code, one who regularly deals in goods of the kind sold in the contract at issue, or holds himself out as having special knowledge or skill relevant to such goods, or who makes the sale through an agent who regularly deals in such goods or claims such knowledge or skill is referred to as merchant.
Fund	Independent accounting entity with a self-balancing set of accounts segregated for the purposes of carrying on specific activities is referred to as a fund.
Customer profile	Description, primarily quantitative, of an individual or segment using specified demographic, lifestyle, and behavioral characteristics is a customer profile.
Credit risk	The risk of loss due to a counterparty defaulting on a contract, or more generally the risk of loss due to some "credit event" is called credit risk.
Discount rate	Discount rate refers to the rate, per year, at which future values are diminished to make them comparable to values in the present. Can be either subjective or objective .

Go to **Cram101.com** for the Practice Tests for this Chapter.

Debit	Debit refers to recording as negative in the balance of payments, any transaction that gives rise to a payment out of the country, such as an import, the purchase of an asset, or lending to foreigners. Opposite of credit.
Smart card	A stored-value card that contains a computer chip that allows it to be loaded with digital cash from the owner's bank account whenever needed is called a smart card.
Micropayment	A payments for electronic purchases so low that it is uneconomical under traditional payment mechanisms like credit cards is a micropayment.
Electronic money	Electronic money refers to money that exists only in electronic form and substitutes for cash as well.
Balance	In banking and accountancy, the outstanding balance is the amount of money owned, (or due), that remains in a deposit account (or a loan account) at a given date, after all past remittances, payments and withdrawal have been accounted for. It can be positive (then, in the balance sheet of a firm, it is an asset) or negative (a liability).
Vendor	A person who sells property to a vendee is a vendor. The words vendor and vendee are more commonly applied to the seller and purchaser of real estate, and the words seller and buyer are more commonly applied to the seller and purchaser of personal property.
Security	Security refers to a claim on the borrower future income that is sold by the borrower to the lender. A security is a type of transferable interest representing financial value.
American Express	From the early 1980s until the late 1990s, American Express was known for cutting its merchant fees (also known as a "discount rate") to fine merchants and restaurants if they only accepted American Express and no other credit or charge cards. This prompted competitors such as Visa and MasterCard to cry foul for a while, as the tactics "locked" restaurants into American Express.
Time horizon	A time horizon is a fixed point of time in the future at which point certain processes will be evaluated or assumed to end. It is necessary in an accounting, finance or risk management regime to assign such a fixed horizon time so that alternatives can be evaluated for performance over the same period of time.
Principal	In agency law, one under whose direction an agent acts and for whose benefit that agent acts is a principal.
Interest	In finance and economics, interest is the price paid by a borrower for the use of a lender's money. In other words, interest is the amount of paid to "rent" money for a period of time.
Security interest	A security interest is a property interest created by agreement or by operation of law over assets to secure the performance of an obligation (usually but not always the payment of a debt) which gives the beneficiary of the security interest certain preferential rights in relation to the assets.
Installment loan	A borrowing arrangement in which a schedule of equal payments are used to pay off a loan is called installment loan.
Collateral	Property that is pledged to the lender to guarantee payment in the event that the borrower is unable to make debt payments is called collateral.
Default	In finance, default occurs when a debtor has not met its legal obligations according to the debt contract, e.g. it has not made a scheduled payment, or violated a covenant (condition) of the debt contract.
Financial institution	A financial institution acts as an agent that provides financial services for its clients. Financial institutions generally fall under financial regulation from a government authority.
Credit union	A credit union is a not-for-profit co-operative financial institution that is owned and

Go to **Cram101.com** for the Practice Tests for this Chapter.
And, **NEVER** highlight a book again!

	controlled by its members, through the election of a volunteer Board of Directors elected from the membership itself.
Union	A worker association that bargains with employers over wages and working conditions is called a union.
Interest income	Interest income refers to payments of income to those who supply the economy with capital.
Contract	A contract is a "promise" or an "agreement" that is enforced or recognized by the law. In the civil law, a contract is considered to be part of the general law of obligations.
Cash discount	Cash discount refers to a discount offered on merchandise sold to encourage prompt payment; offered by sellers of merchandise and represents sales discounts to the seller when they are used and purchase discounts to the purchaser of the merchandise.
Trade credit	Trade credit refers to an amount that is loaned to an exporter to be repaid when the exports are paid for by the foreign importer.

Go to **Cram101.com** for the Practice Tests for this Chapter.

Personal selling	Personal selling is interpersonal communication, often face to face, between a sales representative and an individual or group, usually with the objective of making a sale.
Advertising	Advertising refers to paid, nonpersonal communication through various media by organizations and individuals who are in some way identified in the advertising message.
Promotion	Promotion refers to all the techniques sellers use to motivate people to buy products or services. An attempt by marketers to inform people about products and to persuade them to participate in an exchange.
Publicity	Publicity refers to any information about an individual, product, or organization that's distributed to the public through the media and that's not paid for or controlled by the seller.
Budget	Budget refers to an account, usually for a year, of the planned expenditures and the expected receipts of an entity. For a government, the receipts are tax revenues.
Small business	Small business refers to a business that is independently owned and operated, is not dominant in its field of operation, and meets certain standards of size in terms of employees or annual receipts.
Service	Service refers to a "non tangible product" that is not embodied in a physical good and that typically effects some change in another product, person, or institution. Contrasts with good.
Business plan	A detailed written statement that describes the nature of the business, the target market, the advantages the business will have in relation to competition, and the resources and qualifications of the owner is referred to as a business plan.
Purchasing	Purchasing refers to the function in a firm that searches for quality material resources, finds the best suppliers, and negotiates the best price for goods and services.
Target audience	That group that composes the present and potential prospects for a product or service is called the target audience.
Entrepreneur	The owner/operator. The person who organizes, manages, and assumes the risks of a firm, taking a new idea or a new product and turning it into a successful business is an entrepreneur.
Market	A market is, as defined in economics, a social arrangement that allows buyers and sellers to discover information and carry out a voluntary exchange of goods or services.
Market potential	Market potential refers to maximum total sales of a product by all firms to a segment during a specified time period under specified environmental conditions and marketing efforts of the firms.
Interest	In finance and economics, interest is the price paid by a borrower for the use of a lender's money. In other words, interest is the amount of paid to "rent" money for a period of time.
Unique selling proposition	An advertising strategy that focuses on a product or service attribute that is distinctive to a particular brand and offers an important benefit to the customer is a unique selling proposition.
Firm	An organization that employs resources to produce a good or service for profit and owns and operates one or more plants is referred to as a firm.
Marketing	Promoting and selling products or services to customers, or prospective customers, is referred to as marketing.
Security	Security refers to a claim on the borrower future income that is sold by the borrower to the lender. A security is a type of transferable interest representing financial value.

Business marketing	Business marketing is the practice of organizations, including commercial businesses, governments and institutions, facilitating the sale of their products or services to other companies or organizations that in turn resell them, use them as components in products or services they offer, or use them to support their operations.
Marketing strategy	Marketing strategy refers to the means by which a marketing goal is to be achieved, usually characterized by a specified target market and a marketing program to reach it.
Competitor	Other organizations in the same industry or type of business that provide a good or service to the same set of customers is referred to as a competitor.
Evaluation	The consumer's appraisal of the product or brand on important attributes is called evaluation.
Buying criteria	Buying criteria refers to the factors buying organizations use when evaluating a potential supplier and what it wants to sell.
Appeal	Appeal refers to the act of asking an appellate court to overturn a decision after the trial court's final judgment has been entered.
Warranty	An obligation of a company to replace defective goods or correct any deficiencies in performance or quality of a product is called a warranty.
Coupon	In finance, a coupon is "attached" to a bond, either physically (as with old bonds) or electronically. Each coupon represents a predetermined payment promized to the bond-holder in return for his or her loan of money to the bond-issuer. .
Demographic	A demographic is a term used in marketing and broadcasting, to describe a demographic grouping or a market segment.
Advertisement	Advertisement is the promotion of goods, services, companies and ideas, usually by an identified sponsor. Marketers see advertising as part of an overall promotional strategy.
Closing	The finalization of a real estate sales transaction that passes title to the property from the seller to the buyer is referred to as a closing. Closing is a sales term which refers to the process of making a sale. It refers to reaching the final step, which may be an exchange of money or acquiring a signature.
Relative cost	Relative cost refers to the relationship between the price paid for advertising time or space and the size of the audience delivered; it is used to compare the prices of various media vehicles.
Drawback	Drawback refers to rebate of import duties when the imported good is re-exported or used as input to the production of an exported good.
Margin	A deposit by a buyer in stocks with a seller or a stockbroker, as security to cover fluctuations in the market in reference to stocks that the buyer has purchased but for which he has not paid is a margin. Commodities are also traded on margin.
Continuity	A media scheduling strategy where a continuous pattern of advertising is used over the time span of the advertising campaign is continuity.
Frequency	Frequency refers to the speed of the up and down movements of a fluctuating economic variable; that is, the number of times per unit of time that the variable completes a cycle of up and down movement.
Contract	A contract is a "promise" or an "agreement" that is enforced or recognized by the law. In the civil law, a contract is considered to be part of the general law of obligations.
Discount	The difference between the face value of a bond and its selling price, when a bond is sold for less than its face value it's referred to as a discount.

Go to **Cram101.com** for the Practice Tests for this Chapter.

Target market	One or more specific groups of potential consumers toward which an organization directs its marketing program are a target market.
Users	Users refer to people in the organization who actually use the product or service purchased by the buying center.
Banner ad	A banner ad is a form of advertising on the World Wide Web. This form of online advertising entails embedding an advertisement into a web page.
Direct marketing	Promotional element that uses direct communication with consumers to generate a response in the form of an order, a request for further information, or a visit to a retail outlet is direct marketing.
Average cost	Average cost is equal to total cost divided by the number of goods produced (Quantity-Q). It is also equal to the sum of average variable costs (total variable costs divided by Q) plus average fixed costs (total fixed costs divided by Q).
Complaint	The pleading in a civil case in which the plaintiff states his claim and requests relief is called complaint. In the common law, it is a formal legal document that sets out the basic facts and legal reasons that the filing party (the plaintiffs) believes are sufficient to support a claim against another person, persons, entity or entities (the defendants) that entitles the plaintiff(s) to a remedy (either money damages or injunctive relief).
Credit	Credit refers to a recording as positive in the balance of payments, any transaction that gives rise to a payment into the country, such as an export, the sale of an asset, or borrowing from abroad.
Customer profile	Description, primarily quantitative, of an individual or segment using specified demographic, lifestyle, and behavioral characteristics is a customer profile.
Positioning	The art and science of fitting the product or service to one or more segments of the market in such a way as to set it meaningfully apart from competition is called positioning.
Data mining	The extraction of hidden predictive information from large databases is referred to as data mining.
Invoice	The itemized bill for a transaction, stating the nature of the transaction and its cost. In international trade, the invoice price is often the preferred basis for levying an ad valorem tariff.
Option	A contract that gives the purchaser the option to buy or sell the underlying financial instrument at a specified price, called the exercise price or strike price, within a specific period of time.
Premium	Premium refers to the fee charged by an insurance company for an insurance policy. The rate of losses must be relatively predictable: In order to set the premium (prices) insurers must be able to estimate them accurately.
Business Week	Business Week is a business magazine published by McGraw-Hill. It was first published in 1929 under the direction of Malcolm Muir, who was serving as president of the McGraw-Hill Publishing company at the time. It is considered to be the standard both in industry and among students.
Estate	An estate is the totality of the legal rights, interests, entitlements and obligations attaching to property. In the context of wills and probate, it refers to the totality of the property which the deceased owned or in which some interest was held.
Profit	Profit refers to the return to the resource entrepreneurial ability; total revenue minus total cost.
Targeting	In advertizing, targeting is to select a demographic or other group of people to advertise

Go to **Cram101.com** for the Practice Tests for this Chapter.

	to, and create advertisements appropriately.
Household	An economic unit that provides the economy with resources and uses the income received to purchase goods and services that satisfy economic wants is called household.
Operation	A standardized method or technique that is performed repetitively, often on different materials resulting in different finished goods is called an operation.
Billboard	The most common form of outdoor advertising is called a billboard.
Technology	The body of knowledge and techniques that can be used to combine economic resources to produce goods and services is called technology.
Cost efficiency	Cost efficiency refers to the amount of output associated with an additional dollar spent on input; the MPP of an input divided by its price. Also refers to is a ratio of the excess return over a fund's benchmark, divided by management expenses. It calculates the value added (i.e. the excess over index returns) contributed by each percentage point of management expenses.
Brief	Brief refers to a statement of a party's case or legal arguments, usually prepared by an attorney. Also used to make legal arguments before appellate courts.
Standardization	Standardization, in the context related to technologies and industries, is the process of establishing a technical standard among competing entities in a market, where this will bring benefits without hurting competition.
Regulation	Regulation refers to restrictions state and federal laws place on business with regard to the conduct of its activities.
Extension	Extension refers to an out-of-court settlement in which creditors agree to allow the firm more time to meet its financial obligations. A new repayment schedule will be developed, subject to the acceptance of creditors.
Transit advertising	Advertising targeted to target audiences exposed to commercial transportation facilities, including buses, taxis, trains, elevators, trolleys, airplanes, and subways is called transit advertising.
Corporation	A legal entity chartered by a state or the Federal government that is distinct and separate from the individuals who own it is a corporation. This separation gives the corporation unique powers which other legal entities lack.
Buyer	A buyer refers to a role in the buying center with formal authority and responsibility to select the supplier and negotiate the terms of the contract.
Trade show	A type of exhibition or forum where manufacturers can display their products to current as well as prospective buyers is referred to as trade show.
Industry	A group of firms that produce identical or similar products is an industry. It is also used specifically to refer to an area of economic production focused on manufacturing which involves large amounts of capital investment before any profit can be realized, also called "heavy industry".
Trend	Trend refers to the long-term movement of an economic variable, such as its average rate of increase or decrease over enough years to encompass several business cycles.
Setup cost	A setup cost is any cost necessary to prepare for production and to purchase inventory.
Expense	In accounting, an expense represents an event in which an asset is used up or a liability is incurred. In terms of the accounting equation, expenses reduce owners' equity.
Specialty advertising	An advertising, sales promotion, and motivational communications medium that employs useful articles of merchandise imprinted with an advertiser's name, message, or logo is referred to

Go to **Cram101.com** for the Practice Tests for this Chapter.

205

	as specialty advertising.
Logo	Logo refers to device or other brand name that cannot be spoken.
Advertising specialties	Advertising specialties refers to items used as giveaways to serve as a reminder or stimulate remembrance of a company or brand such as calendars, T-shirts, pens, key tags, and the like. Specialties are usually imprinted with a company or brand name and other identifying marks such as an address and phone number.
Point of Sale	Point of sale can mean a retail shop, a checkout counter in a shop, or a variable location where a transaction occurs.
Fund	Independent accounting entity with a self-balancing set of accounts segregated for the purposes of carrying on specific activities is referred to as a fund.
Tying	Tying is the practice of making the sale of one good (the tying good) to the de facto or de jure customer conditional on the purchase of a second distinctive good.
Advertising objectives	Those specific outcomes that are to be accomplished through advertising are referred to as advertising objectives.
Cooperative advertising	Advertising programs by which a manufacturer pays a percentage of the retailer's local advertising expense for advertising the manufacturer's products are called cooperative advertising.
Cooperative	A business owned and controlled by the people who use it, producers, consumers, or workers with similar needs who pool their resources for mutual gain is called cooperative.
Manufacturing	Production of goods primarily by the application of labor and capital to raw materials and other intermediate inputs, in contrast to agriculture, mining, forestry, fishing, and services a manufacturing.
Shares	Shares refer to an equity security, representing a shareholder's ownership of a corporation. Shares are one of a finite number of equal portions in the capital of a company, entitling the owner to a proportion of distributed, non-reinvested profits known as dividends and to a portion of the value of the company in case of liquidation.
Supply	Supply is the aggregate amount of any material good that can be called into being at a certain price point; it comprises one half of the equation of supply and demand. In classical economic theory, a curve representing supply is one of the factors that produce price.
Standardized product	Standardized product refers to a product whose buyers are indifferent to the seller from whom they purchase it, as long as the price charged by all sellers is the same; a product all units of which are identical and thus are perfect substitutes.
Production	The creation of finished goods and services using the factors of production: land, labor, capital, entrepreneurship, and knowledge.
Gain	In finance, gain is a profit or an increase in value of an investment such as a stock or bond. Gain is calculated by fair market value or the proceeds from the sale of the investment minus the sum of the purchase price and all costs associated with it.
Copywriter	Individual who helps conceive the ideas for ads and commercials and writes the words or copy for them is referred to as copywriter.
Specialist	A specialist is a trader who makes a market in one or several stocks and holds the limit order book for those stocks.
Mistake	In contract law a mistake is incorrect understanding by one or more parties to a contract and may be used as grounds to invalidate the agreement. Common law has identified three different types of mistake in contract: unilateral mistake, mutual mistake, and common mistake.

Go to **Cram101.com** for the Practice Tests for this Chapter.

Chapter 11. Creative Use of Advertising and Promotion

Matching	Matching refers to an accounting concept that establishes when expenses are recognized. Expenses are matched with the revenues they helped to generate and are recognized when those revenues are recognized.
Wall Street Journal	Dow Jones & Company was founded in 1882 by reporters Charles Dow, Edward Jones and Charles Bergstresser. Jones converted the small Customers' Afternoon Letter into The Wall Street Journal, first published in 1889, and began delivery of the Dow Jones News Service via telegraph. The Journal featured the Jones 'Average', the first of several indexes of stock and bond prices on the New York Stock Exchange.
Journal	Book of original entry, in which transactions are recorded in a general ledger system, is referred to as a journal.

Go to **Cram101.com** for the Practice Tests for this Chapter.

Principal	In agency law, one under whose direction an agent acts and for whose benefit that agent acts is a principal.
International trade	The export of goods and services from a country and the import of goods and services into a country is referred to as the international trade.
Economy	The income, expenditures, and resources that affect the cost of running a business and household are called an economy.
Global competition	Global competition exists when competitive conditions across national markets are linked strongly enough to form a true international market and when leading competitors compete head to head in many different countries.
Entrepreneur	The owner/operator. The person who organizes, manages, and assumes the risks of a firm, taking a new idea or a new product and turning it into a successful business is an entrepreneur.
Technology	The body of knowledge and techniques that can be used to combine economic resources to produce goods and services is called technology.
Market potential	Market potential refers to maximum total sales of a product by all firms to a segment during a specified time period under specified environmental conditions and marketing efforts of the firms.
Market	A market is, as defined in economics, a social arrangement that allows buyers and sellers to discover information and carry out a voluntary exchange of goods or services.
Service	Service refers to a "non tangible product" that is not embodied in a physical good and that typically effects some change in another product, person, or institution. Contrasts with good.
Small business	Small business refers to a business that is independently owned and operated, is not dominant in its field of operation, and meets certain standards of size in terms of employees or annual receipts.
Corporation	A legal entity chartered by a state or the Federal government that is distinct and separate from the individuals who own it is a corporation. This separation gives the corporation unique powers which other legal entities lack.
Mistake	In contract law a mistake is incorrect understanding by one or more parties to a contract and may be used as grounds to invalidate the agreement. Common law has identified three different types of mistake in contract: unilateral mistake, mutual mistake, and common mistake.
Domestic	From or in one's own country. A domestic producer is one that produces inside the home country. A domestic price is the price inside the home country. Opposite of 'foreign' or 'world.'.
Realization	Realization is the sale of assets when an entity is being liquidated.
Product life cycle	Product life cycle refers to a series of phases in a product's sales and cash flows over time; these phases, in order of occurrence, are introductory, growth, maturity, and decline.
Maturity stage	The third stage of the product life cycle is called the maturity stage. This is when sales growth slows due to heavy competition, alternative product options or changing buyer or user preferences.
Maturity	Maturity refers to the final payment date of a loan or other financial instrument, after which point no further interest or principal need be paid.
Manufacturing costs	Costs incurred in a manufacturing process, which consist of direct material, direct labor, and manufacturing overhead are referred to as manufacturing costs.

Go to **Cram101.com** for the Practice Tests for this Chapter.

Manufacturing	Production of goods primarily by the application of labor and capital to raw materials and other intermediate inputs, in contrast to agriculture, mining, forestry, fishing, and services a manufacturing.
Fixed cost	The cost that a firm bears if it does not produce at all and that is independent of its output. The presence of a fixed cost tends to imply increasing returns to scale. Contrasts with variable cost.
Industry	A group of firms that produce identical or similar products is an industry. It is also used specifically to refer to an area of economic production focused on manufacturing which involves large amounts of capital investment before any profit can be realized, also called "heavy industry".
Business marketing	Business marketing is the practice of organizations, including commercial businesses, governments and institutions, facilitating the sale of their products or services to other companies or organizations that in turn resell them, use them as components in products or services they offer, or use them to support their operations.
Marketing strategy	Marketing strategy refers to the means by which a marketing goal is to be achieved, usually characterized by a specified target market and a marketing program to reach it.
Family business	A family business is a company owned, controlled, and operated by members of one or several families. Many companies that are now publicly held were founded as family businesses. Many family businesses have non-family members as employees, but, particularly in smaller companies, the top positions are often allocated to family members.
Niche market	A niche market or market niche is a focused, targetable portion of a market. By definition, then, a business that focuses on a niche market is addressing a need for a product or service that is not being addressed by mainstream providers.
Marketing	Promoting and selling products or services to customers, or prospective customers, is referred to as marketing.
Niche	In industry, a niche is a situation or an activity perfectly suited to a person. A niche can imply a working position or an area suited to a person who occupies it. Basically, a job where a person is able to succeed and thrive.
Points	Loan origination fees that may be deductible as interest by a buyer of property. A seller of property who pays points reduces the selling price by the amount of the points paid for the buyer.
Portfolio	In finance, a portfolio is a collection of investments held by an institution or a private individual. Holding but not always a portfolio is part of an investment and risk-limiting strategy called diversification. By owning several assets, certain types of risk (in particular specific risk) can be reduced.
License	A license in the sphere of Intellectual Property Rights (IPR) is a document, contract or agreement giving permission or the 'right' to a legally-definable entity to do something (such as manufacture a product or to use a service), or to apply something (such as a trademark), with the objective of achieving commercial gain.
Contract	A contract is a "promise" or an "agreement" that is enforced or recognized by the law. In the civil law, a contract is considered to be part of the general law of obligations.
Economic growth	Economic growth refers to the increase over time in the capacity of an economy to produce goods and services and to improve the well-being of its citizens.
Preference	The act of a debtor in paying or securing one or more of his creditors in a manner more favorable to them than to other creditors or to the exclusion of such other creditors is a preference. In the absence of statute, a preference is perfectly good, but to be legal it

Go to **Cram101.com** for the Practice Tests for this Chapter.

must be bona fide, and not a mere subterfuge of the debtor to secure a future benefit to himself or to prevent the application of his property to his debts.

Customs	Customs is an authority or agency in a country responsible for collecting customs duties and for controlling the flow of people, animals and goods (including personal effects and hazardous items) in and out of the country.
Commerce	Commerce is the exchange of something of value between two entities. It is the central mechanism from which capitalism is derived.
Exporter	A firm that sells its product in another country is an exporter.
Firm	An organization that employs resources to produce a good or service for profit and owns and operates one or more plants is referred to as a firm.
Innovation	Innovation refers to the first commercially successful introduction of a new product, the use of a new method of production, or the creation of a new form of business organization.
Option	A contract that gives the purchaser the option to buy or sell the underlying financial instrument at a specified price, called the exercise price or strike price, within a specific period of time.
Intermediaries	Intermediaries specialize in information either to bring together two parties to a transaction or to buy in order to sell again.
Joint venture	Joint venture refers to an undertaking by two parties for a specific purpose and duration, taking any of several legal forms.
Franchising	Franchising is a method of doing business wherein a franchisor licenses trademarks and tried and proven methods of doing business to a franchisee in exchange for a recurring payment, and usually a percentage piece of gross sales or gross profits as well as the annual fees. The term " franchising " is used to describe a wide variety of business systems which may or may not fall into the legal definition provided above.
Licensing	Licensing is a form of strategic alliance which involves the sale of a right to use certain proprietary knowledge (so called intellectual property) in a defined way.
Exporting	Selling products to another country is called exporting.
Barter	Barter is a type of trade where goods or services are exchanged for a certain amount of other goods or services; no money is involved in the transaction.
Leadership	Management merely consists of leadership applied to business situations; or in other words: management forms a sub-set of the broader process of leadership.
International Business	International business refers to any firm that engages in international trade or investment.
Microsoft	Microsoft is a multinational computer technology corporation with 2004 global annual sales of US$39.79 billion and 71,553 employees in 102 countries and regions as of July 2006. It develops, manufactures, licenses, and supports a wide range of software products for computing devices.
Acquisition	A company's purchase of the property and obligations of another company is an acquisition.
Converse	Converse is an American shoe company which has been making shoes since the early 20th century. The company's main turning point came in 1917 when the Converse All-Star basketball shoe was introduced. This was a real innovation at the time, considering the sport was only 25 years old.
Subsidiary	A company that is controlled by another company or corporation is a subsidiary.

Users	Users refer to people in the organization who actually use the product or service purchased by the buying center.
Market research	Market research is the process of systematic gathering, recording and analyzing of data about customers, competitors and the market. Market research can help create a business plan, launch a new product or service, fine tune existing products and services, expand into new markets etc. It can be used to determine which portion of the population will purchase the product/service, based on variables like age, gender, location and income level. It can be found out what market characteristics your target market has.
Sales lead	A sales lead is the identity of a person or entity potentially interested in purchasing a product of service, and represents the first stage of a sales process.
Distribution	Distribution in economics, the manner in which total output and income is distributed among individuals or factors.
Management	Management characterizes the process of leading and directing all or part of an organization, often a business, through the deployment and manipulation of resources. Early twentieth-century management writer Mary Parker Follett defined management as "the art of getting things done through people."
Channel	Channel, in communications (sometimes called communications channel), refers to the medium used to convey information from a sender (or transmitter) to a receiver.
Export management company	Export management company refers to export specialists who act as an export-marketing department for client firms.
Export	In economics, an export is any good or commodity, shipped or otherwise transported out of a country, province, town to another part of the world in a legitimate fashion, typically for use in trade or sale.
Merchant	Under the Uniform Commercial Code, one who regularly deals in goods of the kind sold in the contract at issue, or holds himself out as having special knowledge or skill relevant to such goods, or who makes the sale through an agent who regularly deals in such goods or claims such knowledge or skill is referred to as merchant.
Product line	A group of products that are physically similar or are intended for a similar market are called the product line.
Tactic	A short-term immediate decision that, in its totality, leads to the achievement of strategic goals is called a tactic.
Antitrust laws	Legislation that prohibits anticompetitive business activities such as price fixing, bid rigging, monopolization, and tying contracts is referred to as antitrust laws.
Cooperative	A business owned and controlled by the people who use it, producers, consumers, or workers with similar needs who pool their resources for mutual gain is called cooperative.
Antitrust	Government intervention to alter market structure or prevent abuse of market power is called antitrust.
Agent	A person who makes economic decisions for another economic actor. A hired manager operates as an agent for a firm's owner.
Loyalty	Marketers tend to define customer loyalty as making repeat purchases. Some argue that it should be defined attitudinally as a strongly positive feeling about the brand.
Supply	Supply is the aggregate amount of any material good that can be called into being at a certain price point; it comprises one half of the equation of supply and demand. In classical economic theory, a curve representing supply is one of the factors that produce price.

Go to **Cram101.com** for the Practice Tests for this Chapter.

Operation	A standardized method or technique that is performed repetitively, often on different materials resulting in different finished goods is called an operation.
Revenue	Revenue is a U.S. business term for the amount of money that a company receives from its activities, mostly from sales of products and/or services to customers.
Buyer	A buyer refers to a role in the buying center with formal authority and responsibility to select the supplier and negotiate the terms of the contract.
Screening	Screening in economics refers to a strategy of combating adverse selection, one of the potential decision-making complications in cases of asymmetric information.
Trade show	A type of exhibition or forum where manufacturers can display their products to current as well as prospective buyers is referred to as trade show.
Profit	Profit refers to the return to the resource entrepreneurial ability; total revenue minus total cost.
Direct sale	A direct sale is a sale to customers through distributors or self-employed sales people rather than through shops. Includes both personal contact with consumers in their homes (and other nonstore locations such as offices) and phone solicitations initiated by a retailer.
Specialist	A specialist is a trader who makes a market in one or several stocks and holds the limit order book for those stocks.
Advertising	Advertising refers to paid, nonpersonal communication through various media by organizations and individuals who are in some way identified in the advertising message.
Economic development	Increase in the economic standard of living of a country's population, normally accomplished by increasing its stocks of physical and human capital and improving its technology is an economic development.
Export promotion	Export promotion refers to a strategy for economic development that stresses expanding exports, often through policies to assist them such as export subsidies.
Promotion	Promotion refers to all the techniques sellers use to motivate people to buy products or services. An attempt by marketers to inform people about products and to persuade them to participate in an exchange.
Administration	Administration refers to the management and direction of the affairs of governments and institutions; a collective term for all policymaking officials of a government; the execution and implementation of public policy.
Foundation	A Foundation is a type of philanthropic organization set up by either individuals or institutions as a legal entity (either as a corporation or trust) with the purpose of distributing grants to support causes in line with the goals of the foundation.
Marketing Plan	Marketing plan refers to a road map for the marketing activities of an organization for a specified future period of time, such as one year or five years.
Variable	A variable is something measured by a number; it is used to analyze what happens to other things when the size of that number changes.
Preparation	Preparation refers to usually the first stage in the creative process. It includes education and formal training.
Asset	An item of property, such as land, capital, money, a share in ownership, or a claim on others for future payment, such as a bond or a bank deposit is an asset.
Negotiation	Negotiation is the process whereby interested parties resolve disputes, agree upon courses of action, bargain for individual or collective advantage, and/or attempt to craft outcomes which serve their mutual interests.

Go to **Cram101.com** for the Practice Tests for this Chapter.

Chapter 12. Global Marketing Strategies for Entrepreneurs

Go to **Cram101.com** for the Practice Tests for this Chapter.
And, **NEVER** highlight a book again!

Trust	An arrangement in which shareholders of independent firms agree to give up their stock in exchange for trust certificates that entitle them to a share of the trust's common profits.
Business ethics	The study of what makes up good and bad conduct as related to business activities and values is business ethics.
Harvard Business Review	Harvard Business Review is a research-based magazine written for business practitioners, it claims a high ranking business readership and enjoys the reverence of academics, executives, and management consultants. It has been the frequent publishing home for well known scholars and management thinkers.
Body language	Body language is a broad term for forms of communication using body movements or gestures instead of, or in addition to, sounds, verbal language, or other forms of communication.
Countertrade	Countertrade is exchanging goods or services that are paid for, in whole or part, with other goods or services.
Countertrading	The sale of goods or services that are paid for in whole or in part by the transfer of goods or services between seperate countries is called countertrading. Also referred to as bartering.
Complexity	The technical sophistication of the product and hence the amount of understanding required to use it is referred to as complexity. It is the opposite of simplicity.
Convertible currency	Convertible currency refers to a currency that can legally be exchanged for another or for gold.
Exchange	The trade of things of value between buyer and seller so that each is better off after the trade is called the exchange.
Capital	Capital generally refers to financial wealth, especially that used to start or maintain a business. In classical economics, capital is one of four factors of production, the others being land and labor and entrepreneurship.
Business plan	A detailed written statement that describes the nature of the business, the target market, the advantages the business will have in relation to competition, and the resources and qualifications of the owner is referred to as a business plan.
Consultant	A professional that provides expert advice in a particular field or area in which customers occassionaly require this type of knowledge is a consultant.
Freight forwarder	An organization that puts many small shipments together to create a single large shipment that can be transported cost-effectively to the final destination is called freight forwarder.
Regulation	Regulation refers to restrictions state and federal laws place on business with regard to the conduct of its activities.
Credit	Credit refers to a recording as positive in the balance of payments, any transaction that gives rise to a payment into the country, such as an export, the sale of an asset, or borrowing from abroad.
Draft	A signed, written order by which one party instructs another party to pay a specified sum to a third party, at sight or at a specific date is a draft.
Letter of credit	An instrument containing a request to pay to the bearer or person named money, or sell him or her some commodity on credit or give something of value and look to the drawer of the letter for recompense is called letter of credit.
Creditworthiness	Creditworthiness indicates whether a borrower has in the past made loan payments when due.
Financial risk	The risk related to the inability of the firm to meet its debt obligations as they come due

	is called financial risk.
Sight draft	Sight draft refers to a draft or bill that is payable on demand or upon presentation.
Time draft	A draft payable at a designated future date is referred to as time draft.
Forming	The first stage of team development, where the team is formed and the objectives for the team are set is referred to as forming.
Tax treaty	Tax treaty refers to an agreement between the U.S. Department of State and another country, designed to alleviate double taxation of income and asset transfers, and to share administrative information useful to tax agencies in both countries.
Treaties	The first source of international law, consisting of agreements or contracts between two or more nations that are formally signed by an authorized representative and ratified by the supreme power of each nation are called treaties.
Shell	One of the original Seven Sisters, Royal Dutch/Shell is the world's third-largest oil company by revenue, and a major player in the petrochemical industry and the solar energy business. Shell has six core businesses: Exploration and Production, Gas and Power, Downstream, Chemicals, Renewables, and Trading/Shipping, and operates in more than 140 countries.
Shareholder	A shareholder is an individual or company (including a corporation) that legally owns one or more shares of stock in a joined stock company.
Free On Board	Free On Board is an Incoterm. It means that the seller pays for transportation of the goods to the port of shipment, plus loading costs. The buyer pays freight, insurance, unloading costs and transportation from the port of destination to his factory. The passing of risks occurs when the goods pass the ship's rail at the port of shipment.
Insurance	Insurance refers to a system by which individuals can reduce their exposure to risk of large losses by spreading the risks among a large number of persons.
Cost and Freight	Cost and Freight is an Incoterm. It means that the seller pays for transportation to the port of shipment, loading and freight. The buyer pays for the insurance and transportation of the goods from the port of destination to his factory. The passing of risk occurs when the goods pass the ship's rail at the port of shipment.
Journal	Book of original entry, in which transactions are recorded in a general ledger system, is referred to as a journal.
Investment	Investment refers to spending for the production and accumulation of capital and additions to inventories. In a financial sense, buying an asset with the expectation of making a return.
Budget	Budget refers to an account, usually for a year, of the planned expenditures and the expected receipts of an entity. For a government, the receipts are tax revenues.
Free trade	Free trade refers to a situation in which there are no artificial barriers to trade, such as tariffs and quotas. Usually used, often only implicitly, with frictionless trade, so that it implies that there are no barriers to trade of any kind.
Expense	In accounting, an expense represents an event in which an asset is used up or a liability is incurred. In terms of the accounting equation, expenses reduce owners' equity.
Trade barrier	An artificial disincentive to export and/or import, such as a tariff, quota, or other NTB is called a trade barrier.
Target market	One or more specific groups of potential consumers toward which an organization directs its marketing program are a target market.
Global marketing	A strategy of using a common marketing plan and program for all countries in which a company operates, thus selling the product or services the same way everywhere in the world is called

global marketing.

Global marketing strategy	The practice of standardizing marketing activities when there are cultural similarities and adapting them when cultures differ is referred to as global marketing strategy.
Financial institution	A financial institution acts as an agent that provides financial services for its clients. Financial institutions generally fall under financial regulation from a government authority.
Tariff	A tax imposed by a nation on an imported good is called a tariff.
Quota	A government-imposed restriction on quantity, or sometimes on total value, used to restrict the import of something to a specific quantity is called a quota.
Union	A worker association that bargains with employers over wages and working conditions is called a union.
Competitor	Other organizations in the same industry or type of business that provide a good or service to the same set of customers is referred to as a competitor.
Embargo	Embargo refers to the prohibition of some category of trade. May apply to exports and/or imports, of particular products or of all trade, vis a vis the world or a particular country or countries.
Market share	That fraction of an industry's output accounted for by an individual firm or group of firms is called market share.
Dumping	Dumping refers to a practice of charging a very low price in a foreign market for such economic purposes as putting rival suppliers out of business.
Private property	The right of private persons and firms to obtain, own, control, employ, dispose of, and bequeath land, capital, and other property is referred to as private property.
Takeover	A takeover in business refers to one company (the acquirer) purchasing another (the target). Such events resemble mergers, but without the formation of a new company.
Property	Assets defined in the broadest legal sense. Property includes the unrealized receivables of a cash basis taxpayer, but not services rendered.
Human resources	Human resources refers to the individuals within the firm, and to the portion of the firm's organization that deals with hiring, firing, training, and other personnel issues.
Overtime	Overtime is the amount of time someone works beyond normal working hours.
Labor	People's physical and mental talents and efforts that are used to help produce goods and services are called labor.
Labor force	In economics the labor force is the group of people who have a potential for being employed.
Accounting	A system that collects and processes financial information about an organization and reports that information to decision makers is referred to as accounting.
Labor union	A group of workers organized to advance the interests of the group is called a labor union.
Business philosophy	A business philosophy is any of a range of approaches to accounting, marketing, public relations, operations, training, labor relations, executive time management, investment, and/or corporate governance claimed to improve business performance in some measurable or otherwise provable way.
General Agreement on Tariffs and Trade	The General Agreement on Tariffs and Trade was originally created by the Bretton Woods Conference as part of a larger plan for economic recovery after World War II. It included a reduction in tariffs and other international trade barriers and is generally considered the precursor to the World Trade Organization.

225

Uruguay round	The eighth and most recent round of trade negotiations under GATT is referred to as Uruguay round.
Inception	The date and time on which coverage under an insurance policy takes effect is inception. Also refers to the date at which a stock or mutual fund was first traded.
Trend	Trend refers to the long-term movement of an economic variable, such as its average rate of increase or decrease over enough years to encompass several business cycles.
Subsidy	Subsidy refers to government financial assistance to a domestic producer.
Patent	The legal right to the proceeds from and control over the use of an invented product or process, granted for a fixed period of time, usually 20 years. Patent is one form of intellectual property that is subject of the TRIPS agreement.
World Trade Organization	The World Trade Organization is an international, multilateral organization, which sets the rules for the global trading system and resolves disputes between its member states, all of whom are signatories to its approximately 30 agreements.
Trade dispute	Trade dispute refers to any disagreement between nations involving their international trade or trade policies.
North American Free Trade Agreement	A 1993 agreement establishing, over a 15-year period, a free trade zone composed of Canada, Mexico, and the United States is referred to as the North American Free Trade Agreement.
Free trade area	Free trade area refers to a group of countries that adopt free trade on trade among group members, while not necessarily changing the barriers that each member country has on trade with the countries outside the group.
Nontariff barrier	Any policy that interferes with exports or imports other than a simple tariff, prominently including quotas and vers is referred to as nontariff barrier.
Leverage	Leverage is using given resources in such a way that the potential positive or negative outcome is magnified. In finance, this generally refers to borrowing.
Appeal	Appeal refers to the act of asking an appellate court to overturn a decision after the trial court's final judgment has been entered.
Trading bloc	Trading bloc refers to a group of countries that are somehow closely associated in international trade, usually in some sort of PTA.
Gap	In December of 1995, Gap became the first major North American retailer to accept independent monitoring of the working conditions in a contract factory producing its garments. Gap is the largest specialty retailer in the United States.
Trademark	A distinctive word, name, symbol, device, or combination thereof, which enables consumers to identify favored products or services and which may find protection under state or federal law is a trademark.
Copyright	The legal right to the proceeds from and control over the use of a created product, such a written work, audio, video, film, or software is a copyright. This right generally extends over the life of the author plus fifty years.
Franchisor	A company that develops a product concept and sells others the rights to make and sell the products is referred to as a franchisor.
Franchise	A contractual right to sell certain products or services, use certain trademarks, or perform activities in a geographical region is called a franchise.
Interest	In finance and economics, interest is the price paid by a borrower for the use of a lender's money. In other words, interest is the amount of paid to "rent" money for a period of time.

Wall Street Journal

Dow Jones & Company was founded in 1882 by reporters Charles Dow, Edward Jones and Charles Bergstresser. Jones converted the small Customers' Afternoon Letter into The Wall Street Journal, first published in 1889, and began delivery of the Dow Jones News Service via telegraph. The Journal featured the Jones 'Average', the first of several indexes of stock and bond prices on the New York Stock Exchange.

228

Go to **Cram101.com** for the Practice Tests for this Chapter.

229

Go to **Cram101.com** for the Practice Tests for this Chapter.
And, **NEVER** highlight a book again!

Entrepreneur	The owner/operator. The person who organizes, manages, and assumes the risks of a firm, taking a new idea or a new product and turning it into a successful business is an entrepreneur.
Security	Security refers to a claim on the borrower future income that is sold by the borrower to the lender. A security is a type of transferable interest representing financial value.
New economy	New economy, this term was used in the late 1990's to suggest that globalization and/or innovations in information technology had changed the way that the world economy works.
Technology	The body of knowledge and techniques that can be used to combine economic resources to produce goods and services is called technology.
Economy	The income, expenditures, and resources that affect the cost of running a business and household are called an economy.
Business model	A business model is the instrument by which a business intends to generate revenue and profits. It is a summary of how a company means to serve its employees and customers, and involves both strategy (what an business intends to do) as well as an implementation.
Commerce	Commerce is the exchange of something of value between two entities. It is the central mechanism from which capitalism is derived.
Industry	A group of firms that produce identical or similar products is an industry. It is also used specifically to refer to an area of economic production focused on manufacturing which involves large amounts of capital investment before any profit can be realized, also called "heavy industry".
Market	A market is, as defined in economics, a social arrangement that allows buyers and sellers to discover information and carry out a voluntary exchange of goods or services.
Advertising	Advertising refers to paid, nonpersonal communication through various media by organizations and individuals who are in some way identified in the advertising message.
Marketing	Promoting and selling products or services to customers, or prospective customers, is referred to as marketing.
Business opportunity	A business opportunity involves the sale or lease of any product, service, equipment, etc. that will enable the purchaser-licensee to begin a business
Retailing	All activities involved in selling, renting, and providing goods and services to ultimate consumers for personal, family, or household use is referred to as retailing.
Service	Service refers to a "non tangible product" that is not embodied in a physical good and that typically effects some change in another product, person, or institution. Contrasts with good.
Balance	In banking and accountancy, the outstanding balance is the amount of money owned, (or due), that remains in a deposit account (or a loan account) at a given date, after all past remittances, payments and withdrawal have been accounted for. It can be positive (then, in the balance sheet of a firm, it is an asset) or negative (a liability).
Strike	The withholding of labor services by an organized group of workers is referred to as a strike.
Commodity	Could refer to any good, but in trade a commodity is usually a raw material or primary product that enters into international trade, such as metals or basic agricultural products.
Futures	Futures refer to contracts for the sale and future delivery of stocks or commodities, wherein either party may waive delivery, and receive or pay, as the case may be, the difference in market price at the time set for delivery.

Go to **Cram101.com** for the Practice Tests for this Chapter.

Go to **Cram101.com** for the Practice Tests for this Chapter.
And, **NEVER** highlight a book again!

Capital	Capital generally refers to financial wealth, especially that used to start or maintain a business. In classical economics, capital is one of four factors of production, the others being land and labor and entrepreneurship.
Niche	In industry, a niche is a situation or an activity perfectly suited to a person. A niche can imply a working position or an area suited to a person who occupies it. Basically, a job where a person is able to succeed and thrive.
Gross domestic product	Gross domestic product refers to the total value of new goods and services produced in a given year within the borders of a country, regardless of by whom.
Domestic	From or in one's own country. A domestic producer is one that produces inside the home country. A domestic price is the price inside the home country. Opposite of 'foreign' or 'world.'.
Users	Users refer to people in the organization who actually use the product or service purchased by the buying center.
Small business	Small business refers to a business that is independently owned and operated, is not dominant in its field of operation, and meets certain standards of size in terms of employees or annual receipts.
Retail sale	The sale of goods and services to consumers for their own use is a retail sale.
Staffing	Staffing refers to a management function that includes hiring, motivating, and retaining the best people available to accomplish the company's objectives.
Expense	In accounting, an expense represents an event in which an asset is used up or a liability is incurred. In terms of the accounting equation, expenses reduce owners' equity.
Customer service	The ability of logistics management to satisfy users in terms of time, dependability, communication, and convenience is called the customer service.
Preference	The act of a debtor in paying or securing one or more of his creditors in a manner more favorable to them than to other creditors or to the exclusion of such other creditors is a preference. In the absence of statute, a preference is perfectly good, but to be legal it must be bona fide, and not a mere subterfuge of the debtor to secure a future benefit to himself or to prevent the application of his property to his debts.
Appeal	Appeal refers to the act of asking an appellate court to overturn a decision after the trial court's final judgment has been entered.
Generation y	Generation y refers to Americans born after 1976, the year that many baby boomers began having children.
Configuration	An organization's shape, which reflects the division of labor and the means of coordinating the divided tasks is configuration.
Accommodation	Accommodation is a term used to describe a delivery of nonconforming goods meant as a partial performance of a contract for the sale of goods, where a full performance is not possible.
Promotion	Promotion refers to all the techniques sellers use to motivate people to buy products or services. An attempt by marketers to inform people about products and to persuade them to participate in an exchange.
Sales lead	A sales lead is the identity of a person or entity potentially interested in purchasing a product of service, and represents the first stage of a sales process.
Inventory control	Inventory control, in the field of loss prevention, are systems designed to introduce technical barriers to shoplifting.
Control system	A control system is a device or set of devices that manage the behavior of other devices.

	Some devices or systems are not controllable. A control system is an interconnection of components connected or related in such a manner as to command, direct, or regulate itself or another system.
Inventory	Tangible property held for sale in the normal course of business or used in producing goods or services for sale is an inventory.
Market share	That fraction of an industry's output accounted for by an individual firm or group of firms is called market share.
Banner ad	A banner ad is a form of advertising on the World Wide Web. This form of online advertising entails embedding an advertisement into a web page.
Hosting	Internet hosting service is a service that runs Internet servers, allowing organizations and individuals to serve content on the Internet.
Operation	A standardized method or technique that is performed repetitively, often on different materials resulting in different finished goods is called an operation.
Brand	A name, symbol, or design that identifies the goods or services of one seller or group of sellers and distinguishes them from the goods and services of competitors is a brand.
Business marketing	Business marketing is the practice of organizations, including commercial businesses, governments and institutions, facilitating the sale of their products or services to other companies or organizations that in turn resell them, use them as components in products or services they offer, or use them to support their operations.
Marketing strategy	Marketing strategy refers to the means by which a marketing goal is to be achieved, usually characterized by a specified target market and a marketing program to reach it.
Investment	Investment refers to spending for the production and accumulation of capital and additions to inventories. In a financial sense, buying an asset with the expectation of making a return.
Electronic business	Electronic business is any business process that is empowered by an information system. Today, this is mostly done with Web-based technologies.
Business strategy	Business strategy, which refers to the aggregated operational strategies of single business firm or that of an SBU in a diversified corporation refers to the way in which a firm competes in its chosen arenas.
Target audience	That group that composes the present and potential prospects for a product or service is called the target audience.
Merchant	Under the Uniform Commercial Code, one who regularly deals in goods of the kind sold in the contract at issue, or holds himself out as having special knowledge or skill relevant to such goods, or who makes the sale through an agent who regularly deals in such goods or claims such knowledge or skill is referred to as merchant.
Buyer	A buyer refers to a role in the buying center with formal authority and responsibility to select the supplier and negotiate the terms of the contract.
Budget	Budget refers to an account, usually for a year, of the planned expenditures and the expected receipts of an entity. For a government, the receipts are tax revenues.
Channel of distribution	A whole set of marketing intermediaries, such as wholesalers and retailers, who join together to transport and store goods in their path from producers to consumers is referred to as channel of distribution.
Distribution	Distribution in economics, the manner in which total output and income is distributed among individuals or factors.
Channel	Channel, in communications (sometimes called communications channel), refers to the medium

	used to convey information from a sender (or transmitter) to a receiver.
Management	Management characterizes the process of leading and directing all or part of an organization, often a business, through the deployment and manipulation of resources. Early twentieth-century management writer Mary Parker Follett defined management as "the art of getting things done through people."
Warehouse	Warehouse refers to a location, often decentralized, that a firm uses to store, consolidate, age, or mix stock; house product-recall programs; or ease tax burdens.
Supply	Supply is the aggregate amount of any material good that can be called into being at a certain price point; it comprises one half of the equation of supply and demand. In classical economic theory, a curve representing supply is one of the factors that produce price.
Back office	A back office is a part of most corporations where tasks dedicated to running the company itself take place.
Stock	In financial terminology, stock is the capital raized by a corporation, through the issuance and sale of shares.
Transaction cost	A transaction cost is a cost incurred in making an economic exchange. For example, most people, when buying or selling a stock, must pay a commission to their broker; that commission is a transaction cost of doing the stock deal.
Revenue	Revenue is a U.S. business term for the amount of money that a company receives from its activities, mostly from sales of products and/or services to customers.
Productivity	Productivity refers to the total output of goods and services in a given period of time divided by work hours.
Profit	Profit refers to the return to the resource entrepreneurial ability; total revenue minus total cost.
Purchasing	Purchasing refers to the function in a firm that searches for quality material resources, finds the best suppliers, and negotiates the best price for goods and services.
Purchase order	A form on which items or services needed by a business firm are specified and then communicated to the vendor is a purchase order.
Average cost	Average cost is equal to total cost divided by the number of goods produced (Quantity-Q). It is also equal to the sum of average variable costs (total variable costs divided by Q) plus average fixed costs (total fixed costs divided by Q).
Procurement	Procurement is the acquisition of goods or services at the best possible total cost of ownership, in the right quantity, at the right time, in the right place for the direct benefit or use of the governments, corporations, or individuals generally via, but not limited to a contract.
Front office	In Business, front office refers to Sales and Marketing divisions of a company. It may also refer to other divisions in a company that involves interactions with customers.
Cisco Systems	While Cisco Systems was not the first company to develop and sell a router (a device that forwards computer traffic from one network to another), it did create the first commercially successful multi-protocol router to allow previously incompatible computers to communicate using different network protocols.
Raw material	Raw material refers to a good that has not been transformed by production; a primary product.
Raw materials inventory	Raw materials inventory refers to inventory consisting of the basic inputs to the organization's production process.
Option	A contract that gives the purchaser the option to buy or sell the underlying financial

Go to **Cram101.com** for the Practice Tests for this Chapter.

237

	instrument at a specified price, called the exercise price or strike price, within a specific period of time.
Standing	Standing refers to the legal requirement that anyone seeking to challenge a particular action in court must demonstrate that such action substantially affects his legitimate interests before he will be entitled to bring suit.
Credit	Credit refers to a recording as positive in the balance of payments, any transaction that gives rise to a payment into the country, such as an export, the sale of an asset, or borrowing from abroad.
Family business	A family business is a company owned, controlled, and operated by members of one or several families. Many companies that are now publicly held were founded as family businesses. Many family businesses have non-family members as employees, but, particularly in smaller companies, the top positions are often allocated to family members.
Discount	The difference between the face value of a bond and its selling price, when a bond is sold for less than its face value it's referred to as a discount.
Remainder	A remainder in property law is a future interest created in a transferee that is capable of becoming possessory upon the natural termination of a prior estate created by the same instrument.
Marketing cost	Marketing cost refers to the cost incurred in selling goods or services. Includes order-getting costs and order-filling or distribution costs.
Markup	Markup is a term used in marketing to indicate how much the price of a product is above the cost of producing and distributing the product.
Product line	A group of products that are physically similar or are intended for a similar market are called the product line.
Setup cost	A setup cost is any cost necessary to prepare for production and to purchase inventory.
Integration	Economic integration refers to reducing barriers among countries to transactions and to movements of goods, capital, and labor, including harmonization of laws, regulations, and standards. Integrated markets theoretically function as a unified market.
Niche market	A niche market or market niche is a focused, targetable portion of a market. By definition, then, a business that focuses on a niche market is addressing a need for a product or service that is not being addressed by mainstream providers.
Customer profile	Description, primarily quantitative, of an individual or segment using specified demographic, lifestyle, and behavioral characteristics is a customer profile.
Competitor	Other organizations in the same industry or type of business that provide a good or service to the same set of customers is referred to as a competitor.
Interest	In finance and economics, interest is the price paid by a borrower for the use of a lender's money. In other words, interest is the amount of paid to "rent" money for a period of time.
Customer loyalty	Marketers tend to define customer loyalty as making repeat purchases. Some argue that it should be defined attitudinally as a strongly positive feeling about the brand.
Consultant	A professional that provides expert advice in a particular field or area in which customers occassionaly require this type of knowledge is a consultant.
Boston Consulting Group	The Boston Consulting Group is a management consulting firm founded by Harvard Business School alum Bruce Henderson in 1963. In 1965 Bruce Henderson thought that to survive, much less grow, in a competitive landscape occupied by hundreds of larger and better-known consulting firms, a distinctive identity was needed, and pioneered "Business Strategy" as a

Go to **Cram101.com** for the Practice Tests for this Chapter.

Go to **Cram101.com** for the Practice Tests for this Chapter.
And, **NEVER** highlight a book again!

special area of expertise.

Trust	An arrangement in which shareholders of independent firms agree to give up their stock in exchange for trust certificates that entitle them to a share of the trust's common profits.
Credibility	The extent to which a source is perceived as having knowledge, skill, or experience relevant to a communication topic and can be trusted to give an unbiased opinion or present objective information on the issue is called credibility.
Complaint	The pleading in a civil case in which the plaintiff states his claim and requests relief is called complaint. In the common law, it is a formal legal document that sets out the basic facts and legal reasons that the filing party (the plaintiffs) believes are sufficient to support a claim against another person, persons, entity or entities (the defendants) that entitles the plaintiff(s) to a remedy (either money damages or injunctive relief).
Strategic alliance	Strategic alliance refers to a long-term partnership between two or more companies established to help each company build competitive market advantages.
America Online	In 2000 America Online and Time Warner announced plans to merge, and the deal was approved by the Federal Trade Commission on January 11, 2001. This merger was primarily a product of the Internet mania of the late-1990s, known as the Internet bubble. The deal is known as one of the worst corporate mergers in history, destroying over $200 billion in shareholder value.
Administrator	Administrator refers to the personal representative appointed by a probate court to settle the estate of a deceased person who died.
Intel	Intel Corporation, founded in 1968 and based in Santa Clara, California, USA, is the world's largest semiconductor company. Intel is best known for its PC microprocessors, where it maintains roughly 80% market share.
Localization	As an element of wireless marketing strategy, transmitting messages that are relevant to the user's current geographical location are referred to as localization.
Exchange	The trade of things of value between buyer and seller so that each is better off after the trade is called the exchange.
Market research	Market research is the process of systematic gathering, recording and analyzing of data about customers, competitors and the market. Market research can help create a business plan, launch a new product or service, fine tune existing products and services, expand into new markets etc. It can be used to determine which portion of the population will purchase the product/service, based on variables like age, gender, location and income level. It can be found out what market characteristics your target market has.
Yield	The interest rate that equates a future value or an annuity to a given present value is a yield.
Complement	A good that is used in conjunction with another good is a complement. For example, cameras and film would complement eachother.
Layout	Layout refers to the physical arrangement of the various parts of an advertisement including the headline, subheads, illustrations, body copy, and any identifying marks.
Incentive	An incentive is any factor (financial or non-financial) that provides a motive for a particular course of action, or counts as a reason for preferring one choice to the alternatives.
Policy	Similar to a script in that a policy can be a less than completely rational decision-making method. Involves the use of a pre-existing set of decision steps for any problem that presents itself.
Mistake	In contract law a mistake is incorrect understanding by one or more parties to a contract and

Go to **Cram101.com** for the Practice Tests for this Chapter.

may be used as grounds to invalidate the agreement. Common law has identified three different types of mistake in contract: unilateral mistake, mutual mistake, and common mistake.

Browser	A program that allows a user to connect to the World Wide Web by simply typing in a URL is a browser.
Journal	Book of original entry, in which transactions are recorded in a general ledger system, is referred to as a journal.
Leadership	Management merely consists of leadership applied to business situations; or in other words: management forms a sub-set of the broader process of leadership.
Teamwork	That which occurs when group members work together in ways that utilize their skills well to accomplish a purpose is called teamwork.
Publicity	Publicity refers to any information about an individual, product, or organization that's distributed to the public through the media and that's not paid for or controlled by the seller.
Sticky	Sticky is a term used in economics used to describe a situation in which a variable is resistant to change. For example, nominal wages are often said to be sticky.
Marketing channel	Individuals and firms involved in the process of making a product or service available for use or consumption by consumers or industrial users is a marketing channel.
Conversion	Conversion refers to any distinct act of dominion wrongfully exerted over another's personal property in denial of or inconsistent with his rights therein. That tort committed by a person who deals with chattels not belonging to him in a manner that is inconsistent with the ownership of the lawful owner.
Artificial intelligence	Computers or computer enhaned machines that can be programmed to think, learn, and make decisions in a manner similar to people is is the subject of artificial intelligence.
Return on investment	Return on investment refers to the return a businessperson gets on the money he and other owners invest in the firm; for example, a business that earned $100 on a $1,000 investment would have a ROI of 10 percent: 100 divided by 1000.
Federal trade commission	The commission of five members established by the Federal Trade Commission Act of 1914 to investigate unfair competitive practices of firms, to hold hearings on the complaints of such practices, and to issue cease-and-desist orders when firms were found guilty of unfair practices.
Comprehensive	A comprehensive refers to a layout accurate in size, color, scheme, and other necessary details to show how a final ad will look. For presentation only, never for reproduction.
Damages	The sum of money recoverable by a plaintiff who has received a judgment in a civil case is called damages.
Firm	An organization that employs resources to produce a good or service for profit and owns and operates one or more plants is referred to as a firm.
Financial intermediary	Financial intermediary refers to a financial institution, such as a bank or a life insurance company, which directs other people's money into such investments as government and corporate securities.
Fraud	Tax fraud falls into two categories: civil and criminal. Under civil fraud, the IRS may impose as a penalty of an amount equal to as much as 75 percent of the underpayment.
Wall Street Journal	Dow Jones & Company was founded in 1882 by reporters Charles Dow, Edward Jones and Charles Bergstresser. Jones converted the small Customers' Afternoon Letter into The Wall Street Journal, first published in 1889, and began delivery of the Dow Jones News Service via

telegraph. The Journal featured the Jones 'Average', the first of several indexes of stock and bond prices on the New York Stock Exchange.

Estate

An estate is the totality of the legal rights, interests, entitlements and obligations attaching to property. In the context of wills and probate, it refers to the totality of the property which the deceased owned or in which some interest was held.

Forbes

David Churbuck founded online Forbes in 1996. The site drew attention when it uncovered Stephen Glass' journalistic fraud in The New Republic in 1998, a scoop that gave credibility to internet journalism.

244

Go to **Cram101.com** for the Practice Tests for this Chapter.

Personal saving	Personal saving refers to the personal income of households less personal taxes and personal consumption expenditures; disposable income not spent for consumer goods.
Venture capital	Venture capital is capital provided by outside investors for financing of new, growing or struggling businesses. Venture capital investments generally are high risk investments but offer the potential for above average returns.
Equity capital	Equity capital refers to money raized from within the firm or through the sale of ownership in the firm.
Entrepreneur	The owner/operator. The person who organizes, manages, and assumes the risks of a firm, taking a new idea or a new product and turning it into a successful business is an entrepreneur.
Corporation	A legal entity chartered by a state or the Federal government that is distinct and separate from the individuals who own it is a corporation. This separation gives the corporation unique powers which other legal entities lack.
Capital	Capital generally refers to financial wealth, especially that used to start or maintain a business. In classical economics, capital is one of four factors of production, the others being land and labor and entrepreneurship.
Equity	Equity is the name given to the set of legal principles, in countries following the English common law tradition, which supplement strict rules of law where their application would operate harshly, so as to achieve what is sometimes referred to as "natural justice."
Stock	In financial terminology, stock is the capital raized by a corporation, through the issuance and sale of shares.
Security	Security refers to a claim on the borrower future income that is sold by the borrower to the lender. A security is a type of transferable interest representing financial value.
Shares	Shares refer to an equity security, representing a shareholder's ownership of a corporation. Shares are one of a finite number of equal portions in the capital of a company, entitling the owner to a proportion of distributed, non-reinvested profits known as dividends and to a portion of the value of the company in case of liquidation.
Capital market	A financial market in which long-term debt and equity instruments are traded is referred to as a capital market. The capital market includes the stock market and the bond market.
Stock market	An organized marketplace in which common stocks are traded. In the United States, the largest stock market is the New York Stock Exchange, on which are traded the stocks of the largest U.S. companies.
Market	A market is, as defined in economics, a social arrangement that allows buyers and sellers to discover information and carry out a voluntary exchange of goods or services.
Initial public offering	Firms in the process of becoming publicly traded companies will issue shares of stock using an initial public offering, which is merely the process of selling stock for the first time to interested investors.
Tight money	A term to indicate time periods in which financing may be difficult to find and interest rates may be quite high by normal standards is called tight money.
Manufacturing	Production of goods primarily by the application of labor and capital to raw materials and other intermediate inputs, in contrast to agriculture, mining, forestry, fishing, and services a manufacturing.
Distribution	Distribution in economics, the manner in which total output and income is distributed among individuals or factors.

Go to **Cram101.com** for the Practice Tests for this Chapter.

Industry	A group of firms that produce identical or similar products is an industry. It is also used specifically to refer to an area of economic production focused on manufacturing which involves large amounts of capital investment before any profit can be realized, also called "heavy industry".
Economy	The income, expenditures, and resources that affect the cost of running a business and household are called an economy.
Estate	An estate is the totality of the legal rights, interests, entitlements and obligations attaching to property. In the context of wills and probate, it refers to the totality of the property which the deceased owned or in which some interest was held.
Venture capitalists	Venture capitalists refer to individuals or companies that invest in new businesses in exchange for partial ownership of those businesses.
Futures	Futures refer to contracts for the sale and future delivery of stocks or commodities, wherein either party may waive delivery, and receive or pay, as the case may be, the difference in market price at the time set for delivery.
Option	A contract that gives the purchaser the option to buy or sell the underlying financial instrument at a specified price, called the exercise price or strike price, within a specific period of time.
Credit	Credit refers to a recording as positive in the balance of payments, any transaction that gives rise to a payment into the country, such as an export, the sale of an asset, or borrowing from abroad.
Service	Service refers to a "non tangible product" that is not embodied in a physical good and that typically effects some change in another product, person, or institution. Contrasts with good.
Fund	Independent accounting entity with a self-balancing set of accounts segregated for the purposes of carrying on specific activities is referred to as a fund.
Business plan	A detailed written statement that describes the nature of the business, the target market, the advantages the business will have in relation to competition, and the resources and qualifications of the owner is referred to as a business plan.
Lender	Suppliers and financial institutions that lend money to companies is referred to as a lender.
Firm	An organization that employs resources to produce a good or service for profit and owns and operates one or more plants is referred to as a firm.
Venture capital firm	A financial intermediary that pools the resources of its partners and uses the funds to help entrepreneurs start up new businesses is referred to as a venture capital firm.
Inventory	Tangible property held for sale in the normal course of business or used in producing goods or services for sale is an inventory.
Fixed capital	Fixed capital is a concept in economics and accounting, first theoretically analysed in some depth by the economist David Ricardo. It refers to any kind of real or physical capital that is not used up in the production of a product. It is contrasted with circulating capital.
Fixed asset	Fixed asset, also known as property, plant, and equipment (PP&E), is a term used in accountancy for assets and property which cannot easily be converted into cash. This can be compared with current assets such as cash or bank accounts, which are described as liquid assets. In most cases, only tangible assets are referred to as fixed.
Asset	An item of property, such as land, capital, money, a share in ownership, or a claim on others for future payment, such as a bond or a bank deposit is an asset.

Go to **Cram101.com** for the Practice Tests for this Chapter.

Purchasing	Purchasing refers to the function in a firm that searches for quality material resources, finds the best suppliers, and negotiates the best price for goods and services.
Working capital	The dollar difference between total current assets and total current liabilities is called working capital.
Operation	A standardized method or technique that is performed repetitively, often on different materials resulting in different finished goods is called an operation.
Current liability	Current liability refers to a debt that can reasonably be expected to be paid from existing current assets or through the creation of other current liabilities, within one year or the operating cycle, whichever is longer.
Current asset	A current asset is an asset on the balance sheet which is expected to be sold or otherwise used up in the near future, usually within one year.
Liability	A liability is a present obligation of the enterprise arizing from past events, the settlement of which is expected to result in an outflow from the enterprise of resources embodying economic benefits.
Wage	The payment for the service of a unit of labor, per unit time. In trade theory, it is the only payment to labor, usually unskilled labor. In empirical work, wage data may exclude other compenzation, which must be added to get the total cost of employment.
Credit sale	A credit sale occurs when a customer does not pay cash at the time of the sale but instead agrees to pay later. The sale occurs now, with payment from the customer to follow at a later time.
Cash flow	In finance, cash flow refers to the amounts of cash being received and spent by a business during a defined period of time, sometimes tied to a specific project. Most of the time they are being used to determine gaps in the liquid position of a company.
Regulation	Regulation refers to restrictions state and federal laws place on business with regard to the conduct of its activities.
Small business	Small business refers to a business that is independently owned and operated, is not dominant in its field of operation, and meets certain standards of size in terms of employees or annual receipts.
Production	The creation of finished goods and services using the factors of production: land, labor, capital, entrepreneurship, and knowledge.
Capital requirement	The capital requirement is a bank regulation, which sets a framework on how banks and depository institutions must handle their capital. The categorization of assets and capital is highly standardized so that it can be risk weighted.
Investment	Investment refers to spending for the production and accumulation of capital and additions to inventories. In a financial sense, buying an asset with the expectation of making a return.
Equity investment	Equity investment generally refers to the buying and holding of shares of stock on a stock market by individuals and funds in anticipation of income from dividends and capital gain as the value of the stock rises.
Sun Microsystems	Sun Microsystems is most well known for its Unix systems, which have a reputation for system stability and a consistent design philosophy.
Federal Express	The company officially began operations on April 17, 1973, utilizing a network of 14 Dassault Falcon 20s which connected 25 U.S. cities. FedEx, the first cargo airline to use jet aircraft for its services, expanded greatly after the deregulation of the cargo airlines sector. Federal Express use of the hub-spoke distribution paradigm in air freight enabled it to become a world leader in its field.

Go to **Cram101.com** for the Practice Tests for this Chapter.

Microsoft	Microsoft is a multinational computer technology corporation with 2004 global annual sales of US$39.79 billion and 71,553 employees in 102 countries and regions as of July 2006. It develops, manufactures, licenses, and supports a wide range of software products for computing devices.
Intel	Intel Corporation, founded in 1968 and based in Santa Clara, California, USA, is the world's largest semiconductor company. Intel is best known for its PC microprocessors, where it maintains roughly 80% market share.
Yahoo	Yahoo is an American computer services company. It operates an Internet portal, the Yahoo Directory and a host of other services including the popular Yahoo Mail. Yahoo is the most visited website on the Internet today with more than 400 million unique users. The global network of Yahoo! websites received 3.4 billion page views per day on average as of October 2005.
Startup	Any new company can be considered a startup, but the description is usually applied to aggressive young companies that are actively courting private financing from venture capitalists, including wealthy individuals and investment companies.
Shareholder	A shareholder is an individual or company (including a corporation) that legally owns one or more shares of stock in a joined stock company.
Bridge financing	Bridge financing is a method of financing, used by companies before their initial public offering, to obtain necessary cash for the maintenance of operations.
Family business	A family business is a company owned, controlled, and operated by members of one or several families. Many companies that are now publicly held were founded as family businesses. Many family businesses have non-family members as employees, but, particularly in smaller companies, the top positions are often allocated to family members.
Manufacturing business	A business firm that makes the products it sells is called a manufacturing business.
Retained earnings	Cumulative earnings of a company that are not distributed to the owners and are reinvested in the business are called retained earnings.
Accounts receivable	Accounts receivable is one of a series of accounting transactions dealing with the billing of customers which owe money to a person, company or organization for goods and services that have been provided to the customer. This is typically done in a one person organization by writing an invoice and mailing or delivering it to each customer.
Factoring	In mathematics, factorization or factoring is the decomposition of an object into a product of other objects, or factors, which when multiplied together give the original.
Line of credit	Line of credit refers to a given amount of unsecured short-term funds a bank will lend to a business, provided the funds are readily available.
Marketing	Promoting and selling products or services to customers, or prospective customers, is referred to as marketing.
Consultant	A professional that provides expert advice in a particular field or area in which customers occassionaly require this type of knowledge is a consultant.
Bezos	Bezos founded Amazon.com in 1994, and became one of the most prominent dot-com billionaire entrepreneurs. In 2004, he started a human spaceflight start-up company called Blue Origin.
Growth stage	The second stage of the product life cycle characterized by rapid increases in sales and by the appearance of competitors is referred to as the growth stage.
Gap	In December of 1995, Gap became the first major North American retailer to accept independent monitoring of the working conditions in a contract factory producing its garments. Gap is the

Go to **Cram101.com** for the Practice Tests for this Chapter.

253

	largest specialty retailer in the United States.
Oracle	In 2004, sales at Oracle grew at a rate of 14.5% to $6.2 billion, giving it 41.3% and the top share of the relational-database market. Their main competitors in the database arena are IBM DB2 and Microsoft SQL Server, and to a lesser extent Sybase, Teradata, Informix, and MySQL. In the applications arena, their main competitor is SAP.
Investment portfolio	An investment portfolio is an aggregate of investments, such as stocks, bonds, real estate, arts or even fine wines. What distinguishes an investment portfolio from net worth is that some asset classes are not considered investments.
Startup company	A startup company is a company recently formed, usually until IPO or acquisition. Another increasingly prevalent definition differentiates a startup company from a regular business. Whereas a business is usually medium risk and medium return on investment, startup companies usually have lower bootstrapping costs, higher risk, and higher return on investment.
Inherent Risk	Inherent risk is the auditor's assessment that there are material misstatements in the financial statements before considering the effectiveness of internal controls. If the auditor concludes that there is a high likelihood of misstamtement, ignoring internal controls, the auditor would conclude that the inherent risk is high.
Portfolio	In finance, a portfolio is a collection of investments held by an institution or a private individual. Holding but not always a portfolio is part of an investment and risk-limiting strategy called diversification. By owning several assets, certain types of risk (in particular specific risk) can be reduced.
Interest	In finance and economics, interest is the price paid by a borrower for the use of a lender's money. In other words, interest is the amount of paid to "rent" money for a period of time.
Competitive advantage	A business is said to have a competitive advantage when its unique strengths, often based on cost, quality, time, and innovation, offer consumers a greater percieved value and there by differtiating it from its competitors.
Management team	A management team is directly responsible for managing the day-to-day operations (and profitability) of a company.
Management	Management characterizes the process of leading and directing all or part of an organization, often a business, through the deployment and manipulation of resources. Early twentieth-century management writer Mary Parker Follett defined management as "the art of getting things done through people."
Niche	In industry, a niche is a situation or an activity perfectly suited to a person. A niche can imply a working position or an area suited to a person who occupies it. Basically, a job where a person is able to succeed and thrive.
Stockbroker	A registered representative who works as a market intermediary to buy and sell securities for clients is a stockbroker.
Brief	Brief refers to a statement of a party's case or legal arguments, usually prepared by an attorney. Also used to make legal arguments before appellate courts.
Inception	The date and time on which coverage under an insurance policy takes effect is inception. Also refers to the date at which a stock or mutual fund was first traded.
Technology	The body of knowledge and techniques that can be used to combine economic resources to produce goods and services is called technology.
Rate of return	A rate of return is a comparison of the money earned (or lost) on an investment to the amount of money invested.
Limited	A partnership in which some of the partners are limited partners. At least one of the

partnership	partners in a limited partnership must be a general partner.
Partnership	In the common law, a partnership is a type of business entity in which partners share with each other the profits or losses of the business undertaking in which they have all invested.
General partners	Partners in a limited partnership who invest capital, manage the business, and are personally liable for partnership debts are referred to as general partners.
General partner	An owner who has unlimited liability and is active in managing the firm is a general partner. The individual or firm that organizes and manages the limited partnership. For example a hedge fund.
Angel financing	Financing provided by a wealthy individual who believes in the idea for a start-up and provides personal funds and advice to help the business get started is called angel financing.
Nonprofit organization	An organization whose goals do not include making a personal profit for its owners is a nonprofit organization.
Commerce	Commerce is the exchange of something of value between two entities. It is the central mechanism from which capitalism is derived.
Trust	An arrangement in which shareholders of independent firms agree to give up their stock in exchange for trust certificates that entitle them to a share of the trust's common profits.
Common stock	Common stock refers to the basic, normal, voting stock issued by a corporation; called residual equity because it ranks after preferred stock for dividend and liquidation distributions.
Coercion	Economic coercion is when an agent puts economic pressure onto the victim. The most common example of this is cutting off the supply to an essential resource, such as water.
General Electric	In 1876, Thomas Alva Edison opened a new laboratory in Menlo Park, New Jersey. Out of the laboratory was to come perhaps the most famous invention of all—a successful development of the incandescent electric lamp. By 1890, Edison had organized his various businesses into the Edison General Electric Company.
Cisco Systems	While Cisco Systems was not the first company to develop and sell a router (a device that forwards computer traffic from one network to another), it did create the first commercially successful multi-protocol router to allow previously incompatible computers to communicate using different network protocols.
Motorola	The Six Sigma quality system was developed at Motorola even though it became most well known because of its use by General Electric. It was created by engineer Bill Smith, under the direction of Bob Galvin (son of founder Paul Galvin) when he was running the company.
Nokia	Nokia Corporation is the world's largest manufacturer of mobile telephones (as of June 2006), with a global market share of approximately 34% in Q2 of 2006. It produces mobile phones for every major market and protocol, including GSM, CDMA, and W-CDMA (UMTS).
Gain	In finance, gain is a profit or an increase in value of an investment such as a stock or bond. Gain is calculated by fair market value or the proceeds from the sale of the investment minus the sum of the purchase price and all costs associated with it.
Distribution channel	A distribution channel is a chain of intermediaries, each passing a product down the chain to the next organization, before it finally reaches the consumer or end-user.
Channel	Channel, in communications (sometimes called communications channel), refers to the medium used to convey information from a sender (or transmitter) to a receiver.
Credibility	The extent to which a source is perceived as having knowledge, skill, or experience relevant

Go to **Cram101.com** for the Practice Tests for this Chapter.

	to a communication topic and can be trusted to give an unbiased opinion or present objective information on the issue is called credibility.
Enterprise	Enterprise refers to another name for a business organization. Other similar terms are business firm, sometimes simply business, sometimes simply firm, as well as company, and entity.
Foreign corporation	Foreign corporation refers to a corporation incorporated in one state doing business in another state. A corporation doing business in a jurisdiction in which it was not formed.
Strategic partnership	Strategic partnership refers to an association between two firms by which they agree to work together to achieve a strategic goal. This is often associated with long-term supplier-customer relationships.
Ford	Ford is an American company that manufactures and sells automobiles worldwide. Ford introduced methods for large-scale manufacturing of cars, and large-scale management of an industrial workforce, especially elaborately engineered manufacturing sequences typified by the moving assembly lines.
Endowment	Endowment refers to the amount of something that a person or country simply has, rather than their having somehow to acquire it.
Apple Computer	Apple Computer has been a major player in the evolution of personal computing since its founding in 1976. The Apple II microcomputer, introduced in 1977, was a hit with home users.
Browser	A program that allows a user to connect to the World Wide Web by simply typing in a URL is a browser.
Users	Users refer to people in the organization who actually use the product or service purchased by the buying center.
Policy	Similar to a script in that a policy can be a less than completely rational decision-making method. Involves the use of a pre-existing set of decision steps for any problem that presents itself.
Cost structure	The relative proportion of an organization's fixed, variable, and mixed costs is referred to as cost structure.
Screening	Screening in economics refers to a strategy of combating adverse selection, one of the potential decision-making complications in cases of asymmetric information.
Comprehensive	A comprehensive refers to a layout accurate in size, color, scheme, and other necessary details to show how a final ad will look. For presentation only, never for reproduction.
Preferred stock	Stock that has specified rights over common stock is a preferred stock.
Convertible preferred stock	Preferred stock that includes an option for the holder to convert the preferred shares into a fixed number of common shares, usually anytime after a predetermined date is convertible preferred stock.
Allowance	Reduction in the selling price of goods extended to the buyer because the goods are defective or of lower quality than the buyer ordered and to encourage a buyer to keep merchandise that would otherwise be returned is the allowance.
Acquisition	A company's purchase of the property and obligations of another company is an acquisition.
Revenue	Revenue is a U.S. business term for the amount of money that a company receives from its activities, mostly from sales of products and/or services to customers.
Business model	A business model is the instrument by which a business intends to generate revenue and profits. It is a summary of how a company means to serve its employees and customers, and involves both strategy (what an business intends to do) as well as an implementation.

Go to **Cram101.com** for the Practice Tests for this Chapter.

Financial plan	The financial plan section of a business plan consists of three financial statements (the income statement, the cash flow projection, and the balance sheet) and a brief analysis of these three statements.
Budget	Budget refers to an account, usually for a year, of the planned expenditures and the expected receipts of an entity. For a government, the receipts are tax revenues.
Learning curve	Learning curve is a function that measures how labor-hours per unit decline as units of production increase because workers are learning and becoming better at their jobs.
Margin	A deposit by a buyer in stocks with a seller or a stockbroker, as security to cover fluctuations in the market in reference to stocks that the buyer has purchased but for which he has not paid is a margin. Commodities are also traded on margin.
Repositioning	Changing the position an offering occupies in a consumer's mind relative to competitive offerings and so expanding or otherwise altering its potential market is called repositioning.
Market share	That fraction of an industry's output accounted for by an individual firm or group of firms is called market share.
Profit margin	Profit margin is a measure of profitability. It is calculated using a formula and written as a percentage or a number. Profit margin = Net income before tax and interest / Revenue.
Expense	In accounting, an expense represents an event in which an asset is used up or a liability is incurred. In terms of the accounting equation, expenses reduce owners' equity.
Profit	Profit refers to the return to the resource entrepreneurial ability; total revenue minus total cost.
Competitor	Other organizations in the same industry or type of business that provide a good or service to the same set of customers is referred to as a competitor.
Fixed cost	The cost that a firm bears if it does not produce at all and that is independent of its output. The presence of a fixed cost tends to imply increasing returns to scale. Contrasts with variable cost.
Wall Street Journal	Dow Jones & Company was founded in 1882 by reporters Charles Dow, Edward Jones and Charles Bergstresser. Jones converted the small Customers' Afternoon Letter into The Wall Street Journal, first published in 1889, and began delivery of the Dow Jones News Service via telegraph. The Journal featured the Jones 'Average', the first of several indexes of stock and bond prices on the New York Stock Exchange.
Journal	Book of original entry, in which transactions are recorded in a general ledger system, is referred to as a journal.
Exchange	The trade of things of value between buyer and seller so that each is better off after the trade is called the exchange.
Advertising agency	A firm that specializes in the creation, production, and placement of advertising messages and may provide other services that facilitate the marketing communications process is an advertising agency.
Advertising	Advertising refers to paid, nonpersonal communication through various media by organizations and individuals who are in some way identified in the advertising message.
Sales lead	A sales lead is the identity of a person or entity potentially interested in purchasing a product of service, and represents the first stage of a sales process.
Forming	The first stage of team development, where the team is formed and the objectives for the team are set is referred to as forming.

Go to **Cram101.com** for the Practice Tests for this Chapter.

Exit strategy	In entrepreneurship and strategic management an exit strategy is a way to terminate either ones ownership of a company or the operation of some part of the company.
Investment banker	Investment banker refers to a financial organization that specializes in selling primary offerings of securities. Investment bankers can also perform other financial functions, such as advising clients, negotiating mergers and takeovers, and selling secondary offerings.
Innovation	Innovation refers to the first commercially successful introduction of a new product, the use of a new method of production, or the creation of a new form of business organization.
Liaison	An individual who serves as a bridge between groups, tying groups together and facilitating the communication flow needed to integrate group activities is a liaison.
Committee	A long-lasting, sometimes permanent team in the organization structure created to deal with tasks that recur regularly is the committee.
Productivity	Productivity refers to the total output of goods and services in a given period of time divided by work hours.
Public company	A public company is a company owned by the public rather than by a relatively few individuals. There are two different meanings for this term: (1) A company that is owned by stockholders who are members of the general public and trade shares publicly, often through a listing on a stock exchange. Ownership is open to anyone that has the money and inclination to buy shares in the company. It is differentiated from privately held companies where the shares are held by a small group of individuals, who are often members of one or a small group of families or otherwise related individuals, or other companies. The variant of this type of company in the United Kingdom and Ireland is known as a public limited compan, and (2) A government-owned corporation. This meaning of a "public company" comes from the fact that government debt is sometimes referred to as "public debt" although there are no "public bonds", government finance is sometimes called "public finance", among similar uses. This is the less-common meaning.
Net worth	Net worth is the total assets minus total liabilities of an individual or company
Stock option	A stock option is a specific type of option that uses the stock itself as an underlying instrument to determine the option's pay-off and therefore its value.
Loyalty	Marketers tend to define customer loyalty as making repeat purchases. Some argue that it should be defined attitudinally as a strongly positive feeling about the brand.
Employee Stock Ownership Plans	Like profit sharing, Employee Stock Ownership Plans are based on the total organization's performance, but are measured in terms of stock price.
Employee stock ownership plan	Employee Stock Ownership Plan is a qualified employee-benefit plan in which employees are entitled and encouraged to invest in shares of the company's stock and often at a favorable price. The employer's contributions are tax deductible for the employer and tax deferred for the employee.
Stock purchase plan	A stock purchase plan is an organized plan for employees of a company to buy shares of its stock.
Enabling	Enabling refers to giving workers the education and tools they need to assume their new decision-making powers.
Stock exchange	A stock exchange is a corporation or mutual organization which provides facilities for stock brokers and traders, to trade company stocks and other securities.
Market system	All the product and resource markets of a market economy and the relationships among them are called a market system.
Regional stock	Any securities exchange located outside a country's main financial center is a regional stock

exchange	exchange.
Dealer	People who link buyers with sellers by buying and selling securities at stated prices are referred to as a dealer.
NASDAQ	NASDAQ is an American electronic stock exchange. It was founded in 1971 by the National Association of Securities Dealers who divested it in a series of sales in 2000 and 2001.
Takeover	A takeover in business refers to one company (the acquirer) purchasing another (the target). Such events resemble mergers, but without the formation of a new company.
Stockholder	A stockholder is an individual or company (including a corporation) that legally owns one or more shares of stock in a joined stock company. The shareholders are the owners of a corporation. Companies listed at the stock market strive to enhance shareholder value.
Securities and exchange commission	Securities and exchange commission refers to U.S. government agency that determines the financial statements that public companies must provide to stockholders and the measurement rules that they must use in producing those statements.
Raw material	Raw material refers to a good that has not been transformed by production; a primary product.
Prospectus	Prospectus refers to a report detailing a future stock offering containing a set of financial statements; required by the SEC from a company that wishes to make an initial public offering of its stock.
Patent	The legal right to the proceeds from and control over the use of an invented product or process, granted for a fixed period of time, usually 20 years. Patent is one form of intellectual property that is subject of the TRIPS agreement.
Accounting	A system that collects and processes financial information about an organization and reports that information to decision makers is referred to as accounting.
Return on investment	Return on investment refers to the return a businessperson gets on the money he and other owners invest in the firm; for example, a business that earned $100 on a $1,000 investment would have a ROI of 10 percent: 100 divided by 1000.
Fraud	Tax fraud falls into two categories: civil and criminal. Under civil fraud, the IRS may impose as a penalty of an amount equal to as much as 75 percent of the underpayment.
Balance	In banking and accountancy, the outstanding balance is the amount of money owned, (or due), that remains in a deposit account (or a loan account) at a given date, after all past remittances, payments and withdrawal have been accounted for. It can be positive (then, in the balance sheet of a firm, it is an asset) or negative (a liability).
Registration statement	Document that an issuer of securities files with the SEC that contains required information about the issuer, the securities to be issued, and other relevant information so the security may be sold on a national stock exchange is a registration statement.
Underwriting syndicate	Underwriting syndicate refers to a group of investment bankers that is formed to share the risk of a security offering and also to facilitate the distribution of the securities.
Underwriting	The process of selling securities and, at the same time, assuring the seller a specified price is underwriting. Underwriting is done by investment bankers and represents a form of risk taking.
Warrant	A warrant is a security that entitles the holder to buy or sell a certain additional quantity of an underlying security at an agreed-upon price, at the holder's discretion.
Best efforts	Best efforts refer to a distribution in which the investment banker agrees to work for a commission rather than actually underwriting the issue for resale. It is a procedure that is used by smaller investment bankers with relatively unknown companies. The investment banker

Go to **Cram101.com** for the Practice Tests for this Chapter.

is not directly taking the risk for distribution.

Agent	A person who makes economic decisions for another economic actor. A hired manager operates as an agent for a firm's owner.
Underwriters	Investment banks that guarantee prices on securities to corporations and then sell the securities to the public are underwriters.
Aftermarket	The market for a new security offering immediately after it is sold to the public is referred to as aftermarket.
Capital structure	Capital Structure refers to the way a corporation finances itself through some combination of equity sales, equity options, bonds, and loans. Optimal capital structure refers to the particular combination that minimizes the cost of capital while maximizing the stock price.
Corporate finance	Corporate finance is a specific area of finance dealing with the financial decisions corporations make and the tools as well as analyses used to make these decisions. The discipline as a whole may be divided among long-term and short-term decisions and techniques with the primary goal being the enhancing of corporate value by ensuring that return on capital exceeds cost of capital, without taking excessive financial risks.
Publicity	Publicity refers to any information about an individual, product, or organization that's distributed to the public through the media and that's not paid for or controlled by the seller.
Final settlement	Final settlement occurs when the payor bank pays the check in cash, settles for the check without having a right to revoke the settlement, or fails to dishonor the check within certain statutory time periods.
Closing	The finalization of a real estate sales transaction that passes title to the property from the seller to the buyer is referred to as a closing. Closing is a sales term which refers to the process of making a sale. It refers to reaching the final step, which may be an exchange of money or acquiring a signature.
Disclosure	Disclosure means the giving out of information, either voluntarily or to be in compliance with legal regulations or workplace rules.
Total cost	The sum of fixed cost and variable cost is referred to as total cost.
Broker	In commerce, a broker is a party that mediates between a buyer and a seller. A broker who also acts as a seller or as a buyer becomes a principal party to the deal.
Equity financing	Financing that consists of funds that are invested in exchange for ownership in the company is called equity financing.
Disclosure statement	A statement that is presented to the Court and must contain adequate information about the proposed plan of reorganization that is supplied to the creditors and equity holders is called disclosure statement.
Stock warrant	Stock warrant refers to a document authorizing its holder to purchase a stated number of shares of stock at a stated price, usually for a stated period of time; may be freely traded.
Department of Energy	The Department of Energy is a Cabinet-level department of the United States government responsible for energy policy and nuclear safety. Its purview includes the nation's nuclear weapons program, nuclear reactor production for the United States Navy, energy conservation, energy-related research, radioactive waste disposal, and domestic energy production.
Grant	Grant refers to an intergovernmental transfer of funds . Since the New Deal, state and local governments have become increasingly dependent upon federal grants for an almost infinite variety of programs.

Go to **Cram101.com** for the Practice Tests for this Chapter.

Research and development	The use of resources for the deliberate discovery of new information and ways of doing things, together with the application of that information in inventing new products or processes is referred to as research and development.
Advertisement	Advertisement is the promotion of goods, services, companies and ideas, usually by an identified sponsor. Marketers see advertising as part of an overall promotional strategy.
Financial statement	Financial statement refers to a summary of all the transactions that have occurred over a particular period.
Regulatory agency	Regulatory agency refers to an agency, commission, or board established by the Federal government or a state government to regulates businesses in the public interest.
Secondary market	Secondary market refers to the market for securities that have already been issued. It is a market in which investors trade back and forth with each other.
Brokerage firm	A company that conducts various aspects of securities trading, analysis and advisory services is a brokerage firm.
Private placement	Private placement refers to the sale of securities directly to a financial institution by a corporation. This eliminates the middleman and reduces the cost of issue to the corporation.
Early growth	Early growth refers to the first stage of the retail life cycle, when a new outlet emerges as a sharp departure from competitive forms.
Frequency	Frequency refers to the speed of the up and down movements of a fluctuating economic variable; that is, the number of times per unit of time that the variable completes a cycle of up and down movement.
Accredited investor	The U.S. Securities and Exchange Commission will allow only an accredited investor to invest in certain risky, high-yield investments, limited partnerships, and angel investor networks. This accredited investor can be an organization such as a business or retirement plan, or a rich individual. For an individual to be considered an accredited investor he must have a net worth of at least one million US dollars or have made at least $200,000 dollars each year for the last two years ($300,000 with his spouse if married) and have the expectation to make the same amount this year.
Net profit	Net profit is an accounting term which is commonly used in business. It is equal to the gross revenue for a given time period minus associated expenses.
Appeal	Appeal refers to the act of asking an appellate court to overturn a decision after the trial court's final judgment has been entered.
Information system	An information system is a system whether automated or manual, that comprises people, machines, and/or methods organized to collect, process, transmit, and disseminate data that represent user information.
Social responsibility	Social responsibility is a doctrine that claims that an entity whether it is state, government, corporation, organization or individual has a responsibility to society.
Product line	A group of products that are physically similar or are intended for a similar market are called the product line.
Securities market	The securities market is the market for securities, where companies and the government can raise long-term funds.
Limited partner	An owner of a limited partnership who has no right to manage the business but who possesses liability limited to his capital contribution to the business is referred to as limited partner.
Corporate image	A corporate image refers to how a corporation is perceived. It is a generally accepted image

Go to **Cram101.com** for the Practice Tests for this Chapter.

of what a company "stands for".

Financial institution	A financial institution acts as an agent that provides financial services for its clients. Financial institutions generally fall under financial regulation from a government authority.
Administrator	Administrator refers to the personal representative appointed by a probate court to settle the estate of a deceased person who died.
Business development	Business development emcompasses a number of techniques designed to grow an economic enterprise. Such techniques include, but are not limited to, assessments of marketing opportunities and target markets, intelligence gathering on customers and competitors, generating leads for possible sales, followup sales activity, and formal proposal writing.
Forbes	David Churbuck founded online Forbes in 1996. The site drew attention when it uncovered Stephen Glass' journalistic fraud in The New Republic in 1998, a scoop that gave credibility to internet journalism.
Capitalism	Capitalism refers to an economic system in which capital is mostly owned by private individuals and corporations. Contrasts with communism.

Go to **Cram101.com** for the Practice Tests for this Chapter.

Credit	Credit refers to a recording as positive in the balance of payments, any transaction that gives rise to a payment into the country, such as an export, the sale of an asset, or borrowing from abroad.
Administration	Administration refers to the management and direction of the affairs of governments and institutions; a collective term for all policymaking officials of a government; the execution and implementation of public policy.
Small business	Small business refers to a business that is independently owned and operated, is not dominant in its field of operation, and meets certain standards of size in terms of employees or annual receipts.
Economic development	Increase in the economic standard of living of a country's population, normally accomplished by increasing its stocks of physical and human capital and improving its technology is an economic development.
Fund	Independent accounting entity with a self-balancing set of accounts segregated for the purposes of carrying on specific activities is referred to as a fund.
Debt financing	Obtaining financing by borrowing money is debt financing.
Interest	In finance and economics, interest is the price paid by a borrower for the use of a lender's money. In other words, interest is the amount of paid to "rent" money for a period of time.
Capital	Capital generally refers to financial wealth, especially that used to start or maintain a business. In classical economics, capital is one of four factors of production, the others being land and labor and entrepreneurship.
Lender	Suppliers and financial institutions that lend money to companies is referred to as a lender.
Balance sheet	A statement of the assets, liabilities, and net worth of a firm or individual at some given time often at the end of its "fiscal year," is referred to as a balance sheet.
Entrepreneur	The owner/operator. The person who organizes, manages, and assumes the risks of a firm, taking a new idea or a new product and turning it into a successful business is an entrepreneur.
Liability	A liability is a present obligation of the enterprise arizing from past events, the settlement of which is expected to result in an outflow from the enterprise of resources embodying economic benefits.
Balance	In banking and accountancy, the outstanding balance is the amount of money owned, (or due), that remains in a deposit account (or a loan account) at a given date, after all past remittances, payments and withdrawal have been accounted for. It can be positive (then, in the balance sheet of a firm, it is an asset) or negative (a liability).
Interest rate	The rate of return on bonds, loans, or deposits. When one speaks of 'the' interest rate, it is usually in a model where there is only one.
Firm	An organization that employs resources to produce a good or service for profit and owns and operates one or more plants is referred to as a firm.
Prime rate	The rate that a bank charges its most creditworthy customers is referred to as the prime rate.
Points	Loan origination fees that may be deductible as interest by a buyer of property. A seller of property who pays points reduces the selling price by the amount of the points paid for the buyer.
Equity capital	Equity capital refers to money raized from within the firm or through the sale of ownership in the firm.

273

Equity	Equity is the name given to the set of legal principles, in countries following the English common law tradition, which supplement strict rules of law where their application would operate harshly, so as to achieve what is sometimes referred to as "natural justice."
Working capital	The dollar difference between total current assets and total current liabilities is called working capital.
Expense	In accounting, an expense represents an event in which an asset is used up or a liability is incurred. In terms of the accounting equation, expenses reduce owners' equity.
Operating expense	In throughput accounting, the cost accounting aspect of Theory of Constraints (TOC), operating expense is the money spent turning inventory into throughput. In TOC, operating expense is limited to costs that vary strictly with the quantity produced, like raw materials and purchased components.
Productivity	Productivity refers to the total output of goods and services in a given period of time divided by work hours.
Cash flow	In finance, cash flow refers to the amounts of cash being received and spent by a business during a defined period of time, sometimes tied to a specific project. Most of the time they are being used to determine gaps in the liquid position of a company.
Discount	The difference between the face value of a bond and its selling price, when a bond is sold for less than its face value it's referred to as a discount.
Invoice	The itemized bill for a transaction, stating the nature of the transaction and its cost. In international trade, the invoice price is often the preferred basis for levying an ad valorem tariff.
Quality management	Quality management is a method for ensuring that all the activities necessary to design, develop and implement a product or service are effective and efficient with respect to the system and its performance.
Cash discount	Cash discount refers to a discount offered on merchandise sold to encourage prompt payment; offered by sellers of merchandise and represents sales discounts to the seller when they are used and purchase discounts to the purchaser of the merchandise.
Purchasing	Purchasing refers to the function in a firm that searches for quality material resources, finds the best suppliers, and negotiates the best price for goods and services.
Management	Management characterizes the process of leading and directing all or part of an organization, often a business, through the deployment and manipulation of resources. Early twentieth-century management writer Mary Parker Follett defined management as "the art of getting things done through people."
Vendor	A person who sells property to a vendee is a vendor. The words vendor and vendee are more commonly applied to the seller and purchaser of real estate, and the words seller and buyer are more commonly applied to the seller and purchaser of personal property.
Creditor	A person to whom a debt or legal obligation is owed, and who has the right to enforce payment of that debt or obligation is referred to as creditor.
Slowdown	A slowdown is an industrial action in which employees perform their duties but seek to reduce productivity or efficiency in their performance of these duties. A slowdown may be used as either a prelude or an alternative to a strike, as it is seen as less disruptive as well as less risky and costly for workers and their union.
Debt capital	Debt capital refers to funds raized through various forms of borrowing to finance a company that must be repaid.
Complexity	The technical sophistication of the product and hence the amount of understanding required to

Go to **Cram101.com** for the Practice Tests for this Chapter.

use it is referred to as complexity. It is the opposite of simplicity.

Option	A contract that gives the purchaser the option to buy or sell the underlying financial instrument at a specified price, called the exercise price or strike price, within a specific period of time.
Business plan	A detailed written statement that describes the nature of the business, the target market, the advantages the business will have in relation to competition, and the resources and qualifications of the owner is referred to as a business plan.
Financial market	In economics, a financial market is a mechanism which allows people to trade money for securities or commodities such as gold or other precious metals. In general, any commodity market might be considered to be a financial market, if the usual purpose of traders is not the immediate consumption of the commodity, but rather as a means of delaying or accelerating consumption over time.
Commercial bank	A firm that engages in the business of banking is a commercial bank.
Market	A market is, as defined in economics, a social arrangement that allows buyers and sellers to discover information and carry out a voluntary exchange of goods or services.
Collateral	Property that is pledged to the lender to guarantee payment in the event that the borrower is unable to make debt payments is called collateral.
Investment	Investment refers to spending for the production and accumulation of capital and additions to inventories. In a financial sense, buying an asset with the expectation of making a return.
Startup	Any new company can be considered a startup, but the description is usually applied to aggressive young companies that are actively courting private financing from venture capitalists, including wealthy individuals and investment companies.
Asset	An item of property, such as land, capital, money, a share in ownership, or a claim on others for future payment, such as a bond or a bank deposit is an asset.
Default	In finance, default occurs when a debtor has not met its legal obligations according to the debt contract, e.g. it has not made a scheduled payment, or violated a covenant (condition) of the debt contract.
Secured loan	Secured loan refers to a loan backed by something valuable, such as property.
Maturity	Maturity refers to the final payment date of a loan or other financial instrument, after which point no further interest or principal need be paid.
Liquidity	Liquidity refers to the capacity to turn assets into cash, or the amount of assets in a portfolio that have that capacity.
Line of credit	Line of credit refers to a given amount of unsecured short-term funds a bank will lend to a business, provided the funds are readily available.
Operation	A standardized method or technique that is performed repetitively, often on different materials resulting in different finished goods is called an operation.
Micromarketing	How an individual organization direct its marketing activities and allocates its resources to benefit its customers is micromarketing.
Principal	In agency law, one under whose direction an agent acts and for whose benefit that agent acts is a principal.
Interest expense	The cost a business incurs to borrow money. With respect to bonds payable, the interest expense is calculated by multiplying the market rate of interest by the carrying value of the bonds on the date of the payment.

Inventory	Tangible property held for sale in the normal course of business or used in producing goods or services for sale is an inventory.
Estate	An estate is the totality of the legal rights, interests, entitlements and obligations attaching to property. In the context of wills and probate, it refers to the totality of the property which the deceased owned or in which some interest was held.
Grant	Grant refers to an intergovernmental transfer of funds . Since the New Deal, state and local governments have become increasingly dependent upon federal grants for an almost infinite variety of programs.
Term loan	Term loan refers to an intermediate-length loan, in which credit is generally extended from one to seven years. The loan is usually repaid in monthly or quarterly installments over its life, rather than with one single payment.
Covenant	A covenant is a signed written agreement between two or more parties. Also referred to as a contract.
Security interest	A security interest is a property interest created by agreement or by operation of law over assets to secure the performance of an obligation (usually but not always the payment of a debt) which gives the beneficiary of the security interest certain preferential rights in relation to the assets.
Security	Security refers to a claim on the borrower future income that is sold by the borrower to the lender. A security is a type of transferable interest representing financial value.
Amortization schedule	An amortization schedule is a table detailing each periodic payment on a loan (typically a mortgage), as generated by an amortization calculator. They are calculated so that each periodic payment for the entirety of the loan is equal, making the repayment process somewhat simpler under amortization than with other models.
Amortization	Systematic and rational allocation of the acquisition cost of an intangible asset over its useful life is referred to as amortization.
Property	Assets defined in the broadest legal sense. Property includes the unrealized receivables of a cash basis taxpayer, but not services rendered.
Mortgage	Mortgage refers to a note payable issued for property, such as a house, usually repaid in equal installments consisting of part principle and part interest, over a specified period.
Installment contract	A contract that requires or authorizes the goods to be delivered and accepted in separate lots is called an installment contract.
Contract	A contract is a "promise" or an "agreement" that is enforced or recognized by the law. In the civil law, a contract is considered to be part of the general law of obligations.
Pledge	In law a pledge (also pawn) is a bailment of personal property as a security for some debt or engagement.
Contract A	Contract A is a concept applied in Canadian contract law (a Common Law system country) which has recently been applied by courts regarding the fairness and equal treatment of bidders in a contract tendering process. Essentially this concept formalises previously applied precedents and strengthens the protection afforded to Contractors in the tendering process.
Guaranty	An undertaking by one person to be answerable for the payment of some debt, or the due performance of some contract or duty by another person, who remains liable to pay or perform the same is called guaranty.
Gain	In finance, gain is a profit or an increase in value of an investment such as a stock or bond. Gain is calculated by fair market value or the proceeds from the sale of the investment minus the sum of the purchase price and all costs associated with it.

Go to **Cram101.com** for the Practice Tests for this Chapter.

Restructuring	Restructuring is the corporate management term for the act of partially dismantling and reorganizing a company for the purpose of making it more efficient and therefore more profitable.
Exporting	Selling products to another country is called exporting.
Fixture	Fixture refers to a thing that was originally personal property and that has been actually or constructively affixed to the soil itself or to some structure legally a part of the land.
Accounts receivable	Accounts receivable is one of a series of accounting transactions dealing with the billing of customers which owe money to a person, company or organization for goods and services that have been provided to the customer. This is typically done in a one person organization by writing an invoice and mailing or delivering it to each customer.
Direct labor	The earnings of employees who work directly on the products being manufactured are direct labor.
Labor	People's physical and mental talents and efforts that are used to help produce goods and services are called labor.
Export	In economics, an export is any good or commodity, shipped or otherwise transported out of a country, province, town to another part of the world in a legitimate fashion, typically for use in trade or sale.
Applicant	In many tribunal and administrative law suits, the person who initiates the claim is called the applicant.
Retained earnings	Cumulative earnings of a company that are not distributed to the owners and are reinvested in the business are called retained earnings.
International trade	The export of goods and services from a country and the import of goods and services into a country is referred to as the international trade.
National bank	A National bank refers to federally chartered banks. They are an ordinary private bank which operates nationally (as opposed to regionally or locally or even internationally).
Nonprofit organization	An organization whose goals do not include making a personal profit for its owners is a nonprofit organization.
Economic growth	Economic growth refers to the increase over time in the capacity of an economy to produce goods and services and to improve the well-being of its citizens.
Fixed interest rate	Interest rate that does not change over the life of the loan is called the fixed interest rate. A rate that does not fluctuate with general market conditions.
Fixed interest	A fixed interest rate loan is a loan where the interest rate doesn't fluctuate over the life of the loan. This allows the borrower to accurately predict their future payments. When the prevailing interest rate is very low, a fixed rate loan will be slightly higher than variable rate loans because the lender is taking a risk they he could get a higher interest rate by loaning money later.
Supply	Supply is the aggregate amount of any material good that can be called into being at a certain price point; it comprises one half of the equation of supply and demand. In classical economic theory, a curve representing supply is one of the factors that produce price.
Useful life	The length of service of a productive facility or piece of equipment is its useful life. The period of time during which an asset will have economic value and be usable.
Net income	Net income is equal to the income that a firm has after subtracting costs and expenses from the total revenue. Expenses will typically include tax expense.
Net worth	Net worth is the total assets minus total liabilities of an individual or company

Go to **Cram101.com** for the Practice Tests for this Chapter.

281

Tangible	Having a physical existence is referred to as the tangible. Personal property other than real estate, such as cars, boats, stocks, or other assets.
Entrepreneurship	The assembling of resources to produce new or improved products and technologies is referred to as entrepreneurship.
Accion International	ACCION International is a non-profit organization founded in 1961 whose mission it is to provide small loans and technical assistance to those around the world who are under-serviced by local banks.
Intermediaries	Intermediaries specialize in information either to bring together two parties to a transaction or to buy in order to sell again.
Production	The creation of finished goods and services using the factors of production: land, labor, capital, entrepreneurship, and knowledge.
Business development	Business development emcompasses a number of techniques designed to grow an economic enterprise. Such techniques include, but are not limited to, assessments of marketing opportunities and target markets, intelligence gathering on customers and competitors, generating leads for possible sales, followup sales activity, and formal proposal writing.
Holding	The holding is a court's determination of a matter of law based on the issue presented in the particular case. In other words: under this law, with these facts, this result.
Patent	The legal right to the proceeds from and control over the use of an invented product or process, granted for a fixed period of time, usually 20 years. Patent is one form of intellectual property that is subject of the TRIPS agreement.
Industry	A group of firms that produce identical or similar products is an industry. It is also used specifically to refer to an area of economic production focused on manufacturing which involves large amounts of capital investment before any profit can be realized, also called "heavy industry".
Consultant	A professional that provides expert advice in a particular field or area in which customers occassionaly require this type of knowledge is a consultant.
Warrant	A warrant is a security that entitles the holder to buy or sell a certain additional quantity of an underlying security at an agreed-upon price, at the holder's discretion.
Payback period	The amount of time required for a project's after-tax cash inflows to accumulate to an amount that covers the initial investment is a payback period.
Payback	A value that indicates the time period required to recoup an initial investment is a payback. The payback does not include the time-value-of-money concept.
Lien	In its most extensive meaning, it is a charge on property for the payment or discharge of a debt or duty is referred to as lien.
Federal government	Federal government refers to the government of the United States, as distinct from the state and local governments.
Manufacturing	Production of goods primarily by the application of labor and capital to raw materials and other intermediate inputs, in contrast to agriculture, mining, forestry, fishing, and services a manufacturing.
Authority	Authority in agency law, refers to an agent's ability to affect his principal's legal relations with third parties. Also used to refer to an actor's legal power or ability to do something. In addition, sometimes used to refer to a statute, case, or other legal source that justifies a particular result.
Service	Service refers to a "non tangible product" that is not embodied in a physical good and that

Go to **Cram101.com** for the Practice Tests for this Chapter.

typically effects some change in another product, person, or institution. Contrasts with good.

Venture capital	Venture capital is capital provided by outside investors for financing of new, growing or struggling businesses. Venture capital investments generally are high risk investments but offer the potential for above average returns.
Insurance	Insurance refers to a system by which individuals can reduce their exposure to risk of large losses by spreading the risks among a large number of persons.
Policy	Similar to a script in that a policy can be a less than completely rational decision-making method. Involves the use of a pre-existing set of decision steps for any problem that presents itself.
Financial institution	A financial institution acts as an agent that provides financial services for its clients. Financial institutions generally fall under financial regulation from a government authority.
Corporation	A legal entity chartered by a state or the Federal government that is distinct and separate from the individuals who own it is a corporation. This separation gives the corporation unique powers which other legal entities lack.
Enterprise	Enterprise refers to another name for a business organization. Other similar terms are business firm, sometimes simply business, sometimes simply firm, as well as company, and entity.
Commercial finance companies	Organizations that make short-term loans to borrowers who offer tangible assets as collateral are referred to as commercial finance companies.
Factoring	In mathematics, factorization or factoring is the decomposition of an object into a product of other objects, or factors, which when multiplied together give the original.
Face value	The nominal or par value of an instrument as expressed on its face is referred to as the face value.
Gap	In December of 1995, Gap became the first major North American retailer to accept independent monitoring of the working conditions in a contract factory producing its garments. Gap is the largest specialty retailer in the United States.
Lease	A contract for the possession and use of land or other property, including goods, on one side, and a recompense of rent or other income on the other is the lease.
Tying	Tying is the practice of making the sale of one good (the tying good) to the de facto or de jure customer conditional on the purchase of a second distinctive good.
Arthur Andersen	Arthur Andersen was once one of the Big Five accounting firms, performing auditing, tax, and consulting services for large corporations. In 2002 the firm voluntarily surrendered its licenses to practice as Certified Public Accountants in the U.S. pending the result of prosecution by the U.S. Department of Justice over the firm's handling of the auditing of Enron.
Franchise	A contractual right to sell certain products or services, use certain trademarks, or perform activities in a geographical region is called a franchise.
Franchising	Franchising is a method of doing business wherein a franchisor licenses trademarks and tried and proven methods of doing business to a franchisee in exchange for a recurring payment, and usually a percentage piece of gross sales or gross profits as well as the annual fees. The term " franchising " is used to describe a wide variety of business systems which may or may not fall into the legal definition provided above.
Mail fraud	The use of mail to defraud another person is referred to as mail fraud.

Fraud	Tax fraud falls into two categories: civil and criminal. Under civil fraud, the IRS may impose as a penalty of an amount equal to as much as 75 percent of the underpayment.
A share	In finance the term A share has two distinct meanings, both relating to securities. The first is a designation for a 'class' of common or preferred stock. A share of common or preferred stock typically has enhanced voting rights or other benefits compared to the other forms of shares that may have been created. The equity structure, or how many types of shares are offered, is determined by the corporate charter.
Broker	In commerce, a broker is a party that mediates between a buyer and a seller. A broker who also acts as a seller or as a buyer becomes a principal party to the deal.
Credibility	The extent to which a source is perceived as having knowledge, skill, or experience relevant to a communication topic and can be trusted to give an unbiased opinion or present objective information on the issue is called credibility.
Inventory financing	The process of using inventory such as raw materials as collateral for a loan is inventory financing. Lenders may require additional collateral and may require an appraisal by a national appraisal firm acceptable to the lender. Depending on the type of inventory, the lender's advance rate can range from 35% to 80% of the orderly liquidation value of the inventory.
Trade credit	Trade credit refers to an amount that is loaned to an exporter to be repaid when the exports are paid for by the foreign importer.
Savings and loan association	A financial institution that accepts both savings and checking deposits and provides home mortgage loans is referred to as savings and loan association.
Real property	Real property is a legal term encompassing real estate and ownership interests in real estate (immovable property).
Portfolio	In finance, a portfolio is a collection of investments held by an institution or a private individual. Holding but not always a portfolio is part of an investment and risk-limiting strategy called diversification. By owning several assets, certain types of risk (in particular specific risk) can be reduced.
Stock	In financial terminology, stock is the capital raized by a corporation, through the issuance and sale of shares.
Bond	Bond refers to a debt instrument, issued by a borrower and promising a specified stream of payments to the purchaser, usually regular interest payments plus a final repayment of principal.
Block grant	A grant distributed in accordance with a statutory formula for use in a variety of activities within a broad functional area, largely at the recipient's discretion is called block grant.
Economy	The income, expenditures, and resources that affect the cost of running a business and household are called an economy.
Fixed asset	Fixed asset, also known as property, plant, and equipment (PP&E), is a term used in accountancy for assets and property which cannot easily be converted into cash. This can be compared with current assets such as cash or bank accounts, which are described as liquid assets. In most cases, only tangible assets are referred to as fixed.
Innovation	Innovation refers to the first commercially successful introduction of a new product, the use of a new method of production, or the creation of a new form of business organization.
Research and development	The use of resources for the deliberate discovery of new information and ways of doing things, together with the application of that information in inventing new products or

Go to **Cram101.com** for the Practice Tests for this Chapter.

	processes is referred to as research and development.
Complement	A good that is used in conjunction with another good is a complement. For example, cameras and film would complement eachother.
Technology	The body of knowledge and techniques that can be used to combine economic resources to produce goods and services is called technology.
Administrator	Administrator refers to the personal representative appointed by a probate court to settle the estate of a deceased person who died.
Exporter	A firm that sells its product in another country is an exporter.

Service	Service refers to a "non tangible product" that is not embodied in a physical good and that typically effects some change in another product, person, or institution. Contrasts with good.
Option	A contract that gives the purchaser the option to buy or sell the underlying financial instrument at a specified price, called the exercise price or strike price, within a specific period of time.
Business incubator	An innovation that provides shared office space, management support services, and management advice to entrepreneurs is a business incubator.
Americans with Disabilities Act	The Americans with Disabilities Act of 1990 is a wide-ranging civil rights law that prohibits discrimination based on disability.
Consideration	Consideration in contract law, a basic requirement for an enforceable agreement under traditional contract principles, defined in this text as legal value, bargained for and given in exchange for an act or promise. In corporation law, cash or property contributed to a corporation in exchange for shares, or a promise to contribute such cash or property.
Layout	Layout refers to the physical arrangement of the various parts of an advertisement including the headline, subheads, illustrations, body copy, and any identifying marks.
Entrepreneur	The owner/operator. The person who organizes, manages, and assumes the risks of a firm, taking a new idea or a new product and turning it into a successful business is an entrepreneur.
Bookkeeping	The recording of business transactions is called bookkeeping.
Small business	Small business refers to a business that is independently owned and operated, is not dominant in its field of operation, and meets certain standards of size in terms of employees or annual receipts.
Demographic	A demographic is a term used in marketing and broadcasting, to describe a demographic grouping or a market segment.
Retailing	All activities involved in selling, renting, and providing goods and services to ultimate consumers for personal, family, or household use is referred to as retailing.
Market	A market is, as defined in economics, a social arrangement that allows buyers and sellers to discover information and carry out a voluntary exchange of goods or services.
Disposable income	Disposable income is income minus taxes. More accurately, income minus direct taxes plus transfer payments; that is, the income available to be spent and saved.
Firm	An organization that employs resources to produce a good or service for profit and owns and operates one or more plants is referred to as a firm.
Industry	A group of firms that produce identical or similar products is an industry. It is also used specifically to refer to an area of economic production focused on manufacturing which involves large amounts of capital investment before any profit can be realized, also called "heavy industry".
Evaluation	The consumer's appraisal of the product or brand on important attributes is called evaluation.
Aid	Assistance provided by countries and by international institutions such as the World Bank to developing countries in the form of monetary grants, loans at low interest rates, in kind, or a combination of these is called aid. Aid can also refer to assistance of any type rendered to benefit some group or individual.

Go to **Cram101.com** for the Practice Tests for this Chapter.
And, **NEVER** highlight a book again!

Trend	Trend refers to the long-term movement of an economic variable, such as its average rate of increase or decrease over enough years to encompass several business cycles.
Interest	In finance and economics, interest is the price paid by a borrower for the use of a lender's money. In other words, interest is the amount of paid to "rent" money for a period of time.
Analyst	Analyst refers to a person or tool with a primary function of information analysis, generally with a more limited, practical and short term set of goals than a researcher.
Comprehensive	A comprehensive refers to a layout accurate in size, color, scheme, and other necessary details to show how a final ad will look. For presentation only, never for reproduction.
Economy	The income, expenditures, and resources that affect the cost of running a business and household are called an economy.
Marketing	Promoting and selling products or services to customers, or prospective customers, is referred to as marketing.
Income distribution	A description of the fractions of a population that are at various levels of income. The larger these differences in income, the 'worse' the income distribution is usually said to be, the smaller the 'better.'
Distribution	Distribution in economics, the manner in which total output and income is distributed among individuals or factors.
Household	An economic unit that provides the economy with resources and uses the income received to purchase goods and services that satisfy economic wants is called household.
Demographic characteristic	The vital statistics of a population group or a derived sample, such as: age, sex, education, ethnic heritage, education, income, housing is referred to as a demographic characteristic.
Marketing management	Marketing management refers to the process of planning and executing the conception, pricing, promotion, and distribution of ideas, goods, and services to create mutually beneficial exchanges.
Buying power	The dollar amount available to purchase securities on margin is buying power. The amount is calculated by adding the cash held in the brokerage accounts and the amount that could be spent if securities were fully margined to their limit. If an investor uses their buying power, they are purchasing securities on credit.
Retail sale	The sale of goods and services to consumers for their own use is a retail sale.
Management	Management characterizes the process of leading and directing all or part of an organization, often a business, through the deployment and manipulation of resources. Early twentieth-century management writer Mary Parker Follett defined management as "the art of getting things done through people."
Customer profile	Description, primarily quantitative, of an individual or segment using specified demographic, lifestyle, and behavioral characteristics is a customer profile.
Target market	One or more specific groups of potential consumers toward which an organization directs its marketing program are a target market.
Marketing strategy	Marketing strategy refers to the means by which a marketing goal is to be achieved, usually characterized by a specified target market and a marketing program to reach it.
Michael Porter	Michael Porter is a leading contributor to strategic management theory, Porter's main academic objectives focus on how a firm or a region, can build a competitive advantage and develop competitive strategy. Porter's strategic system consists primarily of 5 forces analysis, strategic groups, the value chain, and market positioning stratagies.
Brand	A name, symbol, or design that identifies the goods or services of one seller or group of

sellers and distinguishes them from the goods and services of competitors is a brand.

Accretion	In finance, accretion is the change in the price of a bond bought at a discount between the original price and the par value of the bond.
Synergy	Corporate synergy occurs when corporations interact congruently. A corporate synergy refers to a financial benefit that a corporation expects to realize when it merges with or acquires another corporation.
Core	A core is the set of feasible allocations in an economy that cannot be improved upon by subset of the set of the economy's consumers (a coalition). In construction, when the force in an element is within a certain center section, the core, the element will only be under compression.
Revenue	Revenue is a U.S. business term for the amount of money that a company receives from its activities, mostly from sales of products and/or services to customers.
Market share	That fraction of an industry's output accounted for by an individual firm or group of firms is called market share.
Competitor	Other organizations in the same industry or type of business that provide a good or service to the same set of customers is referred to as a competitor.
Profit	Profit refers to the return to the resource entrepreneurial ability; total revenue minus total cost.
Manufacturing	Production of goods primarily by the application of labor and capital to raw materials and other intermediate inputs, in contrast to agriculture, mining, forestry, fishing, and services a manufacturing.
Wholesale	According to the United Nations Statistics Division Wholesale is the resale of new and used goods to retailers, to industrial, commercial, institutional or professional users, or to other wholesalers, or involves acting as an agent or broker in buying merchandise for, or selling merchandise, to such persons or companies.
Open shop	Open shop refers to a place of employment in which the employer may hire nonunion workers and the workers need not become members of a labor union.
Consultant	A professional that provides expert advice in a particular field or area in which customers occassionaly require this type of knowledge is a consultant.
Capital	Capital generally refers to financial wealth, especially that used to start or maintain a business. In classical economics, capital is one of four factors of production, the others being land and labor and entrepreneurship.
Regulation	Regulation refers to restrictions state and federal laws place on business with regard to the conduct of its activities.
Ordinance	Ordinance refers to a legislative enactment of a county or an incorporated city or town. A law made by a non-sovereign body such as a city council or a colony.
Zoning	Government restrictions on the use of private property in order to ensure the orderly growth and development of a community and to protect the health, safety, and welfare of citizens is called zoning.
Zoning commission	A local administrative body that formulates zoning ordinances, conducts public hearings, and makes recommendations to the city council is called zoning commission.
Variance	Variance refers to a measure of how much an economic or statistical variable varies across values or observations. Its calculation is the same as that of the covariance, being the covariance of the variable with itself.

Appeal	Appeal refers to the act of asking an appellate court to overturn a decision after the trial court's final judgment has been entered.
Tactic	A short-term immediate decision that, in its totality, leads to the achievement of strategic goals is called a tactic.
Grant	Grant refers to an intergovernmental transfer of funds . Since the New Deal, state and local governments have become increasingly dependent upon federal grants for an almost infinite variety of programs.
Compatibility	Compatibility refers to used to describe a product characteristic, it means a good fit with other products used by the consumer or with the consumer's lifestyle. Used in a technical context, it means the ability of systems to work together.
Fixture	Fixture refers to a thing that was originally personal property and that has been actually or constructively affixed to the soil itself or to some structure legally a part of the land.
Preference	The act of a debtor in paying or securing one or more of his creditors in a manner more favorable to them than to other creditors or to the exclusion of such other creditors is a preference. In the absence of statute, a preference is perfectly good, but to be legal it must be bona fide, and not a mere subterfuge of the debtor to secure a future benefit to himself or to prevent the application of his property to his debts.
Inventory	Tangible property held for sale in the normal course of business or used in producing goods or services for sale is an inventory.
Insurance	Insurance refers to a system by which individuals can reduce their exposure to risk of large losses by spreading the risks among a large number of persons.
Utility	Utility refers to the want-satisfying power of a good or service; the satisfaction or pleasure a consumer obtains from the consumption of a good or service.
Jurisdiction	The power of a court to hear and decide a case is called jurisdiction. It is the practical authority granted to a formally constituted body or to a person to deal with and make pronouncements on legal matters and, by implication, to administer justice within a defined area of responsibility.
Raw material	Raw material refers to a good that has not been transformed by production; a primary product.
Labor	People's physical and mental talents and efforts that are used to help produce goods and services are called labor.
Property	Assets defined in the broadest legal sense. Property includes the unrealized receivables of a cash basis taxpayer, but not services rendered.
Variable	A variable is something measured by a number; it is used to analyze what happens to other things when the size of that number changes.
Operation	A standardized method or technique that is performed repetitively, often on different materials resulting in different finished goods is called an operation.
Scope	Scope of a project is the sum total of all projects products and their requirements or features.
Specialist	A specialist is a trader who makes a market in one or several stocks and holds the limit order book for those stocks.
Complementary products	Products that use similar technologies and can coexist in a family of products are called complementary products. They tend to be purchased jointly and whose demands therefore are related.
Screening	Screening in economics refers to a strategy of combating adverse selection, one of the

Go to **Cram101.com** for the Practice Tests for this Chapter.

	potential decision-making complications in cases of asymmetric information.
Breakeven point	Breakeven point refers to quantity of output sold at which total revenues equal total costs, that is where the economic profit is zero.
Key Success Factor	A Key Success Factor is a factor in a given market that is a necessary condition for success.
Success factor	The term success factor refers to the characteristics necessary for high performance; knowledge, skills, abilities, behaviors.
Central business district	The oldest retail setting, the community's downtown area is called central business district.
Warrant	A warrant is a security that entitles the holder to buy or sell a certain additional quantity of an underlying security at an agreed-upon price, at the holder's discretion.
Customer contact	Customer contact refers to a characteristic of services that notes that customers tend to be more involved in the production of services than they are in manufactured goods.
Service business	A business firm that provides services to consumers, such as accounting and legal services, is referred to as a service business.
Gap	In December of 1995, Gap became the first major North American retailer to accept independent monitoring of the working conditions in a contract factory producing its garments. Gap is the largest specialty retailer in the United States.
Starbucks	Although it has endured much criticism for its purported monopoly on the global coffee-bean market, Starbucks purchases only 3% of the coffee beans grown worldwide. In 2000 the company introduced a line of fair trade products and now offers three options for socially conscious coffee drinkers. According to Starbucks, they purchased 4.8 million pounds of Certified Fair Trade coffee in fiscal year 2004 and 11.5 million pounds in 2005.
Complexity	The technical sophistication of the product and hence the amount of understanding required to use it is referred to as complexity. It is the opposite of simplicity.
Community shopping center	A retail location that typically has one primary store and 20 to 40 smaller outlets, serving a population of consumers who are within a 10- to 20-minute drive is called community shopping center.
Tenant	The party to whom the leasehold is transferred is a tenant. A leasehold estate is an ownership interest in land in which a lessee or a tenant holds real property by some form of title from a lessor or landlord.
Power center	A huge shopping strip with a multiple anchor, a convenient location, and a supermarket is called power center.
Anchor stores	Anchor stores refer to the larger stores in a shopping mall, usually a department store in a major retail chain.
Buyer	A buyer refers to a role in the buying center with formal authority and responsibility to select the supplier and negotiate the terms of the contract.
Trademark	A distinctive word, name, symbol, device, or combination thereof, which enables consumers to identify favored products or services and which may find protection under state or federal law is a trademark.
Advertising	Advertising refers to paid, nonpersonal communication through various media by organizations and individuals who are in some way identified in the advertising message.
Technology	The body of knowledge and techniques that can be used to combine economic resources to

Go to **Cram101.com** for the Practice Tests for this Chapter.

produce goods and services is called technology.

Possession	Possession refers to respecting real property, exclusive dominion and control such as owners of like property usually exercise over it. Manual control of personal property either as owner or as one having a qualified right in it.
Warehouse	Warehouse refers to a location, often decentralized, that a firm uses to store, consolidate, age, or mix stock; house product-recall programs; or ease tax burdens.
Zoning ordinances	Local laws that are adopted by municipalities and local governments to regulate land use within their boundaries are zoning ordinances. Zoning ordinances are adopted and enforced to protect the health, safety, morals, and general welfare of the community.
Economies of scale	In economics, returns to scale and economies of scale are related terms that describe what happens as the scale of production increases. They are different terms and not to be used interchangeably.
Foreign trade zone	Foreign trade zone refers to an area within a country where imported goods can be stored or processed without being subject to import duty. Also called a 'free zone,' 'free port,' or 'bonded warehouse.'
Export	In economics, an export is any good or commodity, shipped or otherwise transported out of a country, province, town to another part of the world in a legitimate fashion, typically for use in trade or sale.
Tariff	A tax imposed by a nation on an imported good is called a tariff.
Empowerment	Giving employees the authority and responsibility to respond quickly to customer requests is called empowerment.
Investment	Investment refers to spending for the production and accumulation of capital and additions to inventories. In a financial sense, buying an asset with the expectation of making a return.
Tax credit	Allows a firm to reduce the taxes paid to the home government by the amount of taxes paid to the foreign government is referred to as tax credit.
Credit	Credit refers to a recording as positive in the balance of payments, any transaction that gives rise to a payment into the country, such as an export, the sale of an asset, or borrowing from abroad.
Incentive	An incentive is any factor (financial or non-financial) that provides a motive for a particular course of action, or counts as a reason for preferring one choice to the alternatives.
Economic development	Increase in the economic standard of living of a country's population, normally accomplished by increasing its stocks of physical and human capital and improving its technology is an economic development.
Management consulting	Management consulting refers to both the practice of helping companies to improve performance through analysis of existing business problems and development of future plans, as well as to the firms that specialize in this sort of consulting.
Graduation	Termination of a country's eligibility for GSP tariff preferences on the grounds that it has progressed sufficiently, in terms of per capita income or another measure, that it is no longer in need to special and differential treatment is graduation.
Exporting	Selling products to another country is called exporting.
Failure rate	Failure rate is the frequency with an engineered system or component fails, expressed for example in failures per hour. Failure rate is usually time dependent. In the special case when the likelihood of failure remains constant as time passes, failure rate is simply the

	inverse of the mean time to failure, expressed for example in hours per failure.
Auction	A preexisting business model that operates successfully on the Internet by announcing an item for sale and permitting multiple purchasers to bid on them under specified rules and condition is an auction.
Estate	An estate is the totality of the legal rights, interests, entitlements and obligations attaching to property. In the context of wills and probate, it refers to the totality of the property which the deceased owned or in which some interest was held.
Stock	In financial terminology, stock is the capital raized by a corporation, through the issuance and sale of shares.
Profit margin	Profit margin is a measure of profitability. It is calculated using a formula and written as a percentage or a number. Profit margin = Net income before tax and interest / Revenue.
Net profit	Net profit is an accounting term which is commonly used in business. It is equal to the gross revenue for a given time period minus associated expenses.
Margin	A deposit by a buyer in stocks with a seller or a stockbroker, as security to cover fluctuations in the market in reference to stocks that the buyer has purchased but for which he has not paid is a margin. Commodities are also traded on margin.
Merchant	Under the Uniform Commercial Code, one who regularly deals in goods of the kind sold in the contract at issue, or holds himself out as having special knowledge or skill relevant to such goods, or who makes the sale through an agent who regularly deals in such goods or claims such knowledge or skill is referred to as merchant.
Freelance	A freelance worker is a self-employed person working in a profession or trade in which full-time employment is also common.
Expense	In accounting, an expense represents an event in which an asset is used up or a liability is incurred. In terms of the accounting equation, expenses reduce owners' equity.
Employment discrimination	Inferior treatment in hiring, promotions, work assignments, and such for a particular group of employees, based on criteria that is not controllable, is referred to as employment discrimination.
Accommodation	Accommodation is a term used to describe a delivery of nonconforming goods meant as a partial performance of a contract for the sale of goods, where a full performance is not possible.
Reasonable accommodation	Making facilities readily accessible to and usable by individuals with physical or mental limitations is referred to as reasonable accommodation.
Commerce	Commerce is the exchange of something of value between two entities. It is the central mechanism from which capitalism is derived.
Complement	A good that is used in conjunction with another good is a complement. For example, cameras and film would complement eachother.
Ergonomics	Ergonomics refers to the interface between individuals' physiological characteristics and the physical work environment.
Productivity	Productivity refers to the total output of goods and services in a given period of time divided by work hours.
Occupational Safety and Health Administration	The United States Occupational Safety and Health Administration is an agency of the United States Department of Labor. It was created by Congress under the Occupational Safety and Health Act, signed by President Richard M. Nixon, on December 29, 1970.
Administration	Administration refers to the management and direction of the affairs of governments and

303

institutions; a collective term for all policymaking officials of a government; the execution and implementation of public policy.

Budget	Budget refers to an account, usually for a year, of the planned expenditures and the expected receipts of an entity. For a government, the receipts are tax revenues.
Consumption	In Keynesian economics consumption refers to personal consumption expenditure, i.e., the purchase of currently produced goods and services out of income, out of savings (net worth), or from borrowed funds. It refers to that part of disposable income that does not go to saving.
Gross margin	Gross margin is an ambiguous phrase that expresses the relationship between gross profit and sales revenue as Gross Margin = Revenue - costs of good sold.
Specialty goods	Items that a consumer makes a special effort to search out and buy are referred to as specialty goods.
Markup	Markup is a term used in marketing to indicate how much the price of a product is above the cost of producing and distributing the product.
Discount	The difference between the face value of a bond and its selling price, when a bond is sold for less than its face value it's referred to as a discount.
Standing	Standing refers to the legal requirement that anyone seeking to challenge a particular action in court must demonstrate that such action substantially affects his legitimate interests before he will be entitled to bring suit.
Customer service	The ability of logistics management to satisfy users in terms of time, dependability, communication, and convenience is called the customer service.
Production	The creation of finished goods and services using the factors of production: land, labor, capital, entrepreneurship, and knowledge.
Facility layout	The physical arrangement of resources in the production process is called facility layout.
Product mix	The combination of product lines offered by a manufacturer is referred to as product mix.
Product design	Product Design is defined as the idea generation, concept development, testing and manufacturing or implementation of a physical object or service. It is possibly the evolution of former discipline name - Industrial Design.
Finished goods	Completed products awaiting sale are called finished goods. An item considered a finished good in a supplying plant might be considered a component or raw material in a receiving plant.
Control activities	Control activities are the activities intended to prevent, detect, and correct errors and irregularities relating to business risks. Policies and procedures used by management to meet its objectives.
Product layout	Product layout refers to a facilities layout in which machines and tasks are arranged according to the sequence of steps in the production of a single product.
Fixed investment	Fixed investment refers to spending by firms on equipment and structures and planned spending on residential housing.
Interdependence	The extent to which departments depend on each other for resources or materials to accomplish their tasks is referred to as interdependence.
Process layout	A method of organizing the elements of a production process, in which similar processes and functions are grouped together is called process layout.
Holding	The holding is a court's determination of a matter of law based on the issue presented in the

Go to **Cram101.com** for the Practice Tests for this Chapter.

	particular case. In other words: under this law, with these facts, this result.
Job satisfaction	Job satisfaction describes how content an individual is with his or her job. It is a relatively recent term since in previous centuries the jobs available to a particular person were often predetermined by the occupation of that person's parent.
Automation	Automation allows machines to do work previously accomplished by people.
Lease	A contract for the possession and use of land or other property, including goods, on one side, and a recompense of rent or other income on the other is the lease.
Fund	Independent accounting entity with a self-balancing set of accounts segregated for the purposes of carrying on specific activities is referred to as a fund.
Operating expense	In throughput accounting, the cost accounting aspect of Theory of Constraints (TOC), operating expense is the money spent turning inventory into throughput. In TOC, operating expense is limited to costs that vary strictly with the quantity produced, like raw materials and purchased components.
Fixed cost	The cost that a firm bears if it does not produce at all and that is independent of its output. The presence of a fixed cost tends to imply increasing returns to scale. Contrasts with variable cost.
Depreciation	Depreciation is an accounting and finance term for the method of attributing the cost of an asset across the useful life of the asset. Depreciation is a reduction in the value of a currency in floating exchange rate.
Depreciate	A nation's currency is said to depreciate when exchange rates change so that a unit of its currency can buy fewer units of foreign currency.
Chapter 11 bankruptcy	Chapter 11 bankruptcy governs the process of reorganization under the bankruptcy laws of the United States. It is an attempt to stay in business while a bankruptcy court supervises the "reorganization" of the company's contractual and debt obligations.
Bankruptcy	Bankruptcy is a legally declared inability or impairment of ability of an individual or organization to pay their creditors.
Cash flow	In finance, cash flow refers to the amounts of cash being received and spent by a business during a defined period of time, sometimes tied to a specific project. Most of the time they are being used to determine gaps in the liquid position of a company.
Overhead cost	An expenses of operating a business over and above the direct costs of producing a product is an overhead cost. They can include utilities (eg, electricity, telephone), advertizing and marketing, and any other costs not billed directly to the client or included in the price of the product.
Contract	A contract is a "promise" or an "agreement" that is enforced or recognized by the law. In the civil law, a contract is considered to be part of the general law of obligations.
Broker	In commerce, a broker is a party that mediates between a buyer and a seller. A broker who also acts as a seller or as a buyer becomes a principal party to the deal.
Disclosure	Disclosure means the giving out of information, either voluntarily or to be in compliance with legal regulations or workplace rules.
Statute of frauds	The statute of frauds refers to a requirement in many common law jurisdictions that certain kinds of contracts, typically contractual obligations, be done in writing.
Statute	A statute is a formal, written law of a country or state, written and enacted by its legislative authority, perhaps to then be ratified by the highest executive in the government, and finally published.

Go to **Cram101.com** for the Practice Tests for this Chapter.

Go to **Cram101.com** for the Practice Tests for this Chapter.
And, **NEVER** highlight a book again!

Fraud	Tax fraud falls into two categories: civil and criminal. Under civil fraud, the IRS may impose as a penalty of an amount equal to as much as 75 percent of the underpayment.
Sublease	Sublease refers to a transfer of some but not all of a tenant's remaining right to possess property under a lease.
Purchasing	Purchasing refers to the function in a firm that searches for quality material resources, finds the best suppliers, and negotiates the best price for goods and services.
Bottom line	The bottom line is net income on the last line of a income statement.
Asset	An item of property, such as land, capital, money, a share in ownership, or a claim on others for future payment, such as a bond or a bank deposit is an asset.
Negotiation	Negotiation is the process whereby interested parties resolve disputes, agree upon courses of action, bargain for individual or collective advantage, and/or attempt to craft outcomes which serve their mutual interests.
Fixed asset	Fixed asset, also known as property, plant, and equipment (PP&E), is a term used in accountancy for assets and property which cannot easily be converted into cash. This can be compared with current assets such as cash or bank accounts, which are described as liquid assets. In most cases, only tangible assets are referred to as fixed.
Wall Street Journal	Dow Jones & Company was founded in 1882 by reporters Charles Dow, Edward Jones and Charles Bergstresser. Jones converted the small Customers' Afternoon Letter into The Wall Street Journal, first published in 1889, and began delivery of the Dow Jones News Service via telegraph. The Journal featured the Jones 'Average', the first of several indexes of stock and bond prices on the New York Stock Exchange.
Journal	Book of original entry, in which transactions are recorded in a general ledger system, is referred to as a journal.
Slowdown	A slowdown is an industrial action in which employees perform their duties but seek to reduce productivity or efficiency in their performance of these duties. A slowdown may be used as either a prelude or an alternative to a strike, as it is seen as less disruptive as well as less risky and costly for workers and their union.
Business ethics	The study of what makes up good and bad conduct as related to business activities and values is business ethics.

Go to **Cram101.com** for the Practice Tests for this Chapter.
And, **NEVER** highlight a book again!

Quality management	Quality management is a method for ensuring that all the activities necessary to design, develop and implement a product or service are effective and efficient with respect to the system and its performance.
Management	Management characterizes the process of leading and directing all or part of an organization, often a business, through the deployment and manipulation of resources. Early twentieth-century management writer Mary Parker Follett defined management as "the art of getting things done through people."
Total quality management	The broad set of management and control processes designed to focus an entire organization and all of its employees on providing products or services that do the best possible job of satisfying the customer is called total quality management.
Economic order quantity	Decision model that calculates the optimal quantity of inventory to order under a set of assumptions is called economic order quantity.
Inventory	Tangible property held for sale in the normal course of business or used in producing goods or services for sale is an inventory.
Discount	The difference between the face value of a bond and its selling price, when a bond is sold for less than its face value it's referred to as a discount.
Vendor	A person who sells property to a vendee is a vendor. The words vendor and vendee are more commonly applied to the seller and purchaser of real estate, and the words seller and buyer are more commonly applied to the seller and purchaser of personal property.
Purchasing	Purchasing refers to the function in a firm that searches for quality material resources, finds the best suppliers, and negotiates the best price for goods and services.
Service	Service refers to a "non tangible product" that is not embodied in a physical good and that typically effects some change in another product, person, or institution. Contrasts with good.
Entrepreneur	The owner/operator. The person who organizes, manages, and assumes the risks of a firm, taking a new idea or a new product and turning it into a successful business is an entrepreneur.
Acquisition	A company's purchase of the property and obligations of another company is an acquisition.
Supply	Supply is the aggregate amount of any material good that can be called into being at a certain price point; it comprises one half of the equation of supply and demand. In classical economic theory, a curve representing supply is one of the factors that produce price.
Stock	In financial terminology, stock is the capital raized by a corporation, through the issuance and sale of shares.
Comprehensive	A comprehensive refers to a layout accurate in size, color, scheme, and other necessary details to show how a final ad will look. For presentation only, never for reproduction.
Small business	Small business refers to a business that is independently owned and operated, is not dominant in its field of operation, and meets certain standards of size in terms of employees or annual receipts.
Accounting	A system that collects and processes financial information about an organization and reports that information to decision makers is referred to as accounting.
Production	The creation of finished goods and services using the factors of production: land, labor, capital, entrepreneurship, and knowledge.
Marketing	Promoting and selling products or services to customers, or prospective customers, is referred to as marketing.

Go to **Cram101.com** for the Practice Tests for this Chapter.

Customer satisfaction	Customer satisfaction is a business term which is used to capture the idea of measuring how satisfied an enterprise's customers are with the organization's efforts in a marketplace.
Customer retention	Customer retention refers to the percentage of customers who return to a service provider or continue to purchase a manufactured product.
Market share	That fraction of an industry's output accounted for by an individual firm or group of firms is called market share.
Market	A market is, as defined in economics, a social arrangement that allows buyers and sellers to discover information and carry out a voluntary exchange of goods or services.
Turnover	Turnover in a financial context refers to the rate at which a provider of goods cycles through its average inventory. Turnover in a human resources context refers to the characteristic of a given company or industry, relative to rate at which an employer gains and loses staff.
Competitive advantage	A business is said to have a competitive advantage when its unique strengths, often based on cost, quality, time, and innovation, offer consumers a greater percieved value and there by differtiating it from its competitors.
Continuous improvement	The constant effort to eliminate waste, reduce response time, simplify the design of both products and processes, and improve quality and customer service is referred to as continuous improvement.
Kaizen	Kaizen (Japanese for "change for the better" or "improvement") is an approach to productivity improvement originating in applications of the work of American experts such as Frederick Winslow Taylor, Frank Bunker Gilbreth, Walter Shewhart, and of the War Department's Training Within Industry program by Japanese manufacturers after World War II.
Bankruptcy	Bankruptcy is a legally declared inability or impairment of ability of an individual or organization to pay their creditors.
Operation	A standardized method or technique that is performed repetitively, often on different materials resulting in different finished goods is called an operation.
Manufacturing	Production of goods primarily by the application of labor and capital to raw materials and other intermediate inputs, in contrast to agriculture, mining, forestry, fishing, and services a manufacturing.
Credit	Credit refers to a recording as positive in the balance of payments, any transaction that gives rise to a payment into the country, such as an export, the sale of an asset, or borrowing from abroad.
Preference	The act of a debtor in paying or securing one or more of his creditors in a manner more favorable to them than to other creditors or to the exclusion of such other creditors is a preference. In the absence of statute, a preference is perfectly good, but to be legal it must be bona fide, and not a mere subterfuge of the debtor to secure a future benefit to himself or to prevent the application of his property to his debts.
Productivity	Productivity refers to the total output of goods and services in a given period of time divided by work hours.
Corporation	A legal entity chartered by a state or the Federal government that is distinct and separate from the individuals who own it is a corporation. This separation gives the corporation unique powers which other legal entities lack.
ISO 9000	ISO 9000 is a family of ISO standards for Quality Management Systems. It does not guarantee the quality of end products and services; rather, it certifies that consistent business processes are being applied.

Go to **Cram101.com** for the Practice Tests for this Chapter.

Consultant	A professional that provides expert advice in a particular field or area in which customers occassionaly require this type of knowledge is a consultant.
Firm	An organization that employs resources to produce a good or service for profit and owns and operates one or more plants is referred to as a firm.
Interest	In finance and economics, interest is the price paid by a borrower for the use of a lender's money. In other words, interest is the amount of paid to "rent" money for a period of time.
Incentive	An incentive is any factor (financial or non-financial) that provides a motive for a particular course of action, or counts as a reason for preferring one choice to the alternatives.
Quality assurance	Those activities associated with assuring the quality of a product or service is called quality assurance.
Average cost	Average cost is equal to total cost divided by the number of goods produced (Quantity-Q). It is also equal to the sum of average variable costs (total variable costs divided by Q) plus average fixed costs (total fixed costs divided by Q).
Expense	In accounting, an expense represents an event in which an asset is used up or a liability is incurred. In terms of the accounting equation, expenses reduce owners' equity.
Audit	An examination of the financial reports to ensure that they represent what they claim and conform with generally accepted accounting principles is referred to as audit.
Quality improvement	Quality is inversely proportional to variability thus quality Improvement is the reduction of variability in products and processes.
Gain	In finance, gain is a profit or an increase in value of an investment such as a stock or bond. Gain is calculated by fair market value or the proceeds from the sale of the investment minus the sum of the purchase price and all costs associated with it.
Teamwork	That which occurs when group members work together in ways that utilize their skills well to accomplish a purpose is called teamwork.
Authority	Authority in agency law, refers to an agent's ability to affect his principal's legal relations with third parties. Also used to refer to an actor's legal power or ability to do something. In addition, sometimes used to refer to a statute, case, or other legal source that justifies a particular result.
Raw material	Raw material refers to a good that has not been transformed by production; a primary product.
Partnership	In the common law, a partnership is a type of business entity in which partners share with each other the profits or losses of the business undertaking in which they have all invested.
Industry	A group of firms that produce identical or similar products is an industry. It is also used specifically to refer to an area of economic production focused on manufacturing which involves large amounts of capital investment before any profit can be realized, also called "heavy industry".
Incentive system	An incentive system refers to plans in which employees can earn additional compenzation in return for certain types of performance.
Profit	Profit refers to the return to the resource entrepreneurial ability; total revenue minus total cost.
Knowledge base	Knowledge base refers to a database that includes decision rules for use of the data, which may be qualitative as well as quantitative.
Learning organization	A firm, which values continuous learning and is consistently looking to adapt and change with its environment is referred to as learning organization.

Go to **Cram101.com** for the Practice Tests for this Chapter.

315

Statistical process control	Statistical process control is a method for achieving quality control in manufacturing processes. It is a set of methods using statistical tools such as mean, variance and others, to detect whether the process observed is under control.
Control charts	Control charts refer to tools for monitoring process variation.
Control chart	The control chart, also known as the 'Shewhart chart' or 'process-behavior chart' is a statistical tool intended to assess the nature of variation in a process and to facilitate forecasting and management. The control chart is one of the seven basic tools of quality control, which include the histogram, Pareto chart, check sheet, control chart, cause-and-effect diagram, flowchart, and scatter diagram.
Pareto chart	Chart used to identify and prioritize problems to be solved is a pareto chart. It is a special type of bar chart where the values being plotted are arranged in descending order.
Customer focus	Customer focus acknowledges that the more a company understands and meets the real needs of its consumers, the more likely it is to have happy customers who come back for more, and tell their friends.
Mistake	In contract law a mistake is incorrect understanding by one or more parties to a contract and may be used as grounds to invalidate the agreement. Common law has identified three different types of mistake in contract: unilateral mistake, mutual mistake, and common mistake.
Investment	Investment refers to spending for the production and accumulation of capital and additions to inventories. In a financial sense, buying an asset with the expectation of making a return.
Deming	Deming is widely credited with improving production in the United States during World War II, although he is perhaps best known for his work in Japan. There, from 1950 onward he taught top management how to improve design (and thus service), product quality, testing and sales (the latter through global markets).
Innovation	Innovation refers to the first commercially successful introduction of a new product, the use of a new method of production, or the creation of a new form of business organization.
Points	Loan origination fees that may be deductible as interest by a buyer of property. A seller of property who pays points reduces the selling price by the amount of the points paid for the buyer.
Supervisor	A Supervisor is an employee of an organization with some of the powers and responsibilities of management, occupying a role between true manager and a regular employee. A Supervisor position is typically the first step towards being promoted into a management role.
Controlling	A management function that involves determining whether or not an organization is progressing toward its goals and objectives, and taking corrective action if it is not is called controlling.
Working capital	The dollar difference between total current assets and total current liabilities is called working capital.
Cash flow	In finance, cash flow refers to the amounts of cash being received and spent by a business during a defined period of time, sometimes tied to a specific project. Most of the time they are being used to determine gaps in the liquid position of a company.
Capital	Capital generally refers to financial wealth, especially that used to start or maintain a business. In classical economics, capital is one of four factors of production, the others being land and labor and entrepreneurship.
Tying	Tying is the practice of making the sale of one good (the tying good) to the de facto or de jure customer conditional on the purchase of a second distinctive good.
Inventory	Spending by firms on additional holdings of raw materials, parts, and finished goods is

Go to **Cram101.com** for the Practice Tests for this Chapter.

investment	called inventory investment.
Principal	In agency law, one under whose direction an agent acts and for whose benefit that agent acts is a principal.
Holding	The holding is a court's determination of a matter of law based on the issue presented in the particular case. In other words: under this law, with these facts, this result.
Depreciation	Depreciation is an accounting and finance term for the method of attributing the cost of an asset across the useful life of the asset. Depreciation is a reduction in the value of a currency in floating exchange rate.
Insurance	Insurance refers to a system by which individuals can reduce their exposure to risk of large losses by spreading the risks among a large number of persons.
Premium	Premium refers to the fee charged by an insurance company for an insurance policy. The rate of losses must be relatively predictable: In order to set the premium (prices) insurers must be able to estimate them accurately.
Interest expense	The cost a business incurs to borrow money. With respect to bonds payable, the interest expense is calculated by multiplying the market rate of interest by the carrying value of the bonds on the date of the payment.
Inventory control	Inventory control, in the field of loss prevention, are systems designed to introduce technical barriers to shoplifting.
Carrying costs	Carrying costs refers to costs that arise while holding an inventory of goods for sale.
Carrying cost	The cost to hold an asset, usually inventory is called a carrying cost. For inventory, a carrying cost includes such items as interest, warehousing costs, insurance, and material-handling expenses.
Purchase order	A form on which items or services needed by a business firm are specified and then communicated to the vendor is a purchase order.
Ordering costs	Costs of preparing, issuing, and paying purchase orders, plus receiving and inspecting the items included in the orders are ordering costs.
Total cost	The sum of fixed cost and variable cost is referred to as total cost.
Balance	In banking and accountancy, the outstanding balance is the amount of money owned, (or due), that remains in a deposit account (or a loan account) at a given date, after all past remittances, payments and withdrawal have been accounted for. It can be positive (then, in the balance sheet of a firm, it is an asset) or negative (a liability).
Assembly process	Assembly process refers to that part of the production process that puts together components.
Opportunity cost	The cost of something in terms of opportunity foregone. The opportunity cost to a country of producing a unit more of a good, such as for export or to replace an import, is the quantity of some other good that could have been produced instead.
Cumulative quantity discounts	Cumulative quantity discounts refer to the accumulation of purchases of a product over a given time period, typically a year.
Quantity discounts	Quantity discounts refer to reductions in unit costs for a larger order.
Quantity discount	A quantity discount is a price reduction given for a large order.
Cooperative	A business owned and controlled by the people who use it, producers, consumers, or workers

Go to **Cram101.com** for the Practice Tests for this Chapter.

319

with similar needs who pool their resources for mutual gain is called cooperative.

Health insurance	Health insurance is a type of insurance whereby the insurer pays the medical costs of the insured if the insured becomes sick due to covered causes, or due to accidents. The insurer may be a private organization or a government agency.
Cash discount	Cash discount refers to a discount offered on merchandise sold to encourage prompt payment; offered by sellers of merchandise and represents sales discounts to the seller when they are used and purchase discounts to the purchaser of the merchandise.
Invoice	The itemized bill for a transaction, stating the nature of the transaction and its cost. In international trade, the invoice price is often the preferred basis for levying an ad valorem tariff.
Grant	Grant refers to an intergovernmental transfer of funds . Since the New Deal, state and local governments have become increasingly dependent upon federal grants for an almost infinite variety of programs.
Interest rate	The rate of return on bonds, loans, or deposits. When one speaks of 'the' interest rate, it is usually in a model where there is only one.
Remainder	A remainder in property law is a future interest created in a transferee that is capable of becoming possessory upon the natural termination of a prior estate created by the same instrument.
Trade credit	Trade credit refers to an amount that is loaned to an exporter to be repaid when the exports are paid for by the foreign importer.
Accounts payable	A written record of all vendors to whom the business firm owes money is referred to as accounts payable.
Competitive Strategy	An outline of how a business intends to compete with other firms in the same industry is called competitive strategy.
Distribution	Distribution in economics, the manner in which total output and income is distributed among individuals or factors.
Logistics	Those activities that focus on getting the right amount of the right products to the right place at the right time at the lowest possible cost is referred to as logistics.
Warehouse	Warehouse refers to a location, often decentralized, that a firm uses to store, consolidate, age, or mix stock; house product-recall programs; or ease tax burdens.
Labor	People's physical and mental talents and efforts that are used to help produce goods and services are called labor.
Contract	A contract is a "promise" or an "agreement" that is enforced or recognized by the law. In the civil law, a contract is considered to be part of the general law of obligations.
Regulation	Regulation refers to restrictions state and federal laws place on business with regard to the conduct of its activities.
Customs	Customs is an authority or agency in a country responsible for collecting customs duties and for controlling the flow of people, animals and goods (including personal effects and hazardous items) in and out of the country.
Goodwill	Goodwill is an important accounting concept that describes the value of a business entity not directly attributable to its tangible assets and liabilities.
Gap	In December of 1995, Gap became the first major North American retailer to accept independent monitoring of the working conditions in a contract factory producing its garments. Gap is the largest specialty retailer in the United States.

Go to **Cram101.com** for the Practice Tests for this Chapter.

Usage rate	Usage rate refers to quantity consumed or patronage-store visits during a specific period; varies significantly among different customer groups.
Safety stock	Safety stock is additional inventory planned to buffer against the variability in supply and demand plans, that could otherwise result in inventory shortages.
Trust	An arrangement in which shareholders of independent firms agree to give up their stock in exchange for trust certificates that entitle them to a share of the trust's common profits.
Option	A contract that gives the purchaser the option to buy or sell the underlying financial instrument at a specified price, called the exercise price or strike price, within a specific period of time.
Buyer	A buyer refers to a role in the buying center with formal authority and responsibility to select the supplier and negotiate the terms of the contract.
Product line	A group of products that are physically similar or are intended for a similar market are called the product line.
Proactive	To be proactive is to act before a situation becomes a source of confrontation or crisis. It is the opposite of "retroactive," which refers to actions taken after an event.
Evaluation	The consumer's appraisal of the product or brand on important attributes is called evaluation.
Competitor	Other organizations in the same industry or type of business that provide a good or service to the same set of customers is referred to as a competitor.
Trade association	An industry trade group or trade association is generally a public relations organization founded and funded by corporations that operate in a specific industry. Its purpose is generally to promote that industry through PR activities such as advertizing, education, political donations, political pressure, publishing, and astroturfing.
Commerce	Commerce is the exchange of something of value between two entities. It is the central mechanism from which capitalism is derived.
Merchant	Under the Uniform Commercial Code, one who regularly deals in goods of the kind sold in the contract at issue, or holds himself out as having special knowledge or skill relevant to such goods, or who makes the sale through an agent who regularly deals in such goods or claims such knowledge or skill is referred to as merchant.
Agent	A person who makes economic decisions for another economic actor. A hired manager operates as an agent for a firm's owner.
Strike	The withholding of labor services by an organized group of workers is referred to as a strike.
Complaint	The pleading in a civil case in which the plaintiff states his claim and requests relief is called complaint. In the common law, it is a formal legal document that sets out the basic facts and legal reasons that the filing party (the plaintiffs) believes are sufficient to support a claim against another person, persons, entity or entities (the defendants) that entitles the plaintiff(s) to a remedy (either money damages or injunctive relief).
Trend	Trend refers to the long-term movement of an economic variable, such as its average rate of increase or decrease over enough years to encompass several business cycles.
Wholesale	According to the United Nations Statistics Division Wholesale is the resale of new and used goods to retailers, to industrial, commercial, institutional or professional users, or to other wholesalers, or involves acting as an agent or broker in buying merchandise for, or selling merchandise, to such persons or companies.

Go to **Cram101.com** for the Practice Tests for this Chapter.

Channel	Channel, in communications (sometimes called communications channel), refers to the medium used to convey information from a sender (or transmitter) to a receiver.
Liquidation	Liquidation refers to a process whereby the assets of a business are converted to money. The conversion may be coerced by a legal process to pay off the debt of the business, or to satisfy any other business obligation that the business has not voluntarily satisfied.
Wall Street Journal	Dow Jones & Company was founded in 1882 by reporters Charles Dow, Edward Jones and Charles Bergstresser. Jones converted the small Customers' Afternoon Letter into The Wall Street Journal, first published in 1889, and began delivery of the Dow Jones News Service via telegraph. The Journal featured the Jones 'Average', the first of several indexes of stock and bond prices on the New York Stock Exchange.
Journal	Book of original entry, in which transactions are recorded in a general ledger system, is referred to as a journal.
Uniform Commercial Code	Uniform commercial code refers to a comprehensive commercial law adopted by every state in the United States; it covers sales laws and other commercial laws.
Insurable interest	Any interest in property such that the owner would experience a benefit from the continued existence of the property or a loss from its destruction is called insurable interest.
Financial risk	The risk related to the inability of the firm to meet its debt obligations as they come due is called financial risk.
Consignment	Consignment refers to a bailment for sale. The consignee does not undertake the absolute obligation to sell or pay for the goods.
Consignor	Consignor refers to one who sends goods to another on consignment. A shipper or transmitter of goods.
Consignee	A person to whom goods are consigned, shipped, or otherwise transmitted, either for sale or for safekeeping is the consignee.
Yield	The interest rate that equates a future value or an annuity to a given present value is a yield.
Channel of distribution	A whole set of marketing intermediaries, such as wholesalers and retailers, who join together to transport and store goods in their path from producers to consumers is referred to as channel of distribution.
Trade discounts	Trade discounts refer to price reductions to reward wholesalers or retailers for marketing functions they will perform in the future.

Inventory	Tangible property held for sale in the normal course of business or used in producing goods or services for sale is an inventory.
Vendor	A person who sells property to a vendee is a vendor. The words vendor and vendee are more commonly applied to the seller and purchaser of real estate, and the words seller and buyer are more commonly applied to the seller and purchaser of personal property.
Entrepreneur	The owner/operator. The person who organizes, manages, and assumes the risks of a firm, taking a new idea or a new product and turning it into a successful business is an entrepreneur.
Partnership	In the common law, a partnership is a type of business entity in which partners share with each other the profits or losses of the business undertaking in which they have all invested.
Carrying costs	Carrying costs refers to costs that arise while holding an inventory of goods for sale.
Carrying cost	The cost to hold an asset, usually inventory is called a carrying cost. For inventory, a carrying cost includes such items as interest, warehousing costs, insurance, and material-handling expenses.
Personnel	A collective term for all of the employees of an organization. Personnel is also commonly used to refer to the personnel management function or the organizational unit responsible for administering personnel programs.
Insurance	Insurance refers to a system by which individuals can reduce their exposure to risk of large losses by spreading the risks among a large number of persons.
Interest	In finance and economics, interest is the price paid by a borrower for the use of a lender's money. In other words, interest is the amount of paid to "rent" money for a period of time.
Expense	In accounting, an expense represents an event in which an asset is used up or a liability is incurred. In terms of the accounting equation, expenses reduce owners' equity.
Technology	The body of knowledge and techniques that can be used to combine economic resources to produce goods and services is called technology.
Incentive	An incentive is any factor (financial or non-financial) that provides a motive for a particular course of action, or counts as a reason for preferring one choice to the alternatives.
Information system	An information system is a system whether automated or manual, that comprises people, machines, and/or methods organized to collect, process, transmit, and disseminate data that represent user information.
Firm	An organization that employs resources to produce a good or service for profit and owns and operates one or more plants is referred to as a firm.
Inventory control	Inventory control, in the field of loss prevention, are systems designed to introduce technical barriers to shoplifting.
Control system	A control system is a device or set of devices that manage the behavior of other devices. Some devices or systems are not controllable.A control system is an interconnection of components connected or related in such a manner as to command, direct, or regulate itself or another system.
Holding	The holding is a court's determination of a matter of law based on the issue presented in the particular case. In other words: under this law, with these facts, this result.
Balance	In banking and accountancy, the outstanding balance is the amount of money owned, (or due), that remains in a deposit account (or a loan account) at a given date, after all past remittances, payments and withdrawal have been accounted for. It can be positive (then, in

Go to **Cram101.com** for the Practice Tests for this Chapter.

the balance sheet of a firm, it is an asset) or negative (a liability).

Electronic data interchange	Electronic data interchange refers to the direct exchange between organizations of data via a computer-to-computer interface.
Revenue	Revenue is a U.S. business term for the amount of money that a company receives from its activities, mostly from sales of products and/or services to customers.
Stock	In financial terminology, stock is the capital raized by a corporation, through the issuance and sale of shares.
Controlling	A management function that involves determining whether or not an organization is progressing toward its goals and objectives, and taking corrective action if it is not is called controlling.
Perpetual inventory system	A detailed inventory record maintained recording each purchase and sale during the accounting period is called a perpetual inventory system. The accuracy of perpetual inventory records is tested periodically by physical inventories.
Economic order quantity	Decision model that calculates the optimal quantity of inventory to order under a set of assumptions is called economic order quantity.
Yield	The interest rate that equates a future value or an annuity to a given present value is a yield.
Small business	Small business refers to a business that is independently owned and operated, is not dominant in its field of operation, and meets certain standards of size in terms of employees or annual receipts.
Management	Management characterizes the process of leading and directing all or part of an organization, often a business, through the deployment and manipulation of resources. Early twentieth-century management writer Mary Parker Follett defined management as "the art of getting things done through people."
Universal product code	Universal product code refers to a number assigned to identify each product, represented by a series of bars of varying widths for scanning by optical readers.
Bar code	Bar code refers to a printed code that makes use of lines of various widths to encode data about products.
Purchase order	A form on which items or services needed by a business firm are specified and then communicated to the vendor is a purchase order.
Supply	Supply is the aggregate amount of any material good that can be called into being at a certain price point; it comprises one half of the equation of supply and demand. In classical economic theory, a curve representing supply is one of the factors that produce price.
Competitive advantage	A business is said to have a competitive advantage when its unique strengths, often based on cost, quality, time, and innovation, offer consumers a greater percieved value and there by diffetiating it from its competitors.
Market	A market is, as defined in economics, a social arrangement that allows buyers and sellers to discover information and carry out a voluntary exchange of goods or services.
Unit cost	Unit cost refers to cost computed by dividing some amount of total costs by the related number of units. Also called average cost.
Merchant	Under the Uniform Commercial Code, one who regularly deals in goods of the kind sold in the contract at issue, or holds himself out as having special knowledge or skill relevant to such goods, or who makes the sale through an agent who regularly deals in such goods or claims such knowledge or skill is referred to as merchant.

Go to **Cram101.com** for the Practice Tests for this Chapter.

Buyer	A buyer refers to a role in the buying center with formal authority and responsibility to select the supplier and negotiate the terms of the contract.
Negotiation	Negotiation is the process whereby interested parties resolve disputes, agree upon courses of action, bargain for individual or collective advantage, and/or attempt to craft outcomes which serve their mutual interests.
Exchange	The trade of things of value between buyer and seller so that each is better off after the trade is called the exchange.
Auction	A preexisting business model that operates successfully on the Internet by announcing an item for sale and permitting multiple purchasers to bid on them under specified rules and condition is an auction.
Barter	Barter is a type of trade where goods or services are exchanged for a certain amount of other goods or services; no money is involved in the transaction.
Cannibalization	In marketing, cannibalization refers to a reduction in the sales volume, sales revenue, or market share of one product as a result of the introduction of a new product by the same producer.
Distribution	Distribution in economics, the manner in which total output and income is distributed among individuals or factors.
Inventory management	The planning, coordinating, and controlling activities related to the flow of inventory into, through, and out of an organization is referred to as inventory management.
Option	A contract that gives the purchaser the option to buy or sell the underlying financial instrument at a specified price, called the exercise price or strike price, within a specific period of time.
Safety stock	Safety stock is additional inventory planned to buffer against the variability in supply and demand plans, that could otherwise result in inventory shortages.
Quantity discounts	Quantity discounts refer to reductions in unit costs for a larger order.
Quantity discount	A quantity discount is a price reduction given for a large order.
Discount	The difference between the face value of a bond and its selling price, when a bond is sold for less than its face value it's referred to as a discount.
Wholesale	According to the United Nations Statistics Division Wholesale is the resale of new and used goods to retailers, to industrial, commercial, institutional or professional users, or to other wholesalers, or involves acting as an agent or broker in buying merchandise for, or selling merchandise, to such persons or companies.
Service	Service refers to a "non tangible product" that is not embodied in a physical good and that typically effects some change in another product, person, or institution. Contrasts with good.
Industry	A group of firms that produce identical or similar products is an industry. It is also used specifically to refer to an area of economic production focused on manufacturing which involves large amounts of capital investment before any profit can be realized, also called "heavy industry".
Invoice	The itemized bill for a transaction, stating the nature of the transaction and its cost. In international trade, the invoice price is often the preferred basis for levying an ad valorem tariff.

Go to **Cram101.com** for the Practice Tests for this Chapter.

331

Fund	Independent accounting entity with a self-balancing set of accounts segregated for the purposes of carrying on specific activities is referred to as a fund.
Purchasing	Purchasing refers to the function in a firm that searches for quality material resources, finds the best suppliers, and negotiates the best price for goods and services.
Gap	In December of 1995, Gap became the first major North American retailer to accept independent monitoring of the working conditions in a contract factory producing its garments. Gap is the largest specialty retailer in the United States.
Customer service	The ability of logistics management to satisfy users in terms of time, dependability, communication, and convenience is called the customer service.
Competitor	Other organizations in the same industry or type of business that provide a good or service to the same set of customers is referred to as a competitor.
Loyalty	Marketers tend to define customer loyalty as making repeat purchases. Some argue that it should be defined attitudinally as a strongly positive feeling about the brand.
Trust	An arrangement in which shareholders of independent firms agree to give up their stock in exchange for trust certificates that entitle them to a share of the trust's common profits.
Turnover	Turnover in a financial context refers to the rate at which a provider of goods cycles through its average inventory. Turnover in a human resources context refers to the characteristic of a given company or industry, relative to rate at which an employer gains and loses staff.
Inventory turnover ratio	Inventory turnover ratio refers to a ratio that measures the number of times on average the inventory sold during the period; computed by dividing cost of goods sold by the average inventory during the period.
Weber	Weber was a German political economist and sociologist who is considered one of the founders of the modern study of sociology and public administration. His major works deal with rationalization in sociology of religion and government, but he also wrote much in the field of economics. His most popular work is his essay The Protestant Ethic and the Spirit of Capitalism.
Investment	Investment refers to spending for the production and accumulation of capital and additions to inventories. In a financial sense, buying an asset with the expectation of making a return.
Finished goods	Completed products awaiting sale are called finished goods. An item considered a finished good in a supplying plant might be considered a component or raw material in a receiving plant.
Raw material	Raw material refers to a good that has not been transformed by production; a primary product.
Strike	The withholding of labor services by an organized group of workers is referred to as a strike.
Production	The creation of finished goods and services using the factors of production: land, labor, capital, entrepreneurship, and knowledge.
Manufacturing	Production of goods primarily by the application of labor and capital to raw materials and other intermediate inputs, in contrast to agriculture, mining, forestry, fishing, and services a manufacturing.
Warehouse	Warehouse refers to a location, often decentralized, that a firm uses to store, consolidate, age, or mix stock; house product-recall programs; or ease tax burdens.
Instrument	Instrument refers to an economic variable that is controlled by policy makers and can be used to influence other variables, called targets. Examples are monetary and fiscal policies used

Go to **Cram101.com** for the Practice Tests for this Chapter.

to achieve external and internal balance.

Brand	A name, symbol, or design that identifies the goods or services of one seller or group of sellers and distinguishes them from the goods and services of competitors is a brand.
Wall Street Journal	Dow Jones & Company was founded in 1882 by reporters Charles Dow, Edward Jones and Charles Bergstresser. Jones converted the small Customers' Afternoon Letter into The Wall Street Journal, first published in 1889, and began delivery of the Dow Jones News Service via telegraph. The Journal featured the Jones 'Average', the first of several indexes of stock and bond prices on the New York Stock Exchange.
Journal	Book of original entry, in which transactions are recorded in a general ledger system, is referred to as a journal.
Strategic alliance	Strategic alliance refers to a long-term partnership between two or more companies established to help each company build competitive market advantages.
Sony	Sony is a multinational corporation and one of the world's largest media conglomerates founded in Tokyo, Japan. One of its divisions Sony Electronics is one of the leading manufacturers of electronics, video, communications, and information technology products for the consumer and professional markets.
Time Warner	Time Warner is the world's largest media company with major Internet, publishing, film, telecommunications and television divisions.
Subsidiary	A company that is controlled by another company or corporation is a subsidiary.
Cisco Systems	While Cisco Systems was not the first company to develop and sell a router (a device that forwards computer traffic from one network to another), it did create the first commercially successful multi-protocol router to allow previously incompatible computers to communicate using different network protocols.
Logistics	Those activities that focus on getting the right amount of the right products to the right place at the right time at the lowest possible cost is referred to as logistics.
Inventory investment	Spending by firms on additional holdings of raw materials, parts, and finished goods is called inventory investment.
Teamwork	That which occurs when group members work together in ways that utilize their skills well to accomplish a purpose is called teamwork.
Authority	Authority in agency law, refers to an agent's ability to affect his principal's legal relations with third parties. Also used to refer to an actor's legal power or ability to do something. In addition, sometimes used to refer to a statute, case, or other legal source that justifies a particular result.
Operation	A standardized method or technique that is performed repetitively, often on different materials resulting in different finished goods is called an operation.
Extension	Extension refers to an out-of-court settlement in which creditors agree to allow the firm more time to meet its financial obligations. A new repayment schedule will be developed, subject to the acceptance of creditors.
Empowerment	Giving employees the authority and responsibility to respond quickly to customer requests is called empowerment.
Corporation	A legal entity chartered by a state or the Federal government that is distinct and separate from the individuals who own it is a corporation. This separation gives the corporation unique powers which other legal entities lack.
Leakage	Leakage refers to a withdrawal of potential spending from the income-expenditures stream via

Go to **Cram101.com** for the Practice Tests for this Chapter.

	saving, tax payments, or imports; a withdrawal that reduces the lending potential of the banking system.
Consumption	In Keynesian economics consumption refers to personal consumption expenditure, i.e., the purchase of currently produced goods and services out of income, out of savings (net worth), or from borrowed funds. It refers to that part of disposable income that does not go to saving.
Innovation	Innovation refers to the first commercially successful introduction of a new product, the use of a new method of production, or the creation of a new form of business organization.
Productivity	Productivity refers to the total output of goods and services in a given period of time divided by work hours.
Proactive	To be proactive is to act before a situation becomes a source of confrontation or crisis. It is the opposite of "retroactive," which refers to actions taken after an event.
Theory of constraints	A management approach that focuses on identifying and relaxing the constraints that limit an organization's ability to reach a higher level of goal attainment is referred to as the theory of constraints.
Ordering costs	Costs of preparing, issuing, and paying purchase orders, plus receiving and inspecting the items included in the orders are ordering costs.
Cost of goods sold	In accounting, the cost of goods sold describes the direct expenses incurred in producing a particular good for sale, including the actual cost of materials that comprise the good, and direct labor expense in putting the good in salable condition.
Profit	Profit refers to the return to the resource entrepreneurial ability; total revenue minus total cost.
Working capital	The dollar difference between total current assets and total current liabilities is called working capital.
Capital	Capital generally refers to financial wealth, especially that used to start or maintain a business. In classical economics, capital is one of four factors of production, the others being land and labor and entrepreneurship.
Asset	An item of property, such as land, capital, money, a share in ownership, or a claim on others for future payment, such as a bond or a bank deposit is an asset.
Advertising	Advertising refers to paid, nonpersonal communication through various media by organizations and individuals who are in some way identified in the advertising message.
Promotion	Promotion refers to all the techniques sellers use to motivate people to buy products or services. An attempt by marketers to inform people about products and to persuade them to participate in an exchange.
Cash flow	In finance, cash flow refers to the amounts of cash being received and spent by a business during a defined period of time, sometimes tied to a specific project. Most of the time they are being used to determine gaps in the liquid position of a company.
Security	Security refers to a claim on the borrower future income that is sold by the borrower to the lender. A security is a type of transferable interest representing financial value.
Shrinkage	Breakage and theft of merchandise by customers and employees is referred to as shrinkage.
Association of Certified Fraud Examiners	Established in 1988 the Association of Certified Fraud Examiners is the professional organization that governs professional fraud examiners. It's activities include producing fraud information, tools and training. It also governs the professional designation of Certified Fraud Examiner.

Go to **Cram101.com** for the Practice Tests for this Chapter.

Certified Fraud Examiner	Certified Fraud Examiner is a designation awarded by The Association of Certified Fraud Examiners (ACFE). The ACFE is a 35,000 member-based global association dedicated to providing anti-fraud education and training.
Fraud	Tax fraud falls into two categories: civil and criminal. Under civil fraud, the IRS may impose as a penalty of an amount equal to as much as 75 percent of the underpayment.
Creep	Creep is a problem in project management where the initial objectives of the project are jeopardized by a gradual increase in overall objectives as the project progresses.
Policy	Similar to a script in that a policy can be a less than completely rational decision-making method. Involves the use of a pre-existing set of decision steps for any problem that presents itself.
Wage	The payment for the service of a unit of labor, per unit time. In trade theory, it is the only payment to labor, usually unskilled labor. In empirical work, wage data may exclude other compenzation, which must be added to get the total cost of employment.
Code of ethics	A formal statement of ethical principles and rules of conduct is a code of ethics. Some may have the force of law; these are often promulgated by the (quasi-)governmental agency responsible for licensing a profession. Violations of these codes may be subject to administrative (e.g., loss of license), civil or penal remedies.
Regulation	Regulation refers to restrictions state and federal laws place on business with regard to the conduct of its activities.
Audit	An examination of the financial reports to ensure that they represent what they claim and conform with generally accepted accounting principles is referred to as audit.
Trend	Trend refers to the long-term movement of an economic variable, such as its average rate of increase or decrease over enough years to encompass several business cycles.
Screening	Screening in economics refers to a strategy of combating adverse selection, one of the potential decision-making complications in cases of asymmetric information.
Applicant	In many tribunal and administrative law suits, the person who initiates the claim is called the applicant.
Comprehensive	A comprehensive refers to a layout accurate in size, color, scheme, and other necessary details to show how a final ad will look. For presentation only, never for reproduction.
Tangible	Having a physical existence is referred to as the tangible. Personal property other than real estate, such as cars, boats, stocks, or other assets.
Internal controls	A company's policies and procedures designed to reduce the opportunity for fraud and to provide reasonable assurance that its objectives will be accomplished are internal controls.
Internal control	Internal control refers to the plan of organization and all the related methods and measures adopted within a business to safeguard its assets and enhance the accuracy and reliability of its accounting records.
Trademark	A distinctive word, name, symbol, device, or combination thereof, which enables consumers to identify favored products or services and which may find protection under state or federal law is a trademark.
Coalition	An informal alliance among managers who support a specific goal is called coalition.
Holder	A person in possession of a document of title or an instrument payable or indorsed to him, his order, or to bearer is a holder.
Logo	Logo refers to device or other brand name that cannot be spoken.

Go to **Cram101.com** for the Practice Tests for this Chapter.

Customs	Customs is an authority or agency in a country responsible for collecting customs duties and for controlling the flow of people, animals and goods (including personal effects and hazardous items) in and out of the country.
Slander	The defamation action appropriate to oral defamation is referred to as slander.
Loss prevention	Loss prevention is a term used to describe a number of methods used to reduce the amount of all losses and shrinkage often related to retail trade.
Jury	A body of lay persons, selected by lot, or by some other fair and impartial means, to ascertain, under the guidance of the judge, the truth in questions of fact arising either in civil litigation or a criminal process is referred to as jury.
Damages	The sum of money recoverable by a plaintiff who has received a judgment in a civil case is called damages.
Tactic	A short-term immediate decision that, in its totality, leads to the achievement of strategic goals is called a tactic.
Concealment	In contract law, taking active steps to prevent another from learning the truth is referred to as concealment.
Commerce	Commerce is the exchange of something of value between two entities. It is the central mechanism from which capitalism is derived.
Layout	Layout refers to the physical arrangement of the various parts of an advertisement including the headline, subheads, illustrations, body copy, and any identifying marks.
Consideration	Consideration in contract law, a basic requirement for an enforceable agreement under traditional contract principles, defined in this text as legal value, bargained for and given in exchange for an act or promise. In corporation law, cash or property contributed to a corporation in exchange for shares, or a promise to contribute such cash or property.
Publicity	Publicity refers to any information about an individual, product, or organization that's distributed to the public through the media and that's not paid for or controlled by the seller.
Mistake	In contract law a mistake is incorrect understanding by one or more parties to a contract and may be used as grounds to invalidate the agreement. Common law has identified three different types of mistake in contract: unilateral mistake, mutual mistake, and common mistake.
Marketing	Promoting and selling products or services to customers, or prospective customers, is referred to as marketing.
Budget	Budget refers to an account, usually for a year, of the planned expenditures and the expected receipts of an entity. For a government, the receipts are tax revenues.
Liquidated	Damages made certain by the prior agreement of the parties are called liquidated.
Audit procedures	Audit procedures are the tasks the internal auditor undertakes for collecting, analyzing, interpreting, and documenting information during an audit. They are the means to attain audit objectives.
Consultant	A professional that provides expert advice in a particular field or area in which customers occassionaly require this type of knowledge is a consultant.
Agent	A person who makes economic decisions for another economic actor. A hired manager operates as an agent for a firm's owner.
Compaq	Compaq was founded in February 1982 by Rod Canion, Jim Harris and Bill Murto, three senior managers from semiconductor manufacturer Texas Instruments. Each invested $1,000 to form the company. Their first venture capital came from Ben Rosen and Sevin-Rosen partners. It is

Go to **Cram101.com** for the Practice Tests for this Chapter.

often told that the architecture of the original PC was first sketched out on a placemat by the founders while dining in the Houston restaurant, House of Pies.

Adoption

In corporation law, a corporation's acceptance of a pre-incorporation contract by action of its board of directors, by which the corporation becomes liable on the contract, is referred to as adoption.

Forbes

David Churbuck founded online Forbes in 1996. The site drew attention when it uncovered Stephen Glass' journalistic fraud in The New Republic in 1998, a scoop that gave credibility to internet journalism.

Mistake	In contract law a mistake is incorrect understanding by one or more parties to a contract and may be used as grounds to invalidate the agreement. Common law has identified three different types of mistake in contract: unilateral mistake, mutual mistake, and common mistake.
Effective communication	When the intended meaning equals the perceived meaning it is called effective communication.
Entrepreneur	The owner/operator. The person who organizes, manages, and assumes the risks of a firm, taking a new idea or a new product and turning it into a successful business is an entrepreneur.
Variable	A variable is something measured by a number; it is used to analyze what happens to other things when the size of that number changes.
Leadership	Management merely consists of leadership applied to business situations; or in other words: management forms a sub-set of the broader process of leadership.
Firm	An organization that employs resources to produce a good or service for profit and owns and operates one or more plants is referred to as a firm.
Knowledge worker	Employees who own the means of producing a product or service are called a knowledge worker.
Industry	A group of firms that produce identical or similar products is an industry. It is also used specifically to refer to an area of economic production focused on manufacturing which involves large amounts of capital investment before any profit can be realized, also called "heavy industry".
Small business	Small business refers to a business that is independently owned and operated, is not dominant in its field of operation, and meets certain standards of size in terms of employees or annual receipts.
Innovation	Innovation refers to the first commercially successful introduction of a new product, the use of a new method of production, or the creation of a new form of business organization.
Management	Management characterizes the process of leading and directing all or part of an organization, often a business, through the deployment and manipulation of resources. Early twentieth-century management writer Mary Parker Follett defined management as "the art of getting things done through people."
Logistics	Those activities that focus on getting the right amount of the right products to the right place at the right time at the lowest possible cost is referred to as logistics.
Gain	In finance, gain is a profit or an increase in value of an investment such as a stock or bond. Gain is calculated by fair market value or the proceeds from the sale of the investment minus the sum of the purchase price and all costs associated with it.
Interest	In finance and economics, interest is the price paid by a borrower for the use of a lender's money. In other words, interest is the amount of paid to "rent" money for a period of time.
Performance target	A task established for an employee that provides the comparative basis for performance appraisal is a performance target.
Shares	Shares refer to an equity security, representing a shareholder's ownership of a corporation. Shares are one of a finite number of equal portions in the capital of a company, entitling the owner to a proportion of distributed, non-reinvested profits known as dividends and to a portion of the value of the company in case of liquidation.
Corporation	A legal entity chartered by a state or the Federal government that is distinct and separate from the individuals who own it is a corporation. This separation gives the corporation unique powers which other legal entities lack.

Go to **Cram101.com** for the Practice Tests for this Chapter.

Due diligence	Due diligence is the effort made by an ordinarily prudent or reasonable party to avoid harm to another party or himself. Failure to make this effort is considered negligence. Failure to make this effort is considered negligence.
Applicant	In many tribunal and administrative law suits, the person who initiates the claim is called the applicant.
Board of directors	The group of individuals elected by the stockholders of a corporation to oversee its operations is a board of directors.
Management team	A management team is directly responsible for managing the day-to-day operations (and profitability) of a company.
Human resources	Human resources refers to the individuals within the firm, and to the portion of the firm's organization that deals with hiring, firing, training, and other personnel issues.
Comprehensive	A comprehensive refers to a layout accurate in size, color, scheme, and other necessary details to show how a final ad will look. For presentation only, never for reproduction.
Direct cost	A direct cost is a cost that can be identified specifically with a particular sponsored project, an instructional activity, or any other institutional activity, or that can be directly assigned to such activities relatively easily with a high degree of accuracy.
Staffing	Staffing refers to a management function that includes hiring, motivating, and retaining the best people available to accomplish the company's objectives.
Policy	Similar to a script in that a policy can be a less than completely rational decision-making method. Involves the use of a pre-existing set of decision steps for any problem that presents itself.
Holding	The holding is a court's determination of a matter of law based on the issue presented in the particular case. In other words: under this law, with these facts, this result.
Department of Labor	The United States Department of Labor is a Cabinet department of the United States government responsible for occupational safety, wage and hour standards, unemployment insurance benefits, re-employment services, and some economic statistics.
Labor	People's physical and mental talents and efforts that are used to help produce goods and services are called labor.
Financial risk	The risk related to the inability of the firm to meet its debt obligations as they come due is called financial risk.
Turnover	Turnover in a financial context refers to the rate at which a provider of goods cycles through its average inventory. Turnover in a human resources context refers to the characteristic of a given company or industry, relative to rate at which an employer gains and loses staff.
Telecommuting	Telecommuting is a work arrangement in which employees enjoy limited flexibility in working location and hours.
Technology	The body of knowledge and techniques that can be used to combine economic resources to produce goods and services is called technology.
Core	A core is the set of feasible allocations in an economy that cannot be improved upon by subset of the set of the economy's consumers (a coalition). In construction, when the force in an element is within a certain center section, the core, the element will only be under compression.
Option	A contract that gives the purchaser the option to buy or sell the underlying financial instrument at a specified price, called the exercise price or strike price, within a specific

Go to **Cram101.com** for the Practice Tests for this Chapter.

	period of time.
Contract	A contract is a "promise" or an "agreement" that is enforced or recognized by the law. In the civil law, a contract is considered to be part of the general law of obligations.
Common mistake	A common mistake is where both parties hold the same mistaken belief of the facts.
Peak	Peak refers to the point in the business cycle when an economic expansion reaches its highest point before turning down. Contrasts with trough.
Interpersonal skills	Interpersonal skills are used to communicate with, understand, and motivate individuals and groups.
Body language	Body language is a broad term for forms of communication using body movements or gestures instead of, or in addition to, sounds, verbal language, or other forms of communication.
Liability	A liability is a present obligation of the enterprise arizing from past events, the settlement of which is expected to result in an outflow from the enterprise of resources embodying economic benefits.
Employment law	Employment law is the body of laws, administrative rulings, and precedents which addresses the legal rights of, and restrictions on, workers and their organizations.
Employment discrimination	Inferior treatment in hiring, promotions, work assignments, and such for a particular group of employees, based on criteria that is not controllable, is referred to as employment discrimination.
Burden of proof	Used to refer both to the necessity or obligation of proving the facts needed to support a party's claim, and the persuasiveness of the evidence used to do so is a burden of proof. Regarding the second sense of the term, the usual burden of proof in a civil case is a preponderance of the evidence.
Screening	Screening in economics refers to a strategy of combating adverse selection, one of the potential decision-making complications in cases of asymmetric information.
Civil rights act of 1964	The Civil Rights Act of 1964 is a federal law that, in Title VII, outlaws discrimination based on race, color, religion, gender, or national origin in hiring, promoting, and compensating workers.
Americans with Disabilities Act	The Americans with Disabilities Act of 1990 is a wide-ranging civil rights law that prohibits discrimination based on disability.
Aid	Assistance provided by countries and by international institutions such as the World Bank to developing countries in the form of monetary grants, loans at low interest rates, in kind, or a combination of these is called aid. Aid can also refer to assistance of any type rendered to benefit some group or individual.
Logo	Logo refers to device or other brand name that cannot be spoken.
Organizational culture	The mindset of employees, including their shared beliefs, values, and goals is called the organizational culture.
Disney	Disney is one of the largest media and entertainment corporations in the world. Founded on October 16, 1923 by brothers Walt and Roy Disney as a small animation studio, today it is one of the largest Hollywood studios and also owns nine theme parks and several television networks, including the American Broadcasting Company (ABC).
Flexible work schedule	A flexible work schedule is a shedule in which an employee has a forty hour work week but can set their own schedule within the limits set by the employer.
Virtual team	A group of physically dispersed people who work as a team via alternative communication modes

Go to **Cram101.com** for the Practice Tests for this Chapter.

is called virtual team.

Empowerment	Giving employees the authority and responsibility to respond quickly to customer requests is called empowerment.
Balance	In banking and accountancy, the outstanding balance is the amount of money owned, (or due), that remains in a deposit account (or a loan account) at a given date, after all past remittances, payments and withdrawal have been accounted for. It can be positive (then, in the balance sheet of a firm, it is an asset) or negative (a liability).
Operation	A standardized method or technique that is performed repetitively, often on different materials resulting in different finished goods is called an operation.
Maturity	Maturity refers to the final payment date of a loan or other financial instrument, after which point no further interest or principal need be paid.
Organizational structure	Organizational structure is the way in which the interrelated groups of an organization are constructed. From a managerial point of view the main concerns are ensuring effective communication and coordination.
Investment	Investment refers to spending for the production and accumulation of capital and additions to inventories. In a financial sense, buying an asset with the expectation of making a return.
Capital	Capital generally refers to financial wealth, especially that used to start or maintain a business. In classical economics, capital is one of four factors of production, the others being land and labor and entrepreneurship.
Cash flow	In finance, cash flow refers to the amounts of cash being received and spent by a business during a defined period of time, sometimes tied to a specific project. Most of the time they are being used to determine gaps in the liquid position of a company.
Expense	In accounting, an expense represents an event in which an asset is used up or a liability is incurred. In terms of the accounting equation, expenses reduce owners' equity.
Service	Service refers to a "non tangible product" that is not embodied in a physical good and that typically effects some change in another product, person, or institution. Contrasts with good.
Market	A market is, as defined in economics, a social arrangement that allows buyers and sellers to discover information and carry out a voluntary exchange of goods or services.
Generation x	Generation x refers to the 15 percent of the U.S. population born between 1965 and 1976 a period also known as the baby bust.
Loyalty	Marketers tend to define customer loyalty as making repeat purchases. Some argue that it should be defined attitudinally as a strongly positive feeling about the brand.
Brief	Brief refers to a statement of a party's case or legal arguments, usually prepared by an attorney. Also used to make legal arguments before appellate courts.
Public relations	Public relations refers to the management function that evaluates public attitudes, changes policies and procedures in response to the public's requests, and executes a program of action and information to earn public understanding and acceptance.
Assignment	A transfer of property or some right or interest is referred to as assignment.
Preference	The act of a debtor in paying or securing one or more of his creditors in a manner more favorable to them than to other creditors or to the exclusion of such other creditors is a preference. In the absence of statute, a preference is perfectly good, but to be legal it must be bona fide, and not a mere subterfuge of the debtor to secure a future benefit to himself or to prevent the application of his property to his debts.

Go to **Cram101.com** for the Practice Tests for this Chapter.

Performance appraisal	An evaluation in which the performance level of employees is measured against established standards to make decisions about promotions, compenzation, additional training, or firing is referred to as performance appraisal.
Appeal	Appeal refers to the act of asking an appellate court to overturn a decision after the trial court's final judgment has been entered.
Organization chart	Organization chart refers to a visual device, which shows the relationship and divides the organization's work; it shows who is accountable for the completion of specific work and who reports to whom.
Operating expense	In throughput accounting, the cost accounting aspect of Theory of Constraints (TOC), operating expense is the money spent turning inventory into throughput. In TOC, operating expense is limited to costs that vary strictly with the quantity produced, like raw materials and purchased components.
Incentive	An incentive is any factor (financial or non-financial) that provides a motive for a particular course of action, or counts as a reason for preferring one choice to the alternatives.
Authority	Authority in agency law, refers to an agent's ability to affect his principal's legal relations with third parties. Also used to refer to an actor's legal power or ability to do something. In addition, sometimes used to refer to a statute, case, or other legal source that justifies a particular result.
Business opportunity	A business opportunity involves the sale or lease of any product, service, equipment, etc. that will enable the purchaser-licensee to begin a business
Scope	Scope of a project is the sum total of all projects products and their requirements or features.
Partnership	In the common law, a partnership is a type of business entity in which partners share with each other the profits or losses of the business undertaking in which they have all invested.
Complement	A good that is used in conjunction with another good is a complement. For example, cameras and film would complement eachother.
Productivity	Productivity refers to the total output of goods and services in a given period of time divided by work hours.
Raw material	Raw material refers to a good that has not been transformed by production; a primary product.
Purchasing	Purchasing refers to the function in a firm that searches for quality material resources, finds the best suppliers, and negotiates the best price for goods and services.
Budget	Budget refers to an account, usually for a year, of the planned expenditures and the expected receipts of an entity. For a government, the receipts are tax revenues.
Facilitator	A facilitator is someone who skilfully helps a group of people understand their common objectives and plan to achieve them without personally taking any side of the argument.
Customer satisfaction	Customer satisfaction is a business term which is used to capture the idea of measuring how satisfied an enterprise's customers are with the organization's efforts in a marketplace.
Organization structure	The system of task, reporting, and authority relationships within which the organization does its work is referred to as the organization structure.
Estate	An estate is the totality of the legal rights, interests, entitlements and obligations attaching to property. In the context of wills and probate, it refers to the totality of the property which the deceased owned or in which some interest was held.
Teamwork	That which occurs when group members work together in ways that utilize their skills well to

accomplish a purpose is called teamwork.

Openness	Openness refers to the extent to which an economy is open, often measured by the ratio of its trade to GDP.
Upward communication	A communication channel that allows for relatively free movement of messages from those lower in the organization to those at higher levels is an upward communication.
Nonverbal communication	The many additional ways that communication is accomplished beyond the oral or written word is referred to as nonverbal communication.
Receiver	A person that is appointed as a custodian of other people's property by a court of law or a creditor of the owner, pending a lawsuit or reorganization is called a receiver.
Analyst	Analyst refers to a person or tool with a primary function of information analysis, generally with a more limited, practical and short term set of goals than a researcher.
Credibility	The extent to which a source is perceived as having knowledge, skill, or experience relevant to a communication topic and can be trusted to give an unbiased opinion or present objective information on the issue is called credibility.
Production	The creation of finished goods and services using the factors of production: land, labor, capital, entrepreneurship, and knowledge.
Communication network	A communication network refer to networks that form spontaneously and naturally as the interactions among workers continue over time.
Consultant	A professional that provides expert advice in a particular field or area in which customers occassionaly require this type of knowledge is a consultant.
Partition	Partition refers to proceeding the object of which is to enable those who own property as joint tenants or tenants in common to put an end to the tenancy so as to vest in each a sole estate in specific property or an allotment of the lands and tenements. If a division of the estate is impracticable, the estate ought to be sold and the proceeds divided.
Job simplification	Job simplification involves breaking complex jobs down into a sequence of specialized tasks to be conducted by different employees, resulting in clearly defined jobs characterized by limited skill requirements and little autonomy or responsibility.
Assembly line	An assembly line is a manufacturing process in which interchangeable parts are added to a product in a sequential manner to create a finished product.
Intrinsic reward	Motivating events which occur as a natural part of the learning experience is a intrinsic reward.
Job enlargement	A job enrichment strategy that involves combining a series of tasks into one challenging and interesting assignment is referred to as job enlargement.
Job enrichment	A motivational strategy that emphasizes motivating the worker through the job itself is called job enrichment.
Job rotation	A job enrichment strategy that involves moving employees from one job to another is a job rotation.
Controlling	A management function that involves determining whether or not an organization is progressing toward its goals and objectives, and taking corrective action if it is not is called controlling.
Task significance	The measure of how much of a job has a substantial impact on the lives of other people, whether these people are in the immediate organization or in the world at large is task significance.

Go to **Cram101.com** for the Practice Tests for this Chapter.

Integration	Economic integration refers to reducing barriers among countries to transactions and to movements of goods, capital, and labor, including harmonization of laws, regulations, and standards. Integrated markets theoretically function as a unified market.
Economy	The income, expenditures, and resources that affect the cost of running a business and household are called an economy.
Job sharing	Situation in which the duties and hours of one job position are carried out by two people is job sharing.
Flextime	A scheduling method that gives employees control over their work schedule is flextime; usually involves some 'core' times when employees must be at work, and a set of 'flextime' that can be adjustable for various employees.
Strike	The withholding of labor services by an organized group of workers is referred to as a strike.
Insurance	Insurance refers to a system by which individuals can reduce their exposure to risk of large losses by spreading the risks among a large number of persons.
Cabinet	The heads of the executive departments of a jurisdiction who report to and advise its chief executive; examples would include the president's cabinet, the governor's cabinet, and the mayor's cabinet.
Extrinsic reward	Extrinsic reward refers to something given to you by someone else as recognition for good work; extrinsic rewards include pay increases, praise, and promotions.
Trust	An arrangement in which shareholders of independent firms agree to give up their stock in exchange for trust certificates that entitle them to a share of the trust's common profits.
Net income	Net income is equal to the income that a firm has after subtracting costs and expenses from the total revenue. Expenses will typically include tax expense.
Bad debt	In accounting and finance, bad debt is the portion of receivables that can no longer be collected, typically from accounts receivable or loans. Bad debt in accounting is considered an expense.
Customer service	The ability of logistics management to satisfy users in terms of time, dependability, communication, and convenience is called the customer service.
Promotion	Promotion refers to all the techniques sellers use to motivate people to buy products or services. An attempt by marketers to inform people about products and to persuade them to participate in an exchange.
Security	Security refers to a claim on the borrower future income that is sold by the borrower to the lender. A security is a type of transferable interest representing financial value.
Matching	Matching refers to an accounting concept that establishes when expenses are recognized. Expenses are matched with the revenues they helped to generate and are recognized when those revenues are recognized.
Specific performance	A contract remedy whereby the defendant is ordered to perform according to the terms of his contract is referred to as specific performance.
Points	Loan origination fees that may be deductible as interest by a buyer of property. A seller of property who pays points reduces the selling price by the amount of the points paid for the buyer.
Feedback loop	Feedback loop consists of a response and feedback. It is a system where outputs are fed back into the system as inputs, increasing or decreasing effects.
Higher law	The notion that no matter what the laws of a state are, there remains a higher law, to which

	a person has an even greater obligation. A higher law is often appealed to by those who wish to attack an existing law or practice that courts or legislators are unlikely or unwilling to change.
Financial measure	A financial measure is often used as a very simple mechanism to describe the performance of a business or investment. Because they are easily calculated they can not only be used to compare year on year results but also to compare and set norms for a particular type of business or investment.
Profit margin	Profit margin is a measure of profitability. It is calculated using a formula and written as a percentage or a number. Profit margin = Net income before tax and interest / Revenue.
Profit	Profit refers to the return to the resource entrepreneurial ability; total revenue minus total cost.
Margin	A deposit by a buyer in stocks with a seller or a stockbroker, as security to cover fluctuations in the market in reference to stocks that the buyer has purchased but for which he has not paid is a margin. Commodities are also traded on margin.
Tangible	Having a physical existence is referred to as the tangible. Personal property other than real estate, such as cars, boats, stocks, or other assets.
Brainstorming	Brainstorming refers to a technique designed to overcome our natural tendency to evaluate and criticize ideas and thereby reduce the creative output of those ideas. People are encouraged to produce ideas/options without criticizing, often at a very fast pace to minimize our natural tendency to criticize.
Gap	In December of 1995, Gap became the first major North American retailer to accept independent monitoring of the working conditions in a contract factory producing its garments. Gap is the largest specialty retailer in the United States.
Performance gap	This represents the difference in actual performance shown as compared to the desired standard of performance. In employee performance management efforts, this performance gap is often described in terms of needed knowledge and skills which become training and development goals for the employee.
Financial control	A process in which a firm periodically compares its actual revenues, costs, and expenses with its projected ones is called financial control.
Complaint	The pleading in a civil case in which the plaintiff states his claim and requests relief is called complaint. In the common law, it is a formal legal document that sets out the basic facts and legal reasons that the filing party (the plaintiffs) believes are sufficient to support a claim against another person, persons, entity or entities (the defendants) that entitles the plaintiff(s) to a remedy (either money damages or injunctive relief).
Evaluation	The consumer's appraisal of the product or brand on important attributes is called evaluation.
Upward feedback	In leadership development and management development, upward feedback (also known as subordinate appraisal) is a structured process of delivering feedback from subordinates to managers, intended to identify ways to increase management effectiveness and enhance organizational performance.
Retaliation	The use of an increased trade barrier in response to another country increasing its trade barrier, either as a way of undoing the adverse effects of the latter's action or of punishing it is retaliation.
Company culture	Company culture is the term given to the values and practices shared by the employees of a firm.

Go to **Cram101.com** for the Practice Tests for this Chapter.

Social responsibility	Social responsibility is a doctrine that claims that an entity whether it is state, government, corporation, organization or individual has a responsibility to society.
Change agent	A change agent is someone who engages either deliberately or whose behavior results in social, cultural or behavioral change. This can be studied scientifically and effective techniques can be discovered and employed.
Agent	A person who makes economic decisions for another economic actor. A hired manager operates as an agent for a firm's owner.
Employment test	A written or computerbased test designed to measure a particular attribute such as intelligence or aptitude is an employment test.
Yahoo	Yahoo is an American computer services company. It operates an Internet portal, the Yahoo Directory and a host of other services including the popular Yahoo Mail. Yahoo is the most visited website on the Internet today with more than 400 million unique users. The global network of Yahoo! websites received 3.4 billion page views per day on average as of October 2005.
Manufacturing	Production of goods primarily by the application of labor and capital to raw materials and other intermediate inputs, in contrast to agriculture, mining, forestry, fishing, and services a manufacturing.

Go to **Cram101.com** for the Practice Tests for this Chapter.

Exit strategy	In entrepreneurship and strategic management an exit strategy is a way to terminate either ones ownership of a company or the operation of some part of the company.
Entrepreneur	The owner/operator. The person who organizes, manages, and assumes the risks of a firm, taking a new idea or a new product and turning it into a successful business is an entrepreneur.
Option	A contract that gives the purchaser the option to buy or sell the underlying financial instrument at a specified price, called the exercise price or strike price, within a specific period of time.
Management	Management characterizes the process of leading and directing all or part of an organization, often a business, through the deployment and manipulation of resources. Early twentieth-century management writer Mary Parker Follett defined management as "the art of getting things done through people."
Insurance	Insurance refers to a system by which individuals can reduce their exposure to risk of large losses by spreading the risks among a large number of persons.
Small business	Small business refers to a business that is independently owned and operated, is not dominant in its field of operation, and meets certain standards of size in terms of employees or annual receipts.
Regulation	Regulation refers to restrictions state and federal laws place on business with regard to the conduct of its activities.
Wage	The payment for the service of a unit of labor, per unit time. In trade theory, it is the only payment to labor, usually unskilled labor. In empirical work, wage data may exclude other compenzation, which must be added to get the total cost of employment.
Gross domestic product	Gross domestic product refers to the total value of new goods and services produced in a given year within the borders of a country, regardless of by whom.
Domestic	From or in one's own country. A domestic producer is one that produces inside the home country. A domestic price is the price inside the home country. Opposite of 'foreign' or 'world.'.
Family business	A family business is a company owned, controlled, and operated by members of one or several families. Many companies that are now publicly held were founded as family businesses. Many family businesses have non-family members as employees, but, particularly in smaller companies, the top positions are often allocated to family members.
Firm	An organization that employs resources to produce a good or service for profit and owns and operates one or more plants is referred to as a firm.
Continuity	A media scheduling strategy where a continuous pattern of advertising is used over the time span of the advertising campaign is continuity.
Wall Street Journal	Dow Jones & Company was founded in 1882 by reporters Charles Dow, Edward Jones and Charles Bergstresser. Jones converted the small Customers' Afternoon Letter into The Wall Street Journal, first published in 1889, and began delivery of the Dow Jones News Service via telegraph. The Journal featured the Jones 'Average', the first of several indexes of stock and bond prices on the New York Stock Exchange.
Journal	Book of original entry, in which transactions are recorded in a general ledger system, is referred to as a journal.
Credibility	The extent to which a source is perceived as having knowledge, skill, or experience relevant to a communication topic and can be trusted to give an unbiased opinion or present objective information on the issue is called credibility.

Go to **Cram101.com** for the Practice Tests for this Chapter.
And, **NEVER** highlight a book again!

Interest	In finance and economics, interest is the price paid by a borrower for the use of a lender's money. In other words, interest is the amount of paid to "rent" money for a period of time.
Production	The creation of finished goods and services using the factors of production: land, labor, capital, entrepreneurship, and knowledge.
Marketing	Promoting and selling products or services to customers, or prospective customers, is referred to as marketing.
Bond	Bond refers to a debt instrument, issued by a borrower and promising a specified stream of payments to the purchaser, usually regular interest payments plus a final repayment of principal.
Foundation	A Foundation is a type of philanthropic organization set up by either individuals or institutions as a legal entity (either as a corporation or trust) with the purpose of distributing grants to support causes in line with the goals of the foundation.
Leadership	Management merely consists of leadership applied to business situations; or in other words: management forms a sub-set of the broader process of leadership.
Trust	An arrangement in which shareholders of independent firms agree to give up their stock in exchange for trust certificates that entitle them to a share of the trust's common profits.
Competitive advantage	A business is said to have a competitive advantage when its unique strengths, often based on cost, quality, time, and innovation, offer consumers a greater percieved value and there by differtiating it from its competitors.
Scope	Scope of a project is the sum total of all projects products and their requirements or features.
Openness	Openness refers to the extent to which an economy is open, often measured by the ratio of its trade to GDP.
Arthur Andersen	Arthur Andersen was once one of the Big Five accounting firms, performing auditing, tax, and consulting services for large corporations. In 2002 the firm voluntarily surrendered its licenses to practice as Certified Public Accountants in the U.S. pending the result of prosecution by the U.S. Department of Justice over the firm's handling of the auditing of Enron.
Preparation	Preparation refers to usually the first stage in the creative process. It includes education and formal training.
Strike	The withholding of labor services by an organized group of workers is referred to as a strike.
Buyer	A buyer refers to a role in the buying center with formal authority and responsibility to select the supplier and negotiate the terms of the contract.
Employee stock ownership plan	Employee Stock Ownership Plan is a qualified employee-benefit plan in which employees are entitled and encouraged to invest in shares of the company's stock and often at a favorable price. The employer's contributions are tax deductible for the employer and tax deferred for the employee.
Buyout	A buyout is an investment transaction by which the entire or a controlling part of the stock of a company is sold. A firm buysout the stake of the company to strengthen its influence on the company's decision making body. A buyout can take the forms of a leveraged buyout or a management buyout.
Leveraged buyout	An attempt by employees, management, or a group of investors to purchase an organization primarily through borrowing is a leveraged buyout.

Go to **Cram101.com** for the Practice Tests for this Chapter.

Stock	In financial terminology, stock is the capital raized by a corporation, through the issuance and sale of shares.
Promissory note	Commercial paper or instrument in which the maker promises to pay a specific sum of money to another person, to his order, or to bearer is referred to as a promissory note.
Security	Security refers to a claim on the borrower future income that is sold by the borrower to the lender. A security is a type of transferable interest representing financial value.
Capital gain	Capital gain refers to the gain in value that the owner of an asset experiences when the price of the asset rises, including when the currency in which the asset is denominated appreciates.
Liability	A liability is a present obligation of the enterprise arizing from past events, the settlement of which is expected to result in an outflow from the enterprise of resources embodying economic benefits.
Capital	Capital generally refers to financial wealth, especially that used to start or maintain a business. In classical economics, capital is one of four factors of production, the others being land and labor and entrepreneurship.
Gain	In finance, gain is a profit or an increase in value of an investment such as a stock or bond. Gain is calculated by fair market value or the proceeds from the sale of the investment minus the sum of the purchase price and all costs associated with it.
Board of directors	The group of individuals elected by the stockholders of a corporation to oversee its operations is a board of directors.
Estate	An estate is the totality of the legal rights, interests, entitlements and obligations attaching to property. In the context of wills and probate, it refers to the totality of the property which the deceased owned or in which some interest was held.
Lease	A contract for the possession and use of land or other property, including goods, on one side, and a recompense of rent or other income on the other is the lease.
Financial institution	A financial institution acts as an agent that provides financial services for its clients. Financial institutions generally fall under financial regulation from a government authority.
Operation	A standardized method or technique that is performed repetitively, often on different materials resulting in different finished goods is called an operation.
Closing	The finalization of a real estate sales transaction that passes title to the property from the seller to the buyer is referred to as a closing. Closing is a sales term which refers to the process of making a sale. It refers to reaching the final step, which may be an exchange of money or acquiring a signature.
Drawback	Drawback refers to rebate of import duties when the imported good is re-exported or used as input to the production of an exported good.
Bankruptcy	Bankruptcy is a legally declared inability or impairment of ability of an individual or organization to pay their creditors.
Mistake	In contract law a mistake is incorrect understanding by one or more parties to a contract and may be used as grounds to invalidate the agreement. Common law has identified three different types of mistake in contract: unilateral mistake, mutual mistake, and common mistake.
Economy	The income, expenditures, and resources that affect the cost of running a business and household are called an economy.
Incentive	An incentive is any factor (financial or non-financial) that provides a motive for a particular course of action, or counts as a reason for preferring one choice to the

367

	alternatives.
Subsidiary	A company that is controlled by another company or corporation is a subsidiary.
International Harvester	International Harvester was an American corporation based in Chicago that produced a multitude of agricultural machinery and vehicles. In 1924, International Harvester introduced the Farmall tractor, a smaller general-purpose tractor, to fend off competition from the Ford Motor Company's Fordson tractors. The Farmall was the first tractor in the United States to incorporate a tricycle-like design (or row-crop front axle), which could be used on tall crops such as cotton and corn.
Corporation	A legal entity chartered by a state or the Federal government that is distinct and separate from the individuals who own it is a corporation. This separation gives the corporation unique powers which other legal entities lack.
Industry	A group of firms that produce identical or similar products is an industry. It is also used specifically to refer to an area of economic production focused on manufacturing which involves large amounts of capital investment before any profit can be realized, also called "heavy industry".
Employee Stock Ownership Plans	Like profit sharing, Employee Stock Ownership Plans are based on the total organization's performance, but are measured in terms of stock price.
Purchasing	Purchasing refers to the function in a firm that searches for quality material resources, finds the best suppliers, and negotiates the best price for goods and services.
Shares	Shares refer to an equity security, representing a shareholder's ownership of a corporation. Shares are one of a finite number of equal portions in the capital of a company, entitling the owner to a proportion of distributed, non-reinvested profits known as dividends and to a portion of the value of the company in case of liquidation.
Controlling	A management function that involves determining whether or not an organization is progressing toward its goals and objectives, and taking corrective action if it is not is called controlling.
Succession planning	Succession planning refers to the identification and tracking of high-potential employees capable of filling higher-level managerial positions.
Goodwill	Goodwill is an important accounting concept that describes the value of a business entity not directly attributable to its tangible assets and liabilities.
Service	Service refers to a "non tangible product" that is not embodied in a physical good and that typically effects some change in another product, person, or institution. Contrasts with good.
Exchange	The trade of things of value between buyer and seller so that each is better off after the trade is called the exchange.
Medium of exchange	Medium of exchange refers to any item sellers generally accept and buyers generally use to pay for a good or service; money; a convenient means of exchanging goods and services without engaging in barter.
Graduation	Termination of a country's eligibility for GSP tariff preferences on the grounds that it has progressed sufficiently, in terms of per capita income or another measure, that it is no longer in need to special and differential treatment is graduation.
Apprenticeship	A work-study training method with both on-the-job and classroom training is an apprenticeship.Most of their training is on the job, working for an employer who helps the apprentices learn their trade, art or craft. Less formal, theoretical education is involved.
Competitor	Other organizations in the same industry or type of business that provide a good or service

Go to **Cram101.com** for the Practice Tests for this Chapter.

	to the same set of customers is referred to as a competitor.
Technology	The body of knowledge and techniques that can be used to combine economic resources to produce goods and services is called technology.
Authority	Authority in agency law, refers to an agent's ability to affect his principal's legal relations with third parties. Also used to refer to an actor's legal power or ability to do something. In addition, sometimes used to refer to a statute, case, or other legal source that justifies a particular result.
Profit	Profit refers to the return to the resource entrepreneurial ability; total revenue minus total cost.
Assessment	Collecting information and providing feedback to employees about their behavior, communication style, or skills is an assessment.
Distribution	Distribution in economics, the manner in which total output and income is distributed among individuals or factors.
Trend	Trend refers to the long-term movement of an economic variable, such as its average rate of increase or decrease over enough years to encompass several business cycles.
Inventory	Tangible property held for sale in the normal course of business or used in producing goods or services for sale is an inventory.
Supply	Supply is the aggregate amount of any material good that can be called into being at a certain price point; it comprises one half of the equation of supply and demand. In classical economic theory, a curve representing supply is one of the factors that produce price.
Assignment	A transfer of property or some right or interest is referred to as assignment.
Mentor	An experienced employee who supervises, coaches, and guides lower-level employees by introducing them to the right people and generally being their organizational sponsor is a mentor.
Staffing	Staffing refers to a management function that includes hiring, motivating, and retaining the best people available to accomplish the company's objectives.
Loyalty	Marketers tend to define customer loyalty as making repeat purchases. Some argue that it should be defined attitudinally as a strongly positive feeling about the brand.
Heir	In common law jurisdictions an heir is a person who is entitled to receive a share of the decedent's property via the rules of inheritance in the jurisdiction where the decedent died or owned property at the time of his death.
Key Success Factor	A Key Success Factor is a factor in a given market that is a necessary condition for success.
Success factor	The term success factor refers to the characteristics necessary for high performance; knowledge, skills, abilities, behaviors.
Policy	Similar to a script in that a policy can be a less than completely rational decision-making method. Involves the use of a pre-existing set of decision steps for any problem that presents itself.
Job analysis	Job analysis refers to a study of what is done by employees who hold various job titles. It refers to various methodologies for analyzing the requirements of a job.
Creditor	A person to whom a debt or legal obligation is owed, and who has the right to enforce payment of that debt or obligation is referred to as creditor.
Estate tax	A tax imposed on the right to transfer property by death. Thus, an estate tax is levied on

	the decedent's estate and not on the heir receiving the property.
Asset	An item of property, such as land, capital, money, a share in ownership, or a claim on others for future payment, such as a bond or a bank deposit is an asset.
Underwriters	Investment banks that guarantee prices on securities to corporations and then sell the securities to the public are underwriters.
Consultant	A professional that provides expert advice in a particular field or area in which customers occassionaly require this type of knowledge is a consultant.
Contract	A contract is a "promise" or an "agreement" that is enforced or recognized by the law. In the civil law, a contract is considered to be part of the general law of obligations.
Direct marketing	Promotional element that uses direct communication with consumers to generate a response in the form of an order, a request for further information, or a visit to a retail outlet is direct marketing.
Exempt	Employees who are not covered by the Fair Labor Standards Act are exempt. Exempt employees are not eligible for overtime pay.
Beneficiary	The person for whose benefit an insurance policy, trust, will, or contract is established is a beneficiary. In the case of a contract, the beneficiary is called a third-party beneficiary.
Property	Assets defined in the broadest legal sense. Property includes the unrealized receivables of a cash basis taxpayer, but not services rendered.
Trustee	An independent party appointed to represent the bondholders is referred to as a trustee.
Grantor	A transferor of property. The creator of a trust is usually referred to as the grantor of the trust. In a franchise agreement, for example, the party selling the franchise is the grantor
Principal	In agency law, one under whose direction an agent acts and for whose benefit that agent acts is a principal.
Annuity	A contract to make regular payments to a person for life or for a fixed period is an annuity.
Gift tax	Gift tax refers to a tax imposed on the transfer of property by gift. The tax is imposed upon the donor of a gift and is based on the fair market value of the property on the date of the gift.
Expense	In accounting, an expense represents an event in which an asset is used up or a liability is incurred. In terms of the accounting equation, expenses reduce owners' equity.
Preferred stock	Stock that has specified rights over common stock is a preferred stock.
Common stock	Common stock refers to the basic, normal, voting stock issued by a corporation; called residual equity because it ranks after preferred stock for dividend and liquidation distributions.
Market value	Market value refers to the price of an asset agreed on between a willing buyer and a willing seller; the price an asset could demand if it is sold on the open market.
Market	A market is, as defined in economics, a social arrangement that allows buyers and sellers to discover information and carry out a voluntary exchange of goods or services.
Appreciation	Appreciation refers to a rise in the value of a country's currency on the exchange market, relative either to a particular other currency or to a weighted average of other currencies. The currency is said to appreciate. Opposite of 'depreciation.' Appreciation can also refer to the increase in value of any asset.
Dividend	Amount of corporate profits paid out for each share of stock is referred to as dividend.

Go to **Cram101.com** for the Practice Tests for this Chapter.
And, **NEVER** highlight a book again!

Limited partnership	A partnership in which some of the partners are limited partners. At least one of the partners in a limited partnership must be a general partner.
Partnership	In the common law, a partnership is a type of business entity in which partners share with each other the profits or losses of the business undertaking in which they have all invested.
Partnership interest	A partners share of the profits and losses of a limited partnership and the right to receive payments on partnership assets is a partnership interest.
General partnership	A partnership that is owned by one or more general partners. Creditors of a general partnership can collect amounts owed them from both the partnership assets and the assets of the partners individually.
Limited partner	An owner of a limited partnership who has no right to manage the business but who possesses liability limited to his capital contribution to the business is referred to as limited partner.
General partners	Partners in a limited partnership who invest capital, manage the business, and are personally liable for partnership debts are referred to as general partners.
General partner	An owner who has unlimited liability and is active in managing the firm is a general partner. The individual or firm that organizes and manages the limited partnership. For example a hedge fund.
Discount	The difference between the face value of a bond and its selling price, when a bond is sold for less than its face value it's referred to as a discount.
Agent	A person who makes economic decisions for another economic actor. A hired manager operates as an agent for a firm's owner.
Credit	Credit refers to a recording as positive in the balance of payments, any transaction that gives rise to a payment into the country, such as an export, the sale of an asset, or borrowing from abroad.
Retailing	All activities involved in selling, renting, and providing goods and services to ultimate consumers for personal, family, or household use is referred to as retailing.
Brand	A name, symbol, or design that identifies the goods or services of one seller or group of sellers and distinguishes them from the goods and services of competitors is a brand.
Forbes	David Churbuck founded online Forbes in 1996. The site drew attention when it uncovered Stephen Glass' journalistic fraud in The New Republic in 1998, a scoop that gave credibility to internet journalism.
Points	Loan origination fees that may be deductible as interest by a buyer of property. A seller of property who pays points reduces the selling price by the amount of the points paid for the buyer.
Anticipation	In finance, anticipation is where debts are paid off early, generally in order to pay less interest.
Fund	Independent accounting entity with a self-balancing set of accounts segregated for the purposes of carrying on specific activities is referred to as a fund.
Best efforts	Best efforts refer to a distribution in which the investment banker agrees to work for a commission rather than actually underwriting the issue for resale. It is a procedure that is used by smaller investment bankers with relatively unknown companies. The investment banker is not directly taking the risk for distribution.
Premium	Premium refers to the fee charged by an insurance company for an insurance policy. The rate of losses must be relatively predictable: In order to set the premium (prices) insurers must

	be able to estimate them accurately.
Dealer	People who link buyers with sellers by buying and selling securities at stated prices are referred to as a dealer.
Health insurance	Health insurance is a type of insurance whereby the insurer pays the medical costs of the insured if the insured becomes sick due to covered causes, or due to accidents. The insurer may be a private organization or a government agency.
Allocate	Allocate refers to the assignment of income for various tax purposes. A multistate corporation's nonbusiness income usually is distributed to the state where the nonbusiness assets are located; it is not apportioned with the rest of the entity's income.
Manufacturing	Production of goods primarily by the application of labor and capital to raw materials and other intermediate inputs, in contrast to agriculture, mining, forestry, fishing, and services a manufacturing.
Liability insurance	Liability insurance is designed to offer specific protection against third party claims, i.e., payment is not typically made to the insured, but rather to someone suffering loss who is not a party to the insurance contract.
Tangible asset	Assets that have physical substance that cannot easily be converted into cash are referd to as a tangible asset.
Tangible	Having a physical existence is referred to as the tangible. Personal property other than real estate, such as cars, boats, stocks, or other assets.
Replacement cost	The current purchase price of replacing a property damaged or lost with similar property is the replacement cost.
Building code	A building code is a set of rules that specify the minimum acceptable level of safety for constructed objects such as buildings and nonbuilding structures. Their main purpose is to protect public health, safety and general welfare as they relate to the construction and occupancy of buildings and structures.
Surety	A person who promises to perform the same obligation as another person and who is jointly liable along with the principal for that obligation's performance is referred to as surety.
Data processing	Data processing refers to a name for business technology in the 1970s; included technology that supported an existing business and was primarily used to improve the flow of financial information.
Electronic data processing	Electronic data processing can refer to the use of automated methods to process commercial data. Typically, this uses relatively simple, repetitive activities to process large volumes of similar information.
Finished goods	Completed products awaiting sale are called finished goods. An item considered a finished good in a supplying plant might be considered a component or raw material in a receiving plant.
Raw material	Raw material refers to a good that has not been transformed by production; a primary product.
Marine insurance	Insurance that owners of vessels purchase to insure against loss or damage to the vessel and its cargo caused by perils at sea is referred to as the marine insurance.
In transit	A state in which goods are in the possession of a bailee or carrier and not in the hands of the buyer, seller, lessee, or lessor is referred to as in transit.
Insurance broker	An insurance broker sources (brokes) contracts of insurance on behalf of their customers.The term Insurance Broker became a regulated term under the Insurance Brokers (Registration) Act 1977 which was designed to thwart the bogus practices of firms holding themselves as brokers

377

but in fact acting as representative of one or more favoured insurance companies.

Broker	In commerce, a broker is a party that mediates between a buyer and a seller. A broker who also acts as a seller or as a buyer becomes a principal party to the deal.
Cash value	The cash value of an insurance policy is the amount available to the policy holder in cash upon cancellation of the policy. This term is normally used with a whole life policy in which a portion of the premiums go toward an investment. The cash value is the value of this investment at any particular time.
Fidelity bond	Insurance policy that a company buys to insure itself against loss due to employee dishonesty is called fidelity bond.
Embezzlement	Embezzlement is the fraudulent appropriation by a person to his own use of property or money entrusted to that person's care but owned by someone else.
Forgery	Forgery is the process of making or adapting objects or documents, with the intention to deceive. The similar crime of fraud is the crime of deceiving another, including through the use of objects obtained through forgery. Copies, studio replicas, and reproductions are not considered forgeries, though they may later become forgeries through knowing and willful mis-attributions.
Personnel	A collective term for all of the employees of an organization. Personnel is also commonly used to refer to the personnel management function or the organizational unit responsible for administering personnel programs.
Working capital	The dollar difference between total current assets and total current liabilities is called working capital.
Annuities	Financial contracts under which a customer pays an annual premium in exchange for a future stream of annual payments beginning at a set age, say 65, and ending when the person dies are annuities.
Pension	A pension is a steady income given to a person (usually after retirement). Pensions are typically payments made in the form of a guaranteed annuity to a retired or disabled employee.
Gap	In December of 1995, Gap became the first major North American retailer to accept independent monitoring of the working conditions in a contract factory producing its garments. Gap is the largest specialty retailer in the United States.
Preferred provider organization	A group of health care providers who contract with employers, insurance companies, and so forth to provide health care at a reduced fee is called preferred provider organization.
Health maintenance organization	A Health Maintenance Organization is a fixed, prepaid health care plan that provides comprehensive benefits for employees who are required to use a network of participating providers for all health services.
Remainder	A remainder in property law is a future interest created in a transferee that is capable of becoming possessory upon the natural termination of a prior estate created by the same instrument.
Individual Retirement Account	Traditionally, a tax-deferred investment plan that enables you to save part of your income for retirement is an individual retirement account.
Contribution	In business organization law, the cash or property contributed to a business by its owners is referred to as contribution.
Deductible	The dollar sum of costs that an insured individual must pay before the insurer begins to pay

	is called deductible.
Cash flow	In finance, cash flow refers to the amounts of cash being received and spent by a business during a defined period of time, sometimes tied to a specific project. Most of the time they are being used to determine gaps in the liquid position of a company.
Red tape	Red tape is a derisive term for excessive regulations or rigid conformity to formal rules that are considered redundant or bureaucratic and hinders or prevents action or decision-making.
Productivity	Productivity refers to the total output of goods and services in a given period of time divided by work hours.
Just In Time	Just In Time is an inventory strategy implemented to improve the return on investment of a business by reducing in-process inventory and its associated costs. The process is driven by a series of signals, or Kanban that tell production processes to make the next part.
Product liability	Part of tort law that holds businesses liable for harm that results from the production, design, sale, or use of products they market is referred to as product liability.
Damages	The sum of money recoverable by a plaintiff who has received a judgment in a civil case is called damages.
Americans with Disabilities Act	The Americans with Disabilities Act of 1990 is a wide-ranging civil rights law that prohibits discrimination based on disability.
Family and Medical Leave Act	The Family and Medical Leave Act of 1993 is a United States labor law allowing an employee to take unpaid leave due to illness or to care for a sick family member.
Wrongful termination	Wrongful termination refers to the termination of an agency contract in violation of the terms of the agency contract. The nonbreaching party may recover damages from the breaching party.
Sexual harassment	Unwelcome sexual advances, requests for sexual favors, and other conduct of a sexual nature is called sexual harassment.
Termination	The ending of a corporation that occurs only after the winding-up of the corporation's affairs, the liquidation of its assets, and the distribution of the proceeds to the claimants are referred to as a termination.
Employment discrimination	Inferior treatment in hiring, promotions, work assignments, and such for a particular group of employees, based on criteria that is not controllable, is referred to as employment discrimination.
Employment law	Employment law is the body of laws, administrative rulings, and precedents which addresses the legal rights of, and restrictions on, workers and their organizations.
Human resources	Human resources refers to the individuals within the firm, and to the portion of the firm's organization that deals with hiring, firing, training, and other personnel issues.
Consideration	Consideration in contract law, a basic requirement for an enforceable agreement under traditional contract principles, defined in this text as legal value, bargained for and given in exchange for an act or promise. In corporation law, cash or property contributed to a corporation in exchange for shares, or a promise to contribute such cash or property.
Balance	In banking and accountancy, the outstanding balance is the amount of money owned, (or due), that remains in a deposit account (or a loan account) at a given date, after all past remittances, payments and withdrawal have been accounted for. It can be positive (then, in the balance sheet of a firm, it is an asset) or negative (a liability).

Go to **Cram101.com** for the Practice Tests for this Chapter.

Trade association	An industry trade group or trade association is generally a public relations organization founded and funded by corporations that operate in a specific industry. Its purpose is generally to promote that industry through PR activities such as advertizing, education, political donations, political pressure, publishing, and astroturfing.
Commerce	Commerce is the exchange of something of value between two entities. It is the central mechanism from which capitalism is derived.
Utilization review	Utilization review is a technique used by some insurers and employers to evaluate health care on the basis of appropriateness, necessity, and quality.
Leverage	Leverage is using given resources in such a way that the potential positive or negative outcome is magnified. In finance, this generally refers to borrowing.
Personal finance	Personal finance is the application of the principles of financial economics to an individual's (or a family's) financial decisions.

Bid	A bid price is a price offered by a buyer when he/she buys a good. In the context of stock trading on a stock exchange, the bid price is the highest price a buyer of a stock is willing to pay for a share of that given stock.
Value system	A value system refers to how an individual or a group of individuals organize their ethical or ideological values. A well-defined value system is a moral code.
Entrepreneur	The owner/operator. The person who organizes, manages, and assumes the risks of a firm, taking a new idea or a new product and turning it into a successful business is an entrepreneur.
Interest	In finance and economics, interest is the price paid by a borrower for the use of a lender's money. In other words, interest is the amount of paid to "rent" money for a period of time.
Investment	Investment refers to spending for the production and accumulation of capital and additions to inventories. In a financial sense, buying an asset with the expectation of making a return.
Profit	Profit refers to the return to the resource entrepreneurial ability; total revenue minus total cost.
Social responsibility	Social responsibility is a doctrine that claims that an entity whether it is state, government, corporation, organization or individual has a responsibility to society.
Shareholder	A shareholder is an individual or company (including a corporation) that legally owns one or more shares of stock in a joined stock company.
Lender	Suppliers and financial institutions that lend money to companies is referred to as a lender.
Business ethics	The study of what makes up good and bad conduct as related to business activities and values is business ethics.
Stakeholder	A stakeholder is an individual or group with a vested interest in or expectation for organizational performance. Usually stakeholders can either have an effect on or are affected by an organization.
Foundation	A Foundation is a type of philanthropic organization set up by either individuals or institutions as a legal entity (either as a corporation or trust) with the purpose of distributing grants to support causes in line with the goals of the foundation.
Appeal	Appeal refers to the act of asking an appellate court to overturn a decision after the trial court's final judgment has been entered.
Evaluation	The consumer's appraisal of the product or brand on important attributes is called evaluation.
Small business	Small business refers to a business that is independently owned and operated, is not dominant in its field of operation, and meets certain standards of size in terms of employees or annual receipts.
Complexity	The technical sophistication of the product and hence the amount of understanding required to use it is referred to as complexity. It is the opposite of simplicity.
Firm	An organization that employs resources to produce a good or service for profit and owns and operates one or more plants is referred to as a firm.
Ethical dilemma	An ethical dilemma is a situation that often involves an apparent conflict between moral imperatives, in which to obey one would result in transgressing another.
Context	The effect of the background under which a message often takes on more and richer meaning is a context. Context is especially important in cross-cultural interactions because some cultures are said to be high context or low context.

Go to **Cram101.com** for the Practice Tests for this Chapter.

Maturity	Maturity refers to the final payment date of a loan or other financial instrument, after which point no further interest or principal need be paid.
Socialization	Socialization is the process by which human beings or animals learn to adopt the behavior patterns of the community in which they live. For both humans and animals, this is typically thought to occur during the early stages of life, during which individuals develop the skills and knowledge necessary to function within their culture and environment.
Corporate culture	The whole collection of beliefs, values, and behaviors of a firm that send messages to those within and outside the company about how business is done is the corporate culture.
Corporate policy	Dimension of social responsibility that refers to the position a firm takes on social and political issues is referred to as corporate policy.
Management	Management characterizes the process of leading and directing all or part of an organization, often a business, through the deployment and manipulation of resources. Early twentieth-century management writer Mary Parker Follett defined management as "the art of getting things done through people."
Policy	Similar to a script in that a policy can be a less than completely rational decision-making method. Involves the use of a pre-existing set of decision steps for any problem that presents itself.
Case study	A case study is a particular method of qualitative research. Rather than using large samples and following a rigid protocol to examine a limited number of variables, case study methods involve an in-depth, longitudinal examination of a single instance or event: a case. They provide a systematic way of looking at events, collecting data, analyzing information, and reporting the results.
Utilitarian approach	The ethical concept that moral behaviors produce the greatest good for the greatest number is an utilitarian approach.
Balance	In banking and accountancy, the outstanding balance is the amount of money owned, (or due), that remains in a deposit account (or a loan account) at a given date, after all past remittances, payments and withdrawal have been accounted for. It can be positive (then, in the balance sheet of a firm, it is an asset) or negative (a liability).
Justice approach	Justice approach refers to the ethical concept that moral decisions must be based on standards of equity, fairness, and impartiality.
Distribution	Distribution in economics, the manner in which total output and income is distributed among individuals or factors.
Business opportunity	A business opportunity involves the sale or lease of any product, service, equipment, etc. that will enable the purchaser-licensee to begin a business
Option	A contract that gives the purchaser the option to buy or sell the underlying financial instrument at a specified price, called the exercise price or strike price, within a specific period of time.
Chief executive officer	A chief executive officer is the highest-ranking corporate officer or executive officer of a corporation, or agency. In closely held corporations, it is general business culture that the office chief executive officer is also the chairman of the board.
Stockholder	A stockholder is an individual or company (including a corporation) that legally owns one or more shares of stock in a joined stock company. The shareholders are the owners of a corporation. Companies listed at the stock market strive to enhance shareholder value.
Security	Security refers to a claim on the borrower future income that is sold by the borrower to the lender. A security is a type of transferable interest representing financial value.

Company culture	Company culture is the term given to the values and practices shared by the employees of a firm.
Gain	In finance, gain is a profit or an increase in value of an investment such as a stock or bond. Gain is calculated by fair market value or the proceeds from the sale of the investment minus the sum of the purchase price and all costs associated with it.
Standards of conduct	Standards of conduct refers to a compendium of ethical norms promulgated by an organization to guide the behavior of its members. Many government agencies have formal codes of conduct for their employees.
Due process	Due process of law is a legal concept that ensures the government will respect all of a person's legal rights instead of just some or most of those legal rights when the government deprives a person of life, liberty, or property.
Leadership	Management merely consists of leadership applied to business situations; or in other words: management forms a sub-set of the broader process of leadership.
Rationalization	Rationalization in economics is an attempt to change a pre-existing ad-hoc workflow into one that is based on a set of published rules.
Corporate citizenship	A theory of responsibility that says a business has a responsibility to do good is corporate citizenship. Terms used in the business sector to refer to business giving, ie. business relationships and partnerships with not-for-profit organizations.
Compromise	Compromise occurs when the interaction is moderately important to meeting goals and the goals are neither completely compatible nor completely incompatible.
Consultant	A professional that provides expert advice in a particular field or area in which customers occassionaly require this type of knowledge is a consultant.
Generally accepted accounting principles	Generally accepted accounting principles refers to the standard framework of guidelines for financial accounting. It includes the standards, conventions, and rules accountants follow in recording and summarizing transactions, and in the preparation of financial statements.
Accounting	A system that collects and processes financial information about an organization and reports that information to decision makers is referred to as accounting.
Mistake	In contract law a mistake is incorrect understanding by one or more parties to a contract and may be used as grounds to invalidate the agreement. Common law has identified three different types of mistake in contract: unilateral mistake, mutual mistake, and common mistake.
Bottom line	The bottom line is net income on the last line of a income statement.
Core	A core is the set of feasible allocations in an economy that cannot be improved upon by subset of the set of the economy's consumers (a coalition). In construction, when the force in an element is within a certain center section, the core, the element will only be under compression.
Contribution	In business organization law, the cash or property contributed to a business by its owners is referred to as contribution.
Mentor	An experienced employee who supervises, coaches, and guides lower-level employees by introducing them to the right people and generally being their organizational sponsor is a mentor.
Competitor	Other organizations in the same industry or type of business that provide a good or service to the same set of customers is referred to as a competitor.
Revenue	Revenue is a U.S. business term for the amount of money that a company receives from its

activities, mostly from sales of products and/or services to customers.

Market	A market is, as defined in economics, a social arrangement that allows buyers and sellers to discover information and carry out a voluntary exchange of goods or services.
Entrepreneurship	The assembling of resources to produce new or improved products and technologies is referred to as entrepreneurship.
Globalization	The increasing world-wide integration of markets for goods, services and capital that attracted special attention in the late 1990s is called globalization.
Property	Assets defined in the broadest legal sense. Property includes the unrealized receivables of a cash basis taxpayer, but not services rendered.
Auction	A preexisting business model that operates successfully on the Internet by announcing an item for sale and permitting multiple purchasers to bid on them under specified rules and condition is an auction.
Code of ethics	A formal statement of ethical principles and rules of conduct is a code of ethics. Some may have the force of law; these are often promulgated by the (quasi-)governmental agency responsible for licensing a profession. Violations of these codes may be subject to administrative (e.g., loss of license), civil or penal remedies.
Undue influence	Undue influence is an equitable doctrine that involves one person taking advantage of a position of power over another person.
Concealment	In contract law, taking active steps to prevent another from learning the truth is referred to as concealment.
Privilege	Generally, a legal right to engage in conduct that would otherwise result in legal liability is a privilege. Privileges are commonly classified as absolute or conditional. Occasionally, privilege is also used to denote a legal right to refrain from particular behavior.
Authority	Authority in agency law, refers to an agent's ability to affect his principal's legal relations with third parties. Also used to refer to an actor's legal power or ability to do something. In addition, sometimes used to refer to a statute, case, or other legal source that justifies a particular result.
Service	Service refers to a "non tangible product" that is not embodied in a physical good and that typically effects some change in another product, person, or institution. Contrasts with good.
Compliance	A type of influence process where a receiver accepts the position advocated by a source to obtain favorable outcomes or to avoid punishment is the compliance.
Ethics training	Training programs to help employees deal with ethical questions and values are called ethics training.
Insurance	Insurance refers to a system by which individuals can reduce their exposure to risk of large losses by spreading the risks among a large number of persons.
Audit	An examination of the financial reports to ensure that they represent what they claim and conform with generally accepted accounting principles is referred to as audit.
Negotiable	A negotiable instrument is one that can be bought and sold after being issued - in other words, it is a tradable instrument.
Organizational Behavior	The study of human behavior in organizational settings, the interface between human behavior and the organization, and the organization itself is called organizational behavior.
Enterprise	Enterprise refers to another name for a business organization. Other similar terms are business firm, sometimes simply business, sometimes simply firm, as well as company, and

entity.

Free enterprise	Free enterprise refers to a system in which economic agents are free to own property and engage in commercial transactions.
Commerce	Commerce is the exchange of something of value between two entities. It is the central mechanism from which capitalism is derived.
Controlling	A management function that involves determining whether or not an organization is progressing toward its goals and objectives, and taking corrective action if it is not is called controlling.
Vendor	A person who sells property to a vendee is a vendor. The words vendor and vendee are more commonly applied to the seller and purchaser of real estate, and the words seller and buyer are more commonly applied to the seller and purchaser of personal property.
Gap	In December of 1995, Gap became the first major North American retailer to accept independent monitoring of the working conditions in a contract factory producing its garments. Gap is the largest specialty retailer in the United States.
Contract	A contract is a "promise" or an "agreement" that is enforced or recognized by the law. In the civil law, a contract is considered to be part of the general law of obligations.
Wall Street Journal	Dow Jones & Company was founded in 1882 by reporters Charles Dow, Edward Jones and Charles Bergstresser. Jones converted the small Customers' Afternoon Letter into The Wall Street Journal, first published in 1889, and began delivery of the Dow Jones News Service via telegraph. The Journal featured the Jones 'Average', the first of several indexes of stock and bond prices on the New York Stock Exchange.
Journal	Book of original entry, in which transactions are recorded in a general ledger system, is referred to as a journal.
Buying criteria	Buying criteria refers to the factors buying organizations use when evaluating a potential supplier and what it wants to sell.
Manufacturing	Production of goods primarily by the application of labor and capital to raw materials and other intermediate inputs, in contrast to agriculture, mining, forestry, fishing, and services a manufacturing.
Customer service	The ability of logistics management to satisfy users in terms of time, dependability, communication, and convenience is called the customer service.
Productivity	Productivity refers to the total output of goods and services in a given period of time divided by work hours.
Competitive advantage	A business is said to have a competitive advantage when its unique strengths, often based on cost, quality, time, and innovation, offer consumers a greater percieved value and there by diffetiating it from its competitors.
Asset	An item of property, such as land, capital, money, a share in ownership, or a claim on others for future payment, such as a bond or a bank deposit is an asset.
Starbucks	Although it has endured much criticism for its purported monopoly on the global coffee-bean market, Starbucks purchases only 3% of the coffee beans grown worldwide. In 2000 the company introduced a line of fair trade products and now offers three options for socially conscious coffee drinkers. According to Starbucks, they purchased 4.8 million pounds of Certified Fair Trade coffee in fiscal year 2004 and 11.5 million pounds in 2005.
Industry	A group of firms that produce identical or similar products is an industry. It is also used specifically to refer to an area of economic production focused on manufacturing which involves large amounts of capital investment before any profit can be realized, also called

Go to **Cram101.com** for the Practice Tests for this Chapter.

	"heavy industry".
Turnover	Turnover in a financial context refers to the rate at which a provider of goods cycles through its average inventory. Turnover in a human resources context refers to the characteristic of a given company or industry, relative to rate at which an employer gains and loses staff.
Demographic	A demographic is a term used in marketing and broadcasting, to describe a demographic grouping or a market segment.
Prejudice	Prejudice is, as the name implies, the process of "pre-judging" something. It implies coming to a judgment on a subject before learning where the preponderance of evidence actually lies, or forming a judgment without direct experience.
Diversity training	Diversity training refers to training designed to change employee attitudes about diversity and/or develop skills needed to work with a diverse workforce.
Assessment	Collecting information and providing feedback to employees about their behavior, communication style, or skills is an assessment.
Promotion	Promotion refers to all the techniques sellers use to motivate people to buy products or services. An attempt by marketers to inform people about products and to persuade them to participate in an exchange.
Management team	A management team is directly responsible for managing the day-to-day operations (and profitability) of a company.
Disclosure	Disclosure means the giving out of information, either voluntarily or to be in compliance with legal regulations or workplace rules.
Human resources	Human resources refers to the individuals within the firm, and to the portion of the firm's organization that deals with hiring, firing, training, and other personnel issues.
Liability	A liability is a present obligation of the enterprise arizing from past events, the settlement of which is expected to result in an outflow from the enterprise of resources embodying economic benefits.
Alignment	Term that refers to optimal coordination among disparate departments and divisions within a firm is referred to as alignment.
Middle management	Middle management refers to the level of management that includes general managers, division managers, and branch and plant managers who are responsible for tactical planning and controlling.
Valuing diversity	Valuing diversity refers to putting an end to the assumption that everyone who is not a member of the dominant group must assimilate. The first step is to recognize that diversity exists in organizations so that we can begin to manage it.
Supervisor	A Supervisor is an employee of an organization with some of the powers and responsibilities of management, occupying a role between true manager and a regular employee. A Supervisor position is typically the first step towards being promoted into a management role.
Applicant	In many tribunal and administrative law suits, the person who initiates the claim is called the applicant.
Employee assistance program	Programs offered by companies to help employees deal with job stress and with personal problems that may have developed from the stress or other sources are referred to as an employee assistance program.
Aid	Assistance provided by countries and by international institutions such as the World Bank to developing countries in the form of monetary grants, loans at low interest rates, in kind, or

Go to **Cram101.com** for the Practice Tests for this Chapter.
And, **NEVER** highlight a book again!

	a combination of these is called aid. Aid can also refer to assistance of any type rendered to benefit some group or individual.
Strike	The withholding of labor services by an organized group of workers is referred to as a strike.
Economy	The income, expenditures, and resources that affect the cost of running a business and household are called an economy.
Americans with Disabilities Act	The Americans with Disabilities Act of 1990 is a wide-ranging civil rights law that prohibits discrimination based on disability.
Accommodation	Accommodation is a term used to describe a delivery of nonconforming goods meant as a partial performance of a contract for the sale of goods, where a full performance is not possible.
Reasonable accommodation	Making facilities readily accessible to and usable by individuals with physical or mental limitations is referred to as reasonable accommodation.
Openness	Openness refers to the extent to which an economy is open, often measured by the ratio of its trade to GDP.
Flexible work schedule	A flexible work schedule is a shedule in which an employee has a forty hour work week but can set their own schedule within the limits set by the employer.
Restructuring	Restructuring is the corporate management term for the act of partially dismantling and reorganizing a company for the purpose of making it more efficient and therefore more profitable.
Purchasing	Purchasing refers to the function in a firm that searches for quality material resources, finds the best suppliers, and negotiates the best price for goods and services.
Sexual harassment	Unwelcome sexual advances, requests for sexual favors, and other conduct of a sexual nature is called sexual harassment.
Legal system	Legal system refers to system of rules that regulate behavior and the processes by which the laws of a country are enforced and through which redress of grievances is obtained.
Civil rights act of 1964	The Civil Rights Act of 1964 is a federal law that, in Title VII, outlaws discrimination based on race, color, religion, gender, or national origin in hiring, promoting, and compensating workers.
Jury	A body of lay persons, selected by lot, or by some other fair and impartial means, to ascertain, under the guidance of the judge, the truth in questions of fact arising either in civil litigation or a criminal process is referred to as jury.
Verdict	Usually, the decision made by a jury and reported to the judge on the matters or questions submitted to it at trial is a verdict. In some situations, however, the judge may be the party issuing a verdict.
Hostile work environment	A hostile work environment exists when an employee experiences workplace harassment and fears going to work because of the offensive, intimidating, or oppressive atmosphere generated by the harasser. Hostile work environment is also one of the two legal categories of sexual harassment.
Complaint	The pleading in a civil case in which the plaintiff states his claim and requests relief is called complaint. In the common law, it is a formal legal document that sets out the basic facts and legal reasons that the filing party (the plaintiffs) believes are sufficient to support a claim against another person, persons, entity or entities (the defendants) that entitles the plaintiff(s) to a remedy (either money damages or injunctive relief).

Allegation	An allegation is a statement of a fact by a party in a pleading, which the party claims it will prove. Allegations remain assertions without proof, only claims until they are proved.
Punitive damages	Damages received or paid by the taxpayer can be classified as compensatory damages or as punitive damages. Punitive damages are those awarded to punish the defendant for gross negligence or the intentional infliction of harm. Such damages are includible.
Punitive	Damages designed to punish flagrant wrongdoers and to deter them and others from engaging in similar conduct in the future are called punitive.
Damages	The sum of money recoverable by a plaintiff who has received a judgment in a civil case is called damages.
Tangible	Having a physical existence is referred to as the tangible. Personal property other than real estate, such as cars, boats, stocks, or other assets.
Channel	Channel, in communications (sometimes called communications channel), refers to the medium used to convey information from a sender (or transmitter) to a receiver.
Points	Loan origination fees that may be deductible as interest by a buyer of property. A seller of property who pays points reduces the selling price by the amount of the points paid for the buyer.
Technology	The body of knowledge and techniques that can be used to combine economic resources to produce goods and services is called technology.
Resource management	Resource management is the efficient and effective deployment of an organization's resources when they are needed. Such resources may include financial resources, inventory, human skills, production resources, or information technology.
Human resource management	The process of evaluating human resource needs, finding people to fill those needs, and getting the best work from each employee by providing the right incentives and job environment, all with the goal of meeting the needs of the firm are called human resource management.
Buyer	A buyer refers to a role in the buying center with formal authority and responsibility to select the supplier and negotiate the terms of the contract.
Consumer bill of rights	Codified the ethics of exchange between buyers and sellers, including the right to safety, to be informed, to choose, and to be heard is referred to as consumer bill of rights.
Trust	An arrangement in which shareholders of independent firms agree to give up their stock in exchange for trust certificates that entitle them to a share of the trust's common profits.
Product liability	Part of tort law that holds businesses liable for harm that results from the production, design, sale, or use of products they market is referred to as product liability.
Serious injury	The injury requirement of the escape clause, understood to be more stringent than material injury but otherwise apparently not rigorously defined, is referred to as serious injury.
Litigation	The process of bringing, maintaining, and defending a lawsuit is litigation.
Market economy	A market economy is an economic system in which the production and distribution of goods and services takes place through the mechanism of free markets guided by a free price system rather than by the state in a planned economy.
Free market	A free market is a market where price is determined by the unregulated interchange of supply and demand rather than set by artificial means.
Commodity	Could refer to any good, but in trade a commodity is usually a raw material or primary product that enters into international trade, such as metals or basic agricultural products.

Go to **Cram101.com** for the Practice Tests for this Chapter.

Advertising	Advertising refers to paid, nonpersonal communication through various media by organizations and individuals who are in some way identified in the advertising message.
Ombudsman	An ombudsman is an official, usually appointed by the government or by parliament, who is charged with representing the interests of the public by investigating and addressing complaints reported by individual citizens. An ombudsman need not be appointed by government; they may work for a corporation, a newspaper, an NGO, or even for the general public.
Annual report	An annual report is prepared by corporate management that presents financial information including financial statements, footnotes, and the management discussion and analysis.
Customer satisfaction	Customer satisfaction is a business term which is used to capture the idea of measuring how satisfied an enterprise's customers are with the organization's efforts in a marketplace.
Antitrust policy	The use of the antitrust laws to promote competition and economic efficiency is referred to as antitrust policy.
Free trade	Free trade refers to a situation in which there are no artificial barriers to trade, such as tariffs and quotas. Usually used, often only implicitly, with frictionless trade, so that it implies that there are no barriers to trade of any kind.
Antitrust	Government intervention to alter market structure or prevent abuse of market power is called antitrust.
Sherman Antitrust Act	The Sherman Antitrust Act, formally known as the Act of July 2, 1890 was the first United States federal government action to limit monopolies.
Proactive	To be proactive is to act before a situation becomes a source of confrontation or crisis. It is the opposite of "retroactive," which refers to actions taken after an event.
Fiduciary	Fiduciary refers to one who holds goods in trust for another or one who holds a position of trust and confidence.
Stock	In financial terminology, stock is the capital raized by a corporation, through the issuance and sale of shares.
Precedent	A previously decided court decision that is recognized as authority for the disposition of future decisions is a precedent.
Fraud	Tax fraud falls into two categories: civil and criminal. Under civil fraud, the IRS may impose as a penalty of an amount equal to as much as 75 percent of the underpayment.
Bankruptcy	Bankruptcy is a legally declared inability or impairment of ability of an individual or organization to pay their creditors.
Brief	Brief refers to a statement of a party's case or legal arguments, usually prepared by an attorney. Also used to make legal arguments before appellate courts.
Emerging market	The term emerging market is commonly used to describe business and market activity in industrializing or emerging regions of the world.
Forbes	David Churbuck founded online Forbes in 1996. The site drew attention when it uncovered Stephen Glass' journalistic fraud in The New Republic in 1998, a scoop that gave credibility to internet journalism.
Goodwill	Goodwill is an important accounting concept that describes the value of a business entity not directly attributable to its tangible assets and liabilities.
Personnel	A collective term for all of the employees of an organization. Personnel is also commonly used to refer to the personnel management function or the organizational unit responsible for administering personnel programs.

Go to **Cram101.com** for the Practice Tests for this Chapter.
And, **NEVER** highlight a book again!

Holder	A person in possession of a document of title or an instrument payable or indorsed to him, his order, or to bearer is a holder.

Contract	A contract is a "promise" or an "agreement" that is enforced or recognized by the law. In the civil law, a contract is considered to be part of the general law of obligations.
Uniform Commercial Code	Uniform commercial code refers to a comprehensive commercial law adopted by every state in the United States; it covers sales laws and other commercial laws.
Intellectual property rights	Intellectual property rights, such as patents, copyrights, trademarks, trade secrets, trade names, and domain names are very valuable business assets. Federal and state laws protect intellectual property rights from misappropriation and infringement.
Intellectual property right	Intellectual property right refers to the right to control and derive the benefits from something one has invented, discovered, or created.
Intellectual property	In law, intellectual property is an umbrella term for various legal entitlements which attach to certain types of information, ideas, or other intangibles in their expressed form. The holder of this legal entitlement is generally entitled to exercise various exclusive rights in relation to its subject matter.
Property rights	Bundle of legal rights over the use to which a resource is put and over the use made of any income that may be derived from that resource are referred to as property rights.
Trademark	A distinctive word, name, symbol, device, or combination thereof, which enables consumers to identify favored products or services and which may find protection under state or federal law is a trademark.
Copyright	The legal right to the proceeds from and control over the use of a created product, such a written work, audio, video, film, or software is a copyright. This right generally extends over the life of the author plus fifty years.
Property	Assets defined in the broadest legal sense. Property includes the unrealized receivables of a cash basis taxpayer, but not services rendered.
Patent	The legal right to the proceeds from and control over the use of an invented product or process, granted for a fixed period of time, usually 20 years. Patent is one form of intellectual property that is subject of the TRIPS agreement.
Consumer protection	Consumer protection is government regulation to protect the interests of consumers, for example by requiring businesses to disclose detailed information about products, particularly in areas where safety or public health is an issue, such as food.
Regulation	Regulation refers to restrictions state and federal laws place on business with regard to the conduct of its activities.
Credit	Credit refers to a recording as positive in the balance of payments, any transaction that gives rise to a payment into the country, such as an export, the sale of an asset, or borrowing from abroad.
Business law	Business law is the body of law which governs business and commerce and is often considered to be a branch of civil law and deals both with issues of private law and public law. It regulates corporate contracts, hiring practices, and the manufacture and sales of consumer goods.
Entrepreneur	The owner/operator. The person who organizes, manages, and assumes the risks of a firm, taking a new idea or a new product and turning it into a successful business is an entrepreneur.
Small business	Small business refers to a business that is independently owned and operated, is not dominant in its field of operation, and meets certain standards of size in terms of employees or annual receipts.
Negligence	The omission to do something that a reasonable person, guided by those considerations that

Go to **Cram101.com** for the Practice Tests for this Chapter.

	ordinarily regulate human affairs, would do, or doing something that a prudent and reasonable person would not do is negligence.
Breach of contract	When one party fails to follow the terms of a contract, we have breach of contract.
Raw material	Raw material refers to a good that has not been transformed by production; a primary product.
Product liability	Part of tort law that holds businesses liable for harm that results from the production, design, sale, or use of products they market is referred to as product liability.
Manufacturing	Production of goods primarily by the application of labor and capital to raw materials and other intermediate inputs, in contrast to agriculture, mining, forestry, fishing, and services a manufacturing.
Liability	A liability is a present obligation of the enterprise arizing from past events, the settlement of which is expected to result in an outflow from the enterprise of resources embodying economic benefits.
Cessna	Cessna, located in Wichita, Kansas, is a manufacturer of general aviation aircraft, from small two-seat, single-engine aircraft to business jets. The company traces its history to June 1911, when Clyde Cessna, a farmer in Rago, Kansas, built a wood-and-fabric plane and became the first person to build and fly an aircraft between the Mississippi River and the Rocky Mountains.
Jury	A body of lay persons, selected by lot, or by some other fair and impartial means, to ascertain, under the guidance of the judge, the truth in questions of fact arising either in civil litigation or a criminal process is referred to as jury.
Contract law	Set of laws that specify what constitutes a legally enforceable agreement is called contract
Valid contract	Valid contract refers to a contract that meets all of the essential elements to establish a contract; a contract that is enforceable by at least one of the parties.
Exchange	The trade of things of value between buyer and seller so that each is better off after the trade is called the exchange.
Misrepresent-tion	The assertion of a fact that is not in accord with the truth is misrepresentation. A contract can be rescinded on the ground of misrepresentation when the assertion relates to a material fact or is made fraudulently and the other party actually and justifiably relies on the assertion.
Mistake	In contract law a mistake is incorrect understanding by one or more parties to a contract and may be used as grounds to invalidate the agreement. Common law has identified three different types of mistake in contract: unilateral mistake, mutual mistake, and common mistake.
Fraud	Tax fraud falls into two categories: civil and criminal. Under civil fraud, the IRS may impose as a penalty of an amount equal to as much as 75 percent of the underpayment.
Invoice	The itemized bill for a transaction, stating the nature of the transaction and its cost. In international trade, the invoice price is often the preferred basis for levying an ad valorem tariff.
Dealer	People who link buyers with sellers by buying and selling securities at stated prices are referred to as a dealer.
Objective theory of contracts	A theory that says that the intent to contract is judged by the reasonable person standard and not by the subjective intent of the parties is referred to as objective theory of contracts.
Supply	Supply is the aggregate amount of any material good that can be called into being at a

certain price point; it comprises one half of the equation of supply and demand. In classical economic theory, a curve representing supply is one of the factors that produce price.

Market price	Market price is an economic concept with commonplace familiarity; it is the price that a good or service is offered at, or will fetch, in the marketplace; it is of interest mainly in the study of microeconomics.
Market	A market is, as defined in economics, a social arrangement that allows buyers and sellers to discover information and carry out a voluntary exchange of goods or services.
Common law	The legal system that is based on the judgement and decree of courts rather than legislative action is called common law.
Mailbox rule	A rule that states that an acceptance is effective when it is dispatched, even if it is lost in transmission is the mailbox rule. The mailbox rule is an exception to the general principle. The mailbox rule provides that the contract is formed when the letter of acceptance is placed in the mailbox.
Consideration	Consideration in contract law, a basic requirement for an enforceable agreement under traditional contract principles, defined in this text as legal value, bargained for and given in exchange for an act or promise. In corporation law, cash or property contributed to a corporation in exchange for shares, or a promise to contribute such cash or property.
Swap	In finance a swap is a derivative, where two counterparties exchange one stream of cash flows against another stream. These streams are called the legs of the swap. The cash flows are calculated over a notional principal amount. Swaps are often used to hedge certain risks, for instance interest rate risk. Another use is speculation.
Buyer	A buyer refers to a role in the buying center with formal authority and responsibility to select the supplier and negotiate the terms of the contract.
Promissory estoppel	An equitable doctrine that protects those who foreseeably and reasonably rely on the promises of others by enforcing such promises when enforcement is necessary to avoid injustice, even though one or more of the elements normally required for an enforceable agreement is absent is a promissory estoppel.
Estoppel	That state of affairs that arises when one is forbidden by law from alleging or denying a fact because of his previous action or inaction is referred to as estoppel.
Franchise	A contractual right to sell certain products or services, use certain trademarks, or perform activities in a geographical region is called a franchise.
Grant	Grant refers to an intergovernmental transfer of funds . Since the New Deal, state and local governments have become increasingly dependent upon federal grants for an almost infinite variety of programs.
Asset	An item of property, such as land, capital, money, a share in ownership, or a claim on others for future payment, such as a bond or a bank deposit is an asset.
Undue influence	Undue influence is an equitable doctrine that involves one person taking advantage of a position of power over another person.
Duress	Duress refers to overpowering of the will of a person by force or fear.
Option	A contract that gives the purchaser the option to buy or sell the underlying financial instrument at a specified price, called the exercise price or strike price, within a specific period of time.
Disaffirm	In contract law, a party's exercise of his power to avoid a contract entered before the party reached the age of majority is to disaffirm.

Guardian	A person to whom the law has entrusted the custody and control of the person, or estate, or both, of an incompetent person is a guardian.
Standards of conduct	Standards of conduct refers to a compendium of ethical norms promulgated by an organization to guide the behavior of its members. Many government agencies have formal codes of conduct for their employees.
Public policy	Decision making by government. Governments are constantly concerned about what they should or should not do. And whatever they do or do not do is public policy. public program All those activities designed to implement a public policy; often this calls for the creation of organizations, public agencies, and bureaus.
Policy	Similar to a script in that a policy can be a less than completely rational decision-making method. Involves the use of a pre-existing set of decision steps for any problem that presents itself.
Marketing	Promoting and selling products or services to customers, or prospective customers, is referred to as marketing.
Direct sale	A direct sale is a sale to customers through distributors or self-employed sales people rather than through shops. Includes both personal contact with consumers in their homes (and other nonstore locations such as offices) and phone solicitations initiated by a retailer.
Equity	Equity is the name given to the set of legal principles, in countries following the English common law tradition, which supplement strict rules of law where their application would operate harshly, so as to achieve what is sometimes referred to as "natural justice."
Exculpatory Clause	Exculpatory Clause refers to a clause in a contract or trust instrument that excuses a party from some duty.
Bid	A bid price is a price offered by a buyer when he/she buys a good. In the context of stock trading on a stock exchange, the bid price is the highest price a buyer of a stock is willing to pay for a share of that given stock.
Intentional misrepresent-tion	Intentional misrepresentation is intentionally defrauding another person out of money, property, or something else of value.
Trial	An examination before a competent tribunal, according to the law of the land, of the facts or law put in issue in a cause, for the purpose of determining such issue is a trial. When the court hears and determines any issue of fact or law for the purpose of determining the rights of the parties, it may be considered a trial.
Compensatory damages	Damages received or paid by the taxpayer can be classified as compensatory damages or as punitive damages. Compensatory damages are those paid to compensate one for harm caused by another.
Monetary damages	Monetary damages, in civil law, refers to compenzation given to an injured party by a liable party. Monetary damages may be restitution, a penalty, or both.
Compensatory	Damages that will compensate a part for direct losses due to an injury suffered are referred to as compensatory .
Damages	The sum of money recoverable by a plaintiff who has received a judgment in a civil case is called damages.
Consequential	Damages that do not flow directly and immediately from an act but rather flow from the results of the act are consequential.
Specific performance	A contract remedy whereby the defendant is ordered to perform according to the terms of his contract is referred to as specific performance.

Go to **Cram101.com** for the Practice Tests for this Chapter.

411

Service	Service refers to a "non tangible product" that is not embodied in a physical good and that typically effects some change in another product, person, or institution. Contrasts with good.
Merchant	Under the Uniform Commercial Code, one who regularly deals in goods of the kind sold in the contract at issue, or holds himself out as having special knowledge or skill relevant to such goods, or who makes the sale through an agent who regularly deals in such goods or claims such knowledge or skill is referred to as merchant.
Customs	Customs is an authority or agency in a country responsible for collecting customs duties and for controlling the flow of people, animals and goods (including personal effects and hazardous items) in and out of the country.
Statute	A statute is a formal, written law of a country or state, written and enacted by its legislative authority, perhaps to then be ratified by the highest executive in the government, and finally published.
Personal property	Personal property is a type of property. In the common law systems personal property may also be called chattels. It is distinguished from real property, or real estate.
Tangible	Having a physical existence is referred to as the tangible. Personal property other than real estate, such as cars, boats, stocks, or other assets.
Estate	An estate is the totality of the legal rights, interests, entitlements and obligations attaching to property. In the context of wills and probate, it refers to the totality of the property which the deceased owned or in which some interest was held.
Jurisdiction	The power of a court to hear and decide a case is called jurisdiction. It is the practical authority granted to a formally constituted body or to a person to deal with and make pronouncements on legal matters and, by implication, to administer justice within a defined area of responsibility.
Agent	A person who makes economic decisions for another economic actor. A hired manager operates as an agent for a firm's owner.
Forming	The first stage of team development, where the team is formed and the objectives for the team are set is referred to as forming.
Statute of frauds	The statute of frauds refers to a requirement in many common law jurisdictions that certain kinds of contracts, typically contractual obligations, be done in writing.
Fair dealing	Fair dealing is a doctrine of limitations and exceptions to copyright which is found in many of the common law jurisdictions of the Commonwealth of Nations.
Warehouse	Warehouse refers to a location, often decentralized, that a firm uses to store, consolidate, age, or mix stock; house product-recall programs; or ease tax burdens.
Perfect tender rule	A rule that says if the goods or tender of a delivery fail in any respect to conform to the contract, the buyer may opt either to reject the whole shipment, to accept the whole shipment, or to reject part and accept part of the shipment is called the perfect tender rule.
Tender of delivery	The obligation of the seller to transfer and deliver goods to the buyer in accordance with the sales contract is a tender of delivery.
Tender	An unconditional offer of payment, consisting in the actual production in money or legal tender of a sum not less than the amount due.
Possession	Possession refers to respecting real property, exclusive dominion and control such as owners of like property usually exercise over it. Manual control of personal property either as owner or as one having a qualified right in it.

Go to **Cram101.com** for the Practice Tests for this Chapter.
And, **NEVER** highlight a book again!

Liquidated damages	The stipulation by the parties to a contract of the sum of money to be recovered by the aggrieved party in the event of a breach of the contract by the other party are referred to as liquidated damages.
Liquidated	Damages made certain by the prior agreement of the parties are called liquidated.
Lien	In its most extensive meaning, it is a charge on property for the payment or discharge of a debt or duty is referred to as lien.
Production	The creation of finished goods and services using the factors of production: land, labor, capital, entrepreneurship, and knowledge.
Statute of limitations	Statute of limitations refers to provisions of the law that specify the maximum period of time in which action may be taken on a past event.
Warranty	An obligation of a company to replace defective goods or correct any deficiencies in performance or quality of a product is called a warranty.
Economy	The income, expenditures, and resources that affect the cost of running a business and household are called an economy.
Breach of warranty	A breach of warranty occurs when the promise is broken, i.e., a product is defective or not as should be expected by a reasonable buyer.
Express warranties	Express warranties refer to specific representations by the seller regarding the goods.
Express warranty	An express warranty is a written guarantee from the manufacturer or distributor that specifies the conditions under which the product can be returned,replaced,or repaired.
Warranty of title	The warranty of title implies that the seller of goods has the right to sell them (e.g., they are not stolen, or patent infringements, or already sold to someone else). This theoretically saves a seller from having to "pay twice" for a product, if it is confiscated by the rightful owner, but only if the seller can be found and makes restitution.
Implied warranty of merchantability	Unless properly disclosed, a warranty that is implied that sold or leased goods are fit for the ordinary purpose for which they are sold or leased, and other assurances are called implied warranty of merchantability.
Warranty of merchantability	The warranty of merchantability is implied, unless expressly disclaimed by name, or the sale is identified with the phrase "as is" or "with all faults." To be "merchantable", the goods must reasonably conform to an ordinary buyer's expectations, i.e., they are what they say they are.
Implied warranty	A warranty created by operation of law is called implied warranty.
Implied warranty of fitness for a particular purpose	An implied warranty that information is fit for the licensee's purpose that applies if the licensor knows of any particular purpose for which the computer information is required and knows that the licensee is relying on the licensor's skill or judgment to select or furnish suitable information is the implied warranty of fitness for a particular purpose.
Purchasing	Purchasing refers to the function in a firm that searches for quality material resources, finds the best suppliers, and negotiates the best price for goods and services.
Scope	Scope of a project is the sum total of all projects products and their requirements or features.
Consultant	A professional that provides expert advice in a particular field or area in which customers occassionaly require this type of knowledge is a consultant.
Optimum	Optimum refers to the best. Usually refers to a most preferred choice by consumers subject to

Go to **Cram101.com** for the Practice Tests for this Chapter.
And, **NEVER** highlight a book again!

	a budget constraint or a profit maximizing choice by firms or industry subject to a technological constraint.
Quality assurance	Those activities associated with assuring the quality of a product or service is called quality assurance.
Industry	A group of firms that produce identical or similar products is an industry. It is also used specifically to refer to an area of economic production focused on manufacturing which involves large amounts of capital investment before any profit can be realized, also called "heavy industry".
Punitive damages	Damages received or paid by the taxpayer can be classified as compensatory damages or as punitive damages. Punitive damages are those awarded to punish the defendant for gross negligence or the intentional infliction of harm. Such damages are includible.
Punitive	Damages designed to punish flagrant wrongdoers and to deter them and others from engaging in similar conduct in the future are called punitive.
Chain of distribution	All manufacturers, distributors, wholesalers, retailers, lessors, and subcomponent manufacturers involved in a transaction is called chain of distribution.
Distribution	Distribution in economics, the manner in which total output and income is distributed among individuals or factors.
Misuse	A defense that relieves a seller of product liability if the user abnormally misused the product is called misuse. Products must be designed to protect against foreseeable misuse.
Strict liability	Legal responsibility placed on an individual for the results of his actions irrespective of whether he was culpable or at fault is a strict liability.
Proximate cause	A legal limitation on a negligent wrongdoer's liability for the actual consequences of his actions is a proximate cause. Such wrongdoers are said to be relieved of responsibility for consequences that are too remote or not the proximate result of their actions.
Allegation	An allegation is a statement of a fact by a party in a pleading, which the party claims it will prove. Allegations remain assertions without proof, only claims until they are proved.
Federal government	Federal government refers to the government of the United States, as distinct from the state and local governments.
Innovation	Innovation refers to the first commercially successful introduction of a new product, the use of a new method of production, or the creation of a new form of business organization.
Monopoly	A monopoly is defined as a persistent market situation where there is only one provider of a kind of product or service.
License	A license in the sphere of Intellectual Property Rights (IPR) is a document, contract or agreement giving permission or the 'right' to a legally-definable entity to do something (such as manufacture a product or to use a service), or to apply something (such as a trademark), with the objective of achieving commercial gain.
Business model	A business model is the instrument by which a business intends to generate revenue and profits. It is a summary of how a company means to serve its employees and customers, and involves both strategy (what an business intends to do) as well as an implementation.
Commerce	Commerce is the exchange of something of value between two entities. It is the central mechanism from which capitalism is derived.
Disclosure	Disclosure means the giving out of information, either voluntarily or to be in compliance with legal regulations or workplace rules.
Technology	The body of knowledge and techniques that can be used to combine economic resources to

Go to **Cram101.com** for the Practice Tests for this Chapter.

produce goods and services is called technology.

Warrant	A warrant is a security that entitles the holder to buy or sell a certain additional quantity of an underlying security at an agreed-upon price, at the holder's discretion.
Interest	In finance and economics, interest is the price paid by a borrower for the use of a lender's money. In other words, interest is the amount of paid to "rent" money for a period of time.
Patent infringement	Patent infringement refers to unauthorized use of another's patent. A patent holder may recover damages and other remedies against a patent infringer.
Average cost	Average cost is equal to total cost divided by the number of goods produced (Quantity-Q). It is also equal to the sum of average variable costs (total variable costs divided by Q) plus average fixed costs (total fixed costs divided by Q).
Holder	A person in possession of a document of title or an instrument payable or indorsed to him, his order, or to bearer is a holder.
Logo	Logo refers to device or other brand name that cannot be spoken.
Holding	The holding is a court's determination of a matter of law based on the issue presented in the particular case. In other words: under this law, with these facts, this result.
Brand	A name, symbol, or design that identifies the goods or services of one seller or group of sellers and distinguishes them from the goods and services of competitors is a brand.
Layout	Layout refers to the physical arrangement of the various parts of an advertisement including the headline, subheads, illustrations, body copy, and any identifying marks.
Competitor	Other organizations in the same industry or type of business that provide a good or service to the same set of customers is referred to as a competitor.
Corporation	A legal entity chartered by a state or the Federal government that is distinct and separate from the individuals who own it is a corporation. This separation gives the corporation unique powers which other legal entities lack.
Legal system	Legal system refers to system of rules that regulate behavior and the processes by which the laws of a country are enforced and through which redress of grievances is obtained.
Budget	Budget refers to an account, usually for a year, of the planned expenditures and the expected receipts of an entity. For a government, the receipts are tax revenues.
Tactic	A short-term immediate decision that, in its totality, leads to the achievement of strategic goals is called a tactic.
Principal	In agency law, one under whose direction an agent acts and for whose benefit that agent acts is a principal.
Fiduciary	Fiduciary refers to one who holds goods in trust for another or one who holds a position of trust and confidence.
Trust	An arrangement in which shareholders of independent firms agree to give up their stock in exchange for trust certificates that entitle them to a share of the trust's common profits.
Accounting	A system that collects and processes financial information about an organization and reports that information to decision makers is referred to as accounting.
Profit	Profit refers to the return to the resource entrepreneurial ability; total revenue minus total cost.
Administration	Administration refers to the management and direction of the affairs of governments and institutions; a collective term for all policymaking officials of a government; the execution and implementation of public policy.

Go to **Cram101.com** for the Practice Tests for this Chapter.

Expense	In accounting, an expense represents an event in which an asset is used up or a liability is incurred. In terms of the accounting equation, expenses reduce owners' equity.
Duty to indemnify	A duty that a principal owes to protect the agent for losses the agent suffered during the agency because of the principal's misconduct is called duty to indemnify.
Bankruptcy	Bankruptcy is a legally declared inability or impairment of ability of an individual or organization to pay their creditors.
Business strategy	Business strategy, which refers to the aggregated operational strategies of single business firm or that of an SBU in a diversified corporation refers to the way in which a firm competes in its chosen arenas.
Reorganization	Reorganization occurs, among other instances, when one corporation acquires another in a merger or acquisition, a single corporation divides into two or more entities, or a corporation makes a substantial change in its capital structure.
Liquidation	Liquidation refers to a process whereby the assets of a business are converted to money. The conversion may be coerced by a legal process to pay off the debt of the business, or to satisfy any other business obligation that the business has not voluntarily satisfied.
Firm	An organization that employs resources to produce a good or service for profit and owns and operates one or more plants is referred to as a firm.
Creditor	A person to whom a debt or legal obligation is owed, and who has the right to enforce payment of that debt or obligation is referred to as creditor.
Trustee	An independent party appointed to represent the bondholders is referred to as a trustee.
Stockholder	A stockholder is an individual or company (including a corporation) that legally owns one or more shares of stock in a joined stock company. The shareholders are the owners of a corporation. Companies listed at the stock market strive to enhance shareholder value.
Involuntary petition	Involuntary petition refers to a chapter 7 or 11 bankruptcy petition filed by creditors of the debtor; alleges that the debtor is not paying his or her debts as they become due.
Petition	A petition is a request to an authority, most commonly a government official or public entity. In the colloquial sense, a petition is a document addressed to some official and signed by numerous individuals.
Automatic stay	Under the Bankruptcy Act, the suspension of all litigation against the debtor and his property, which is triggered by the filing of a bankruptcy petition, is called automatic stay.
Attachment	Attachment in general, the process of taking a person's property under an appropriate judicial order by an appropriate officer of the court. Used for a variety of purposes, including the acquisition of jurisdiction over the property seized and the securing of property that may be used to satisfy a debt.
Exempt	Employees who are not covered by the Fair Labor Standards Act are exempt. Exempt employees are not eligible for overtime pay.
Allowance	Reduction in the selling price of goods extended to the buyer because the goods are defective or of lower quality than the buyer ordered and to encourage a buyer to keep merchandise that would otherwise be returned is the allowance.
Household	An economic unit that provides the economy with resources and uses the income received to purchase goods and services that satisfy economic wants is called household.
Fraudulent conveyance	In legal parlance, fraudulent conveyance refers to the illegal transfer of property to another party in order to defer, hinder or defraud creditors. In order to be found guilty of

Go to **Cram101.com** for the Practice Tests for this Chapter.

fraudulent conveyance, it must be proven that the accused's intention for transferring the property was to put it out of reach of a known creditor.

Conveyance	A written instrument transferring the title to land or some interest therein from one person to another is the conveyance.
Chapter 7 bankruptcy	Chapter 7 bankruptcy governs the process of liquidation under the bankruptcy laws of the United States. It is the most common form of bankruptcy in the United States.
Fresh start	The goal of federal bankruptcy law is to discharge the debtor from burdensome debts and allow him or her to begin again, which is called a fresh start.
Remainder	A remainder in property law is a future interest created in a transferee that is capable of becoming possessory upon the natural termination of a prior estate created by the same instrument.
Chapter 11 bankruptcy	Chapter 11 bankruptcy governs the process of reorganization under the bankruptcy laws of the United States. It is an attempt to stay in business while a bankruptcy court supervises the "reorganization" of the company's contractual and debt obligations.
Debtor in possession	A debtor in possession, in the United States bankruptcy law, is a person who is bankrupt, but remains in possession of property upon which a creditor has a lien or similar security interest.
Management	Management characterizes the process of leading and directing all or part of an organization, often a business, through the deployment and manipulation of resources. Early twentieth-century management writer Mary Parker Follett defined management as "the art of getting things done through people."
Operation	A standardized method or technique that is performed repetitively, often on different materials resulting in different finished goods is called an operation.
Interstate commerce commission	A federal regulatory group created by Congress in 1887 to oversee and correct abuses in the railroad industry is an interstate commerce commission.
Great Depression	The period of severe economic contraction and high unemployment that began in 1929 and continued throughout the 1930s is referred to as the Great Depression.
Depression	Depression refers to a prolonged period characterized by high unemployment, low output and investment, depressed business confidence, falling prices, and widespread business failures. A milder form of business downturn is a recession.
Compliance	A type of influence process where a receiver accepts the position advocated by a source to obtain favorable outcomes or to avoid punishment is the compliance.
Complaint	The pleading in a civil case in which the plaintiff states his claim and requests relief is called complaint. In the common law, it is a formal legal document that sets out the basic facts and legal reasons that the filing party (the plaintiffs) believes are sufficient to support a claim against another person, persons, entity or entities (the defendants) that entitles the plaintiff(s) to a remedy (either money damages or injunctive relief).
Competitive market	A market in which no buyer or seller has market power is called a competitive market.
Profit margin	Profit margin is a measure of profitability. It is calculated using a formula and written as a percentage or a number. Profit margin = Net income before tax and interest / Revenue.
Margin	A deposit by a buyer in stocks with a seller or a stockbroker, as security to cover fluctuations in the market in reference to stocks that the buyer has purchased but for which he has not paid is a margin. Commodities are also traded on margin.

Go to **Cram101.com** for the Practice Tests for this Chapter.

Marginal benefit	Marginal benefit refers to the extra benefit of consuming 1 more unit of some good or service; the change in total benefit when 1 more unit is consumed.
Antitrust laws	Legislation that prohibits anticompetitive business activities such as price fixing, bid rigging, monopolization, and tying contracts is referred to as antitrust laws.
Antitrust	Government intervention to alter market structure or prevent abuse of market power is called antitrust.
Sherman Antitrust Act	The Sherman Antitrust Act, formally known as the Act of July 2, 1890 was the first United States federal government action to limit monopolies.
Restraint of trade	Contracts in restraint of trade are contracts which have the effect of restricting a person's freedom to conduct business in a specified or unspecified location for a specified or unspecified length of time.
Monopoly power	Monopoly power is an example of market failure which occurs when one or more of the participants has the ability to influence the price or other outcomes in some general or specialized market.
Clayton act	The Clayton act is a federal antitrust act of 1914 that strengthened the Sherman Act by making it illegal for firms to engage in certain specified practices.
Sales promotion	Sales promotion refers to the promotional tool that stimulates consumer purchasing and dealer interest by means of short-term activities.
Promotion	Promotion refers to all the techniques sellers use to motivate people to buy products or services. An attempt by marketers to inform people about products and to persuade them to participate in an exchange.
Advertising	Advertising refers to paid, nonpersonal communication through various media by organizations and individuals who are in some way identified in the advertising message.
Advertisement	Advertisement is the promotion of goods, services, companies and ideas, usually by an identified sponsor. Marketers see advertising as part of an overall promotional strategy.
Libel	Libel refers to the defamation action appropriate to printed or written defamations, or to those that have a physical form.
Stock	In financial terminology, stock is the capital raized by a corporation, through the issuance and sale of shares.
Price discrimination	Price discrimination refers to the sale by a firm to buyers at two different prices. When this occurs internationally and the lower price is charged for export, it is regarded as dumping.
Exclusive dealing	An arrangement a manufacturer makes with a reseller to handle only its products and not those of competitors is referred to as exclusive dealing.
Tying	Tying is the practice of making the sale of one good (the tying good) to the de facto or de jure customer conditional on the purchase of a second distinctive good.
Board of directors	The group of individuals elected by the stockholders of a corporation to oversee its operations is a board of directors.
Interlocking directorate	Interlocking directorate refers to a situation where one or more members of the board of directors of a corporation are also on the board of directors of a competing corporation; illegal under the Clayton Act.
Federal trade commission act	The federal act of 1914 that established the Federal Trade Commission is referred to as Federal Trade Commission Act.

Go to **Cram101.com** for the Practice Tests for this Chapter.

Federal trade commission	The commission of five members established by the Federal Trade Commission Act of 1914 to investigate unfair competitive practices of firms, to hold hearings on the complaints of such practices, and to issue cease-and-desist orders when firms were found guilty of unfair practices.
Trade regulation rules	Trade regulation rules are industry wide rules that define unfair practices before they occur. Used by the Federal Trade Commission to regulate advertising and promotion.
Cease and desist order	An order issued to a company by the Federal Trade Commission to stop practices it considers unfair is a cease and desist order. It is used in demands for a person or organization to permanently stop doing something.
Commodity	Could refer to any good, but in trade a commodity is usually a raw material or primary product that enters into international trade, such as metals or basic agricultural products.
Merger	Merger refers to the combination of two firms into a single firm.
Food and Drug Administration	The Food and Drug Administration is an agency of the United States Department of Health and Human Services and is responsible for regulating food (human and animal), dietary supplements, drugs (human and animal), cosmetics, medical devices (human and animal) and radiation emitting devices (including non-medical devices), biologics, and blood products in the United States.
Fair Packaging and Labeling Act	The Fair Packaging and Labeling Act is a US law that applies to labels on many consumer products. It requires the label to state the identity of the product, the name and place of business of the manufacturer, packer, or distributor, and the net quantity of contents. Passed under Lyndon B. Johnson in 1966, the law first took effect on July 1, 1967.
Vendor	A person who sells property to a vendee is a vendor. The words vendor and vendee are more commonly applied to the seller and purchaser of real estate, and the words seller and buyer are more commonly applied to the seller and purchaser of personal property.
Product safety	Product safety refers to a multi-step, scientific process to assess the probability that exposure to a product during any stage of its lifecycle will lead to a negative impact on human health or the environment.
Consumer good	Products and services that are ultimately consumed rather than used in the production of another good are a consumer good.
Lender	Suppliers and financial institutions that lend money to companies is referred to as a lender.
Annual percentage rate	Annual percentage rate refers to a measure of the effective rate on a loan. One uses the actuarial method of compound interest when calculating the annual percentage rate.
Relative cost	Relative cost refers to the relationship between the price paid for advertising time or space and the size of the audience delivered; it is used to compare the prices of various media vehicles.
Total cost	The sum of fixed cost and variable cost is referred to as total cost.
Mortgage	Mortgage refers to a note payable issued for property, such as a house, usually repaid in equal installments consisting of part principle and part interest, over a specified period.
Issuer	The company that borrows money from investors by issuing bonds is referred to as issuer. They are legally responsible for the obligations of the issue and for reporting financial conditions, material developments and any other operational activities as required by the regulations of their jurisdictions.
Welfare	Welfare refers to the economic well being of an individual, group, or economy. For individuals, it is conceptualized by a utility function. For groups, including countries and

Go to **Cram101.com** for the Practice Tests for this Chapter.
And, **NEVER** highlight a book again!

the world, it is a tricky philosophical concept, since individuals fare differently.

Resource Conservation and Recovery Act	A federal statute that authorizes the EPA to regulate facilities that generate, treat, store, transport, and dispose of hazardous wastes is a Resource Conservation and Recovery Act.
Clean Water Act	The Clean Water Act, established the symbolic goals of eliminating releases to water of toxic amounts of toxic substances, eliminating additional water pollution by 1985, and ensuring that surface waters would meet standards necessary for human sports and recreation by 1983.
Clean Air Act	A Clean Air Act describes one of a number of pieces of legislation relating to the reduction of smog and atmospheric pollution in general. The United States Congress passed the Clean Air Act in 1963, the Clean Air Act Amendment in 1966, the Clean Air Act Extension in 1970, and Clean Air Act Amendments in 1977 and 1990.
Recovery	Characterized by rizing output, falling unemployment, rizing profits, and increasing economic activity following a decline is a recovery.
Comprehensive	A comprehensive refers to a layout accurate in size, color, scheme, and other necessary details to show how a final ad will look. For presentation only, never for reproduction.
Fund	Independent accounting entity with a self-balancing set of accounts segregated for the purposes of carrying on specific activities is referred to as a fund.
Superfund	A fund authorized by the CERCLA to cover the costs of cleaning up hazardous waste disposal sites whose owners cannot be found or are unwilling or unable to pay for the cleanup is referred to as superfund.
Offer and acceptance	Offer and acceptance analysis is a traditional approach in contract law used to determine whether an agreement exists between two parties. An offer is an indication by one person to another of their willingness to contract on certain terms without further negotiations. A contract is then formed if there is express or implied agreement.
Indemnification	Right of a partner to be reimbursed for expenditures incurred on behalf of the partnership is referred to as indemnification.
Controlling interest	A firm has a controlling interest in another business entity when it owns more than 50 percent of that entity's voting stock.
Controlling	A management function that involves determining whether or not an organization is progressing toward its goals and objectives, and taking corrective action if it is not is called controlling.
Business development	Business development emcompasses a number of techniques designed to grow an economic enterprise. Such techniques include, but are not limited to, assessments of marketing opportunities and target markets, intelligence gathering on customers and competitors, generating leads for possible sales, followup sales activity, and formal proposal writing.
Forbes	David Churbuck founded online Forbes in 1996. The site drew attention when it uncovered Stephen Glass' journalistic fraud in The New Republic in 1998, a scoop that gave credibility to internet journalism.
Wall Street Journal	Dow Jones & Company was founded in 1882 by reporters Charles Dow, Edward Jones and Charles Bergstresser. Jones converted the small Customers' Afternoon Letter into The Wall Street Journal, first published in 1889, and began delivery of the Dow Jones News Service via telegraph. The Journal featured the Jones 'Average', the first of several indexes of stock and bond prices on the New York Stock Exchange.
National bank	A National bank refers to federally chartered banks. They are an ordinary private bank which

Go to **Cram101.com** for the Practice Tests for this Chapter.

operates nationally (as opposed to regionally or locally or even internationally).

Journal | Book of original entry, in which transactions are recorded in a general ledger system, is referred to as a journal.

430

Go to **Cram101.com** for the Practice Tests for this Chapter.

CPSIA information can be obtained at www.ICGtesting.com
Printed in the USA
BVOW10s1958211213

339795BV00001B/15/P